PIMLICO

580

VERBATIM

Erin McKean is the editor of *VERBATIM: The Language Quarterly* and senior editor, US Dictionaries, for Oxford University Press. She lives in Chicago.

VERBATIM

Edited by
ERIN McKEAN

PIMLICO

Published by Pimlico 2003

2 4 6 8 10 9 7 5 3 1

First published in the United States by Harcourt 2001
First published in Great Britain by Pimlico 2003

Pimlico
Random House
20 Vauxhall Bridge Road, London SW1V 2SA

Random House Australia (Pty) Limited
20 Alfred Street, Milsons Point, Sydney, New South Wales 2061, Australia

Random House New Zealand Limited
18 Poland Road, Glenfield, Auckland 10, New Zealand

Random House (Pty) Limited
Endulini, 5A Jubilee Road, Parktown 2193, South Africa

The Random House Group Limited Reg. No. 954009
www.randomhouse.co.uk

A CIP catalogue record for this book is available from the British Library

ISBN 0-7126-4597-7

Papers used by Random House UK Limited are natural,
recyclable products made from wood grown in sustainable forests;
the manufacturing processes conform to the environmental
regulations of the country of origin

Printed and bound in Great Britain by Mackays of Chatham

For Joey and Henry, who make everything possible

Acknowledgments

I certainly haven't done—and couldn't have done—any of this by myself. I'd especially like to thank Dr. Warren Gilson of Middleton, Wisconsin, our benefactor, who recognized that *Verbatim* should be continued and who generously established *Verbatim* as a nonprofit corporation. Paul Heacock, Hazel Hall, and Lorraine Alexson have done more work on shorter deadlines than any three people in the history of the printed word, for which I cannot thank them enough. Also, Nick Humez, Ivan Brunetti, Debbie Posner, Mary Beth Protomastro, Bob Olson, Mat Coward, Richard Bready, Jesse Sheidlower, John Mella, and Tony Hall are all decorated veterans of the *Verbatim* helpfulness campaign, for which I am grateful. But most of all, I want to thank Larry Urdang for conceiving *Verbatim* and for answering my questions, especially the ones I didn't know enough to ask.

Contents

Foreword

In the broad definition of language as a structured, more or less consistent system of communication, we can readily accept that birds, whales, and other species have language. In a narrower sense, one in which language is characterized by diversity and variety, artistic expression, a means by which abstract thought rather than just instinctual leanings are conveyed among its users, it belongs only to people. Speculations about the origins of human language were once as numerous and fanciful as theories of the origin of the universe, ranging from a God-given gift to a legacy from extraterrestrials.

Although some wrote about language millennia ago, it was only relatively recently that the study of linguistics was born, when thoughtful people began to examine the many languages, discern their differences and similarities, then group them into the generally accepted hierarchical arrangement they enjoy today. Archaeolinguistics, the decoding of writing systems of extinct languages, like those of the Mayan and Egyptian hieroglyphs, is a fascinating, specialized field, reconstructing long-dead languages; speech analysis and speech synthesis, reflexes of acoustics, another branch of linguistics coupled with what might be termed anatomical physics, has made advances in recent years leading to voice-activated, hands-free electronic devices; the statistics of responses to advertising yield information about our responses to words; somewhere, a scholar is probably analyzing equivocation and lying as aspects of politics. In myriad overt and subtle ways, language pervades everything we do, how we relate to the people and the things and other forces about us.

Considering its pervasiveness, it is no wonder that many people pay attention to language. In years gone by, great attention was paid in education to ensuring that students were well acquainted with what was considered "good" language, in the sense of 'in keeping with what is regarded as traditional grammar and usage.' Today, less attention is paid to grammar and usage and more to the *effective use* of language: The last half of the twentieth century has seen an abandonment of criteria of taste and art in favor of self-aggrandizement and greed. Consequently, an aspect of language study that focuses on how to employ it to gain the best advantage has come to the fore in popularity. However, as with diet fads, though there be some who lose weight and others who merely gain no more, there are those who use language effectively and those who do not—and the former are not known to be inspired by get-ahead-quick courses. Indeed, advertisements for vocabulary building, once viewed as a key to (financial) success, are rarely seen anymore.

Not all those who are interested in—even fascinated by—language are willing to make the effort to study linguistics, which is probably just as well. Professional linguists guard their domain zealously, often forbidding any untrained "amateur" admittance to the secret annual cabals sponsored by such august institutions as the Linguistics Society of America, the Dialect Society, the American Name Society, and so forth.

Yet language is the "property" of us all, and thoughts and opinions about it must not be reserved for the few who regard themselves as the elite. Besides, language, alongside its peculiarities, has its amusing, entertaining, funny aspects. Beginning publication in the seventeenth century, the British weekly *Gentleman's Magazine* included occasional articles and correspondence dealing with language; in the early nineteenth century, *Notes and Queries,* another British weekly, began publication, and it, too, became a forum for people interested in language, literature, and other cultural elements of life. (*Gentlemen's Magazine* ceased publication decades ago; *Notes and Queries* continues as a small-circulation scholarly quarterly, published now by Oxford University Press.)

In the years after World War II, when I became involved in linguistics and lexicography, I noted that, except for the occasional article in the Sunday newspaper supplement or magazine, there was no regular periodical serving what I perceived to be a general interest in language—not, I hasten to say, in remedial English or techniques for improving one's station in life but merely to satisfy intellectual curiosity.

And so *Verbatim: The Language Quarterly* was born. Its first issue, in 1974, as a newsletter, was to have been four pages in length, but out of control, it grew to six; subsequent issues have numbered as many as sixty-four pages; in book form (octavo), the first twenty-four issues occupy 991 pages of text.

Its contributors of articles, letters, and reviews are diverse, from professional linguists like Dwight Bollinger, Lillian Feinsilver, Frederic G. Cassidy, Garland Cannon, Robert A. Fowkes, Eric Hamp, Tom McArthur, Henry Truby, Dennis Baron, and

Reinhold Aman to lexicographers like Thomas Clark, Bryan Garner, Norman W. Schur, Ed Gates, Sidney Landau, and others. But by far the most important among the contributors are those, too numerous to list here, who simply love words and language, who submit articles on every conceivable subject within the extremely broad reaches of the subject. Efforts have always been made to select from among the submissions those considered the best written, which is especially important to *Verbatim,* for the professional journals are characteristically stuffed with such turgid, obscure, incomprehensibly boring articles that the subject of language itself is suffocated.

It was always my hope that *Verbatim* would emerge as a breath of fresh air for that interested cadre of word lovers who had been forced to endure Sunday-supplement curiosity collections and word puzzles leveled at six-year-olds. Having yielded my editorship in 1997, after twenty-three years, I was particularly delighted to turn over the blue pencil to Erin McKean, a professional lexicographer who has cleaved to the high standards to which I aspired.

—LAURENCE URDANG

Preface

When Dr. Warren Gilson called me (lo these many years ago—last century, in fact) to ask if I would be at all interested in editing *Verbatim*, I was sure it was a joke. I knew about *Verbatim*, and had read it compulsively in high school, at Wake Forest University library, while I should have been researching term papers. But I no more expected that one day I would edit *Verbatim* than I expect to be crowned Queen of Rumania or to "thank the Academy" or to eat pickled eggs. However, some good fairy kept me from hanging up the phone, and "Doc" Gilson made a persuasive case—in short, if these several years have been a joke, it's a hoax on the order of Piltdown man.

I have never worked so hard, stayed up so late, learned so much, or talked to so many interesting people about so many fascinating subjects as I have while editing *Verbatim*. I've been able to do fun things (such as call up writers I admire and ask them to write for *Verbatim*, and read letters from subscribers) and not-so-fun things (such as fill out forms for the U.S. Post Office and reject unsuitable manuscripts). I've been able to do new things (such as put *Verbatim* on the web, at www. verbatimmag.com) and old things (shift, sort, and inventory hundreds and hundreds of back issues).

When people ask me what *Verbatim* is, I say that it's a magazine about all of the fun parts of English and linguistics, written for people who don't necessarily have a Ph.D. *Verbatim* is a magazine that informs you about English usage without making you feel self-conscious or guilty. It entertains you with articles—that aren't wrapped in impenetrable jargon—about the intriguing science of linguistics. It makes you laugh (sometimes in spite of yourself) and leaves you better informed about ideas that matter. And it's been doing so for more than twenty-five years.

Twenty-five years, and there's still no shortage of areas for *Verbatim* to explore. Changes in English are piling up in drifts (*muggles, k3wl d00d,* and "all your base are belong to us" anyone?), and the science of linguistics is becoming more scientific every day, necessitating even more documentation and explanation in our pages. I believe *Verbatim* has a mandate to continue for at least another twenty-five years, on paper, on the web, or beamed directly to the back of your retina or to your wrist-reader, as the technology improves.

Choosing the articles for the book you're holding now was a wild romp. Flipping through the issues (and the hardcover volumes that collect volumes one through six), I scribbled notes madly. So madly, in fact, that I ended up with enough must-include articles to fill a book three times this size. I decided to highlight *Verbatim*'s strengths: great writing about dictionaries, English usage, popular linguistics, and obscenity, with a large helping of humor. (If you blench at seeing four-letter words in print, please put this book down now and get your sal volatile ready.) Perhaps the hardest task was deciding what of Laurence Urdang's amazing collection of writing to include and what to lovingly place back in the archive for next time. I have chosen a few of my favorites, and I hope they become yours as well.

Grammar and Other Lost Arts

When someone starts complaining to me about grammar, I listen intently. Not so much because I'm entranced by yet another rant about the declining grammaticality of speaking and writing today, but because I am sure to hear an error in the speech of the ranter. It's almost inevitable. English is a slippery divil; the rules are lagging far behind the caravan, and the inmates are not only running the asylum, they're instituting managed care and turning a stupendous profit. English is messy, uninhibited, sprawling, and sloppy. That's what I like about it. It's a miracle when a good stylist can take the unmanageable tangle that is our language and craft a sparkling, coherent, evocative sentence out of it. In *Verbatim*, we believe that good writers are good writers not because of the rules of English, but in spite of them.

An Intolerant View of Intolerance

LAURENCE URDANG

Notwithstanding the redundancy in the title, I consider myself—as, I am sure, everyone regards himself—a tolerant human being: I try to avoid prejudice in all things. Yet I must confess to a seemingly uncorrectable, irrepressible foible: I am intolerant of intolerance, especially when it comes to language. Language, as we all know, is an uncommon denominator: Not everyone uses it in the same way. In fact, it is likely that no two people use it in identical ways. When we have been taught that *like* is a preposition, not an adverb or conjunction substitutable for *as* in constructions like *Do as I say, not as I do* and then encounter someone who does just that, the very fact that the other person speaks or writes in that fashion tells us something about him. It may tell us that he is trying to be "in" by being colloquial with his up-to-date slang, or it may tell us that he is an unfortunate who has not had the benefits of our (superior) education. But it cannot be denied that usage informs us about the user. If everyone spoke and wrote in exactly the same way, saying "If I were he" instead of "If I was him," "She doesn't love me" instead of "She don't love me," "Between her and me" instead of "Between she and I," "nuclear" instead of "nucular," and so on, not only would it be difficult to tell one speaker from another in *level* and expressivity, but listening to speech and reading writing would prove an unsupportable bore.

A measure of my irritation with intolerance stems from my general experience with purists who want everyone to speak the way they do (which isn't always formally proper, either, mind you), but the precipitating catalyst of my present dyspepsia is an article by Jean Stafford, "At This Point in Time, TV Is Murdering the English Language," which appeared in the (Sunday) *New York Times*, 15 September 1974. In it, this self-appointed Guardian of the English Language (I must interrupt myself here to point out that everyone who is intolerant of the way others use English is, by definition, a "Guardian of the English Language"; "self-appointed" is a truistic propagandism since such Guardians are seldom appointed by a committee; by this token, I suppose I am an appointed—by implication—Assailant of the English Language. I have a nagging suspicion that either the roles or the titles have got somehow reversed.) Anyway, this Ste. Peter who would bar from the Elysian Fields any who violate the Rules as she sees them condemns a number of grammatical, semantic, and syntactic anomalies which, in her view, spell the doom of civilization. I am tempted to add "as we know it," one of the more boring clichés of our time, but I shall restrain myself.

Here, in (mercifully) abbreviated form, is a selection from those stylistic solecisms that Miss Stafford singled out for vituperative comment:

"[Let us] declare a honeymoon." (Walter Cronkite): *How is a honeymoon declared?*

"Diaper" *has three syllables, not two.* (various commercials)

"Nucular" for *nuclear.* (President Eisenhower)

"Hopefully, . . ." (President Kennedy)

"All aspirin is not alike." (TV commercial)

"Nauseous" for *nauseated.* (TV commercial)

"*Gasid* indigestion." (various commercials)

"You get a lot of dirt with kids; you get a lot of *clean* with Tide." (TV commercial) *When did* clean *become a noun?*

"Adhesive that will really *bond* the denture to the gums." (TV commercial)

"Guesstimate." *Prevalent.*

"A system for learning in depth." (*Britannica* commercial)

"Opt for." *Prevalent cliché.*

"Lifestyle." *Prevalent cliché.*

"Irregardless." *Prevalent tautology.*

"Funded." *Use of noun as verb.*

"Feedback." *Semantic shift.*

"Input." *Semantic shift.*

"Career experiences." *Bureaucratic gobbledygook.*

"Economy doesn't have to be dull." (TV commercial)

"Self-destruct." *Nonword.*

"Enormity" for *hugeness, enormousness, great importance.*

"No-commenting." *Use of phrase as a verb.*

"Stonewalling." *Neologistic cliché.*

"Specificity." *Cliché.*

"At this point in time, . . ." *Wordy cliché for* now, at present.

"Phased out." *Semantic shift and cliché.*

"-wise." *Trite suffix for making nouns into adverbs.*

It would be very dull, indeed, to examine each one of these citations, but a few generalizations seem to be in order. First of all, the problems can be classified into relatively few categories:

1. redundancies and tautologies: *irregardless*

2. boredom of the cliché: *guesstimate, opt for, lifestyle, specificity, stonewalling,-wise, at this point in time,* etc.

3. intentional/unintentional and/or illogical gobbledygook: *career experiences, economy doesn't have to be dull,* etc.

4. metaphor: *declare a honeymoon, in depth, feedback, input, phased out, bond,* etc.

5. linguistic change: *clean, funded, no-commenting,* etc.

6. semantic change: *nauseous, bond, enormity,* etc.

7. neologisms and blends: *guesstimate, self-destruct, stone-walling, gasid (indigestion)*, etc.

As can be seen—and I haven't tried being exhaustive in this superficial analysis—some of the more heinous examples cited by Miss Stafford fall into more than one category. It is noteworthy that except for classifications one, two, and three, which are usually so ephemeral as to have little or no effect on language (however they may affect thinking, patience, and nerves), all these categories are the stuff of which language is made. Change is one of the definitive characteristics of language, despite Miss Stafford's unwillingness to recognize it. Critics of contemporary language have always been among us—Richard Grant White is a famous Victorian example—but the language has survived despite their quixotic failings. In fact, if fifty years later, one examines the solecisms which they often became most excited and scornful about, it often turns out either that the same condemned usages are still the objects of Guardians' censure or that they have become standard, and it is hard to understand what the fuss was all about.

Miss Stafford, self-appointed (and, I suspect, *Times*-supported) Defender of the Faith in the English Language, fails to recognize these elementary facts. After all, if everyone had her gifts, chances are she never would have received her Pulitzer Prize—if one could be awarded at all. If she needs evidence that language changes, let her analyze and compare with Modern English writings of which she approves the writings of Spenser, Chaucer, Shakespeare, Milton, Austen, and other English "masters of style," whose writings need varying degrees of interpretation, depending on their remove from the contemporary reader.

The problem, which seems to elude Miss Stafford, lies not with

TV—which is, after all, merely the medium of expression and not the expression itself—but with the poor *style,* not the poor language. Yet Miss Stafford, either blinded by her contumelious zeal or hanging on for dear life as her runaway hobby horse gallops into the sunset (possibly both), deplores the poverty-stricken imagery that is often the result of a combination of an impoverished imagination and a hyperactive gift of gab instead of ignoring it, comforted by the knowledge that it will all soon dry up and blow away.

In short, she is playing right into the hands of those she criticizes, for all they want is to be attended to and remembered, and, through her articles, Miss Stafford is elevating them to a higher memorial than they could otherwise merit. Come to think of it, I should never have written this article.

Intolerable Intolerance, Redux

ERIN McKEAN

Laurence Urdang, in an article entitled "An Intolerant View of Intolerance" wrote:

"I consider myself—as, I am sure, everyone regards himself—a tolerant human being: I try to avoid prejudice in all things. Yet I must confess to a seemingly uncorrectable, irrepressible foible: I am intolerant of intolerance, especially when it comes to language."

If they are still accepting new members in the ranks of language intolerance intolerators, you can sign me up as well. Nothing is as irksome as to be forced (wearing a polite smile, rapidly souring to a grimace) to listen to someone's tirade, rant, or polemic against "today's English." "No one knows how to speak the King's English anymore," they say (ignoring more than two hundred years of language democracy). They complain about grammar (or if writing or chatting online, usually "grammer"); they complain about spelling; they complain about pronunciation (usually "accent"); they complain about sunspots (no, wait, that's something else)—you get the idea. And, even more irritating, I'm expected to grab their bright banner and run with it. "Language changes!" I say brightly. "Did you know that *nice* used to mean 'stupid'?" Or else I sympathize: "Yes, quite terrible, but what can you do?"

Why don't I fall in with the ranters? Why am I not correcting the speech of those around me (however tempting it might be) and writing letters to the *Chicago Tribune,* seeing as how their writers are incapable of distinguishing *discreet* from *discrete*? It's not because I have a temperate and forgiving nature—for instance, I think that those who throw lit cigarette butts out of car windows should be shot, or, at the very least, set on fire—and it's not because I'm resigned to a future where our children and grandchildren communicate with grunts or exclusively by e-mail. I haven't joined in with the English-is-disintegrating polemicists for several very good reasons.

Perhaps the weakest reason not to spew corrections at every turn is that I am as certain as I can be that my English is not Fowler-perfect. Being a card-swiping member of the electronic age (*q.v.* MTV generation, Generation X), I know that some of the finer subtleties escape me. I think I know the rules, it's just that they just don't fire all the time. It may be cowardice, but the easiest way to put your own utterances under intense scrutiny is to toss off a thoughtless public correction of someone else's. Call it McKean's Law: Any correction of the speech or writing of others will contain at least one grammatical, spelling, or typographical error.

Another reason not to go around citing language offenders, at least out loud, is pragmatic. Bluntly: Some prisoners can be rehabilitated, and some cannot. If you believe that the people you have the itch to correct really *want* to know their errors and learn from them, go ahead. If not, you're risking a punch in the nose or worse. (Maybe this is not a problem in the more lightly armed U.K., but here in the concealed-carry United States, I hesitate to tell strangers in line at Wal-Mart that they should say "fewer bullets" and not "less bullets.")

Caught up in the glow of your own erudition (everyone loves to catch a mistake!), it is easy to forget that no one loves to be caught in a mistake. Correcting someone's English, unless they have specifically asked you to, can be insulting. (N.B., I hereby give all *Verbatim* readers license to correct me at any time, by phone, mail, e-mail, or in person.) Your correction implies (however rightly) that they are stupid, uneducated, or, at the very least, careless. Unless you intend to insult your correctee, such personal corrections—or even minor corrections in print—should be used very sparingly. It's a matter both of politeness and Do-As-You-Would-Be-Done-By.

Such corrections (although we don't talk about this too much in the United States, outside of a few small-circulation magazines) smack of elitism and classism. We're big believers of the perfectibility of persons here in the New World, and we don't like to admit that some may be handicapped by their socioeconomic circumstances, education level, or even their natural gifts. But when these corrections are made, allowances are seldom made for these disadvantages, since we "know" that everyone has an equal chance to pull their own language up by its bootstraps. It's better to stop a minute and think of the circumstances of the speaker or writer before butting in with an "Excuse me . . ." or running for notepaper and a stamped envelope.

Now, I know that *Verbatim* readers, being a polite and mannerly bunch, don't go around correcting total strangers (or even, for the most part, their own relatives), and neither do they fire off letters to the newspaper and popular magazines unless the entire meaning of a statement is changed or unclear because of a misusage. And certainly *Verbatim* readers don't make a point of criticizing people for entirely discredited usage shibboleths, such as the fatal sentence-ending preposition or the dreaded split infinitive. (Just wanted to make that perfectly clear.) *Verbatim* readers merely clip the most hilarious misusages, giggling quietly, and slip them in an envelope to me, to enliven *Verbatim* with SIC! SIC! SIC!s.

Perhaps the most important reason to restrain rampant criticism is because (and it has taken me a long time to accept this) I like that "bad English" exists.

I don't especially like hearing most of it, and I don't especially like reading most of it, and I especially don't like being guilty of producing any of it, but how boring would reading, viewing, and listening be without it? A tedious flat sameness, going on forever. You might as well be reading traffic signs, listening to a radio weather report. "Bad English," including under that broad heading so much of the regional, dialectal, and the speaker's own quirks, gives us so much more to go on than the textbook "good English" held up as the ideal to emulate. All bad-English speakers are bad in their own ways, but the vast majority of good-English speakers, because of limited vocabulary, for the most part, are good in the same way.

Also, most importantly, if it weren't for bad English (as the song goes), there soon wouldn't be any English at all. Bad

English, with all its misusages, mispronunciations, and outright errors, is the cauldron where the new is formed. Every word in English, except perhaps the most obsolete words that were left by the wayside long ago (now tourist traps, for the most part), has been changed by the mouths and pens of those speakers and writers who thought the word was fit to use. The vast web of English has broken strands here and there, but the whole remains strong, and in the meantime the broken strands are being woven back in—not repaired, never repaired, but rewoven.

Insisting on this particular era's "good English" exclusively, for everyone, for ever and ever, amen, would be stultifying and ultimately the death of the language. Sure, we can put fingers in dikes and shore up the bits of the walls that are most precious to us, but it's a hopeless and ultimately unrewarding task. Better to insist on clarity of thought and fight bad style than to fight little battles over bad usage.

SIC! SIC! SIC!

"Naples City Councilmen on Thursday adopted a . . . budget . . . but only after a public hearing in which much rabble was raised. . . ." From the *Naples Daily News,* 16 September 1983. Submitted by Lynn G. Lee, Naples, Florida.

Noun Overuse Phenomenon Article

BRUCE D. PRICE

Have you noticed a new *clunk-clunk* sound in the English language? Phrases such as "patient starter package" for *sample*? "Drug dosage forms" for *pills*? "Health cause" for *sick-*

ness? "Increased labor market participation rates" for *more people working*? This overuse of nouns is a modern trend that has pretty much escaped notice. To put the phenomenon on the intellectual map, I've dubbed it Nounspeak. The allusion is to Newspeak, about which Orwell wrote: "Newspeak was designed not to extend but to diminish the range of thought."

The Germanic languages like to pile up nouns. The Romance languages virtually forbid it. The English lexicon, betwixt and between, has traditionally accepted nouns in pairs with no hesitation. Examples are *book store, love affair, deer crossing,* and *state university.* Three nouns in a row used to be the outer limit and is a rare find in English prose before 1950. Now we daily encounter excrescences like "growth trend pattern" and "consumer price inflation" and even, hold your hat, "U.S. Air Force aircraft fuel systems equipment mechanics course" (from a Long Island newspaper).

Nounspeak is not grammatically wrong. We're concerned here with good style and with clarity and with avoiding problems for ourselves. *Space ship* is not a problem. *Space ship booster rocket* is the beginning of a problem. Most writers would, I trust, try to find alternate phrasing. But more and more we're having to accept decided problems such as *space ship booster rocket ignition system.* I suggest it's time to back up.

Scientists love Nounspeak. Anyone hearing them joust with their mother tongue must lament the change of standards since the Royal Society took as its motto *Nulla in Verba* more than three hundred years ago. Bureaucrats also love Nounspeak. Certainly the military loves Nounspeak. Would you ever guess that *target neutralization requirement* means 'the desired dead'? Or that *airplane delivery systems* might mean 'bombs'? Here's the National Academy of Science discussing military research: "Work has included development of empirical and rational

formulae for aerosal survival, formulae for predicting human lethal dose, and quantification of disease severity." (They're talking
about germs and poisonous gases.) And most of all the "soft sciences," such as psychology, education, sociology, and anthropology, love Nounspeak. A prize of some sardonic sort ought to
be presented to the behaviorist quoted in *Science Digest* who concocted *place for goods purchase.* It takes a minute to realize he's
thinking about 'stores.' The pattern is that people with little to
say turn to Nounspeak for pompous packaging, while those with
something unsavory to say find friendly camouflage in Nounspeak's abstractions and opacities. Who can forget *body count*?

At a glance Nounspeak might seem a natural development, like
the disappearance of the distinction between *who* and *whom* or
the evolution of a slang word into polite speech, but it is only
natural in the sense that foods such as breakfast cereals are a
"natural" development in modern society. Normally, a language
is shaped by the intellectual writers at the top and the great mass
of not-so-intellectual speakers at the bottom. But Nounspeak,
like breakfast cereals, is largely an artificial imposition, perpetrated by that growing multitude in the middle with from one to
four years of college. Not at all restrained by any sense of edu-
cational deficiency, this multitude talks to dazzle its own ears.
And to hell with Sir Quiller-Couch.

People aren't *broke* anymore. They have a *money problem* or
a *bad money situation. Discontented consumers* (real people) have
become *consumer discontent* (an abstraction, like so much Nounspeak). Weathermen don't predict *rain* anymore: now it's *precip-
itation activity.*

There may be a metaphysical dimension here. People often
have the sensation that they aren't being heard. So they keep
lumping noun on noun, as though by saying the same thing two
or three times, they'll be understood across the existential void.

Can you think of another reason for *Newsweek*'s startling duo *inlet cove*? (One can hardly find two more perfectly synonymous words in English. So why use both?) And *rain postponement dates* recently appeared on a sign in the subway in New York City.

Nouns must comfort with their solidity. They seem to pin matters down, to freeze life, to ward off future shock. But it's largely a sham. Life is flux and process. Verbs are truer to this constant change; and expert stylists have always recommended reliance on verbs. Listen to Gertrude Stein railing against nouns in "Lectures in America": "Things once they are named the name does not go on doing anything to them and so why write in nouns. . . . And therefore and I say it again more and more one does not use nouns. . . . Nouns as I say even by definition are completely not interesting." And Gertrude Stein was speaking about nouns in meager doses, not the excesses here labeled Nounspeak.

Poor Gertrude Stein. Alive today, she could not read the front page of any newspaper in the country without finding a surfeit of nouns, many of which can be cut entirely with *no* loss of sense. The favorite freeloaders are *area, situation,* and *problem.* One of Nounspeak's major linguistic discoveries is that you can attach any one, or even two, of these words to any other English word with no change of meaning. The gain in precision is illusory but the loss of clarity is real. "What's your problem area, Jack?"

Nounspeak shares common ground with jargon and bombast and gobbledygook and prolixity and confusion of whatever sort. But Nounspeak does seem to be the most sharply defined of these phenomena and may be the more interesting in exhibiting its own rudimentary "grammar," the devices by which perfectly fine English is "translated" into Nounspeak. (One cannot help thinking of Nounspeak as being almost a dialect of English.)

The first and most obvious of these devices is: Never use one noun when two (or three) can be rummaged up. Contemplate these words: *subject, interim, spending, transition, passengers,* and *contract.* Is not each a sturdy soldier of a word, wholly equipped by itself, and ready for any mission? But these excellent nouns split in Nounspeak to become: *subject matter, interim period, spending total, transition period, passenger volume,* and *contract agreement.* (All examples are from the press.) Note that nothing is added except the extra syllables. Like germs, one noun splits into two, and then one of those can become two again.

A second technique for subverting English into Nounspeak requires changing strong, aggressive verbs into weak nouns. *We control pests* in English. *We accomplish pest control* is Nounspeak. It's hard to see any good reason for this device. But many variations can be found in the press. The idea is to smash those verbs. Mothers don't *feed* infants, they practice *infant feeding*; teachers don't *educate* anymore, they work at *student education*; politicians don't *appeal to voters,* they have *voter appeal*; readers don't *respond,* they show *reader response.*

A third technique diminishes clarity by disdaining the possessive *'s* or *of.* "Nixon had this to say about the Agnew criticism...." Heard on the radio, there is no way of knowing whether Agnew was criticized or criticizing, except by context. Paradigmatically, "B's A" and "A of B" are being changed wholesale into "BA." Thus *rate of change,* which is smooth and flows easily into the brain, becomes *change rate,* which is *clunk-clunk* English and hard to digest.

In the years ahead English will depend much more heavily on nouns than Gertrude Stein might like. But it's reasonable to ask that our writers and editors steer us away from Nounspeak's worst excesses. We'll know the tide has turned when the IRS whittles its *Tax Schedule Rate Chart* down to *Tax Rate Chart,* then to the very sensible *Tax Chart,* then—unlikely victory—to *Taxes,* which is what they were trying to say all along.

Epistola

Price's "Noun Overuse Phenomenon Article" is both welcome and telling. Perhaps its appeal is primarily to the poet, but everyone could profit from it. There are some who might say that it is not nouns so much which are at fault as the failure to use more evocative ones, but that is skirting this issue.

Noun overuse is the result of several invidious modern trends. One is the direct result of teaching adjective avoidance in our English classes. Another is that *not* stringing nouns together takes time, that modern commodity which is so poorly rationed. Good writing calls us to go back over what we have written, crossing out the dross, replacing it with a more acceptable style.

Perhaps we use fewer verbs because we do less. Sitting in an office all day and before a TV set all evening is scarcely conducive to thinking in terms of dynamically active verbs. But of course it is the use of verbs that is the allopathic antidote to excessive noun usage. Our overemphasis on commerce and technology slides us into dreary noncreativity. Even to use adjectives properly requires training in English usage. It's easier to run nouns together than to worry about choosing between difficult alternatives such as, say, *continuous* and *continual.*

For it isn't only more verbs and adjectives that we crave. We should sweat more over grammar. We should explore more carefully all the other parts of speech, and we should cease to neglect our idioms.

If only we were to connect the noun strings with hyphens,

that would be a start. Our writing might not suddenly become clearer, but it would draw attention to noun overuse with an end to facilitating its excision.

Good sentences thrum to an inner rhythm. They don't just galumph along any old way. They describe real processes. They don't list unwieldy impedimenta over which we stumble as over a marine's obstacle course. As Price points out, that is what makes sentences go *clunk-clunk.* We should remember Poe's "Unity of effect" which means that the writer chooses only words that contribute to his whole thought, that enhance that thought or at least that do not distract us from its purpose.

This, however, requires discernment and word-sense, so maybe not everyone should be entitled to call himself a writer simply because he can link words to one another the way a monkey might string bunches of grotesquely unmatched beads together.

As usual, *poeta nascitur non fit.* Why not put all our starving poets to work rewriting the garbage turned out by the whole politics-advertising-academia-technology-military-industry-institution-corpus?

ED REHMUS
San Francisco, California

SIC! SIC! SIC!

"2 DIE IN APPARENT MURDER-SUICIDE. . . . The bodies were found by each other in a house on Shamrock Avenue, said Johnny Shelton of the Surry County Emergency Medical Services, and each had been shot in the chest. . . . Neighbors told investigators that Hawks and Mrs. Jones had been dating since Mrs. Jones' divorce a year ago, but that, following an argument earlier this week, she had told him to pack his thing and leave." From *Winston-Salem Journal,* 7 October 1983. Submitted by W. D. Sanders, Winston-Salem, North Carolina.

Pleonasties

HAROLD J. ELLNER, M.D.

It was minus twenty degrees below zero," tautologically reported the ham operator from Minnesota. Shall we accept this as merely a pleonasm (unnecessary repetition) or nitpickingly consider it a double negative and record the temperature at plus twenty?

Pleonasms pervade every aspect of communication. At times they are intentionally used for emphasis, at times for verbosity, and on other occasions are just honest mistakes. (In that the author is a urologist and a sports fan, note of many of these pleonasms has been made in these areas. They are, however, everywhere.)

It is time to institute the Pleonastic Putdown ("pleonasty") to rebel, as would Edwin Newman and John Simon, against verbosity. It will not earn the putter-down (pleonasticist) much cordiality, but it may help defend the language.

W. C. Fields, who objected to almost everyone, was reputed to have set the style when he refused to work for a studio he thought to be Jewish-run. "No," he was told, "the president is Roman Catholic." "That's the worst kind," rejoined Fields. Prejudicial, yes, but a decisive pleonasty.

[As] Washington's new governor, John Spellman, not above an occasional pleonasm, issued certificates of gratitude to his supporters, ". . . in appreciation and recognition of your significant contribution to my successful election." One wonders what constitutes an unsuccessful election. Shakespeare's Falstaff, in *Henry IV,* referred to "an 'Ebrew Jew," undoubtedly for emphasis.

Here, then, are some pleonasms heard, recorded, and furnished with a suggested pleonasty for each:

Medical

"This room costs $200 to the patient." *To whom else?*

"A positive culture was obtained for Strep." *If Strep was there, it was positive.*

"Scrotal masses in the male." *Yes, they predominate in the male.*

"These tests, when performed, gave normal results." *More so than if they were not performed.*

"The urodynamics of urology." *That's the nicest kind in the whole specialty.*

"Then, appropriate treatment was instituted." *Better than inappropriate any time.*

"A diagnostic X-ray film." *Are any otherwise?*

"The patient had a complicated clinical course." *It would have been worse if nonclinical.*

"Clinically, the pain diminished." *That's the best way for it to happen.*

"He'd undergone a previous prostatectomy." *Most are.*

"It has been shown in the past by Paulsen et al. . . ." *A large number of his findings were in the past. . . .*

"A prior surgeon did it." *Certainly not a future one.*

"He claimed marked subjective improvement." *If he claimed it, it had to be subjective.*

"Under appropriate anesthesia." *We have no inappropriate anesthesiologist.*

"There was still persistent disease." *Still disease? Persistent disease? Take your choice.*

"He gained 14 pounds in weight." *Certainly not in height or in British currency.*

"It was a totally complete excision." *That's how I want my total (or complete) one.*

"Skin rash." *Bad place for one.*

"Dr. James Kildare, M.D." *Which shall we drop, the Dr. or the M.D.?*

"The male prostate gland." *Needless to say . . .*

"Past history." *Ah, yes, much history is found there.*

"His motor movements weren't good." *But wait until you see his sensory ones.*

"Liver cirrhosis." *The worst kind!*

"Some few specimens." *Which shall we drop, some or few?*

"Mentally insane." *Far worse than physically . . .*

Sports

"He made twenty in a row without a miss." *Twenty in a row would be hard to swing with one or two misses.*

(Cosell): "Why do you persist in keeping on playing?" *Well, Howard, I persist in playing because I want to keep on playing.*

"In good field position." *Are there any non-field positions in this game?*

"Face mask." *I'm glad you explained that; I was thinking "elbow mask."*

"He'll try a 44-yard field-goal attempt." *What's wrong with the reverse? Can he attempt a try?*

"This is their first offensive possession" also, "first offensive play from scrimmage." *The defensive team does not possess. Nor does it run any plays from scrimmage.*

"They got a whole full minute time-out." *There are full minutes and full minutes. Give me a whole full minute any time.*

"Five seconds on the clock." *Anywhere else?*

"Deflected away." *Where else can it be deflected?*

"He was awarded the game ball." *As distinguished from the ungame ball?*

General

"To recoil back." *It's the forward recoiling that's dangerous.*

"The ethnic background of the people." *Could it be of anyone else?*

"Past experience has shown . . ." *That's the most enriching kind.*

"The end result." *How final can you get?*

"The sight was pleasing to the eye." *And to none of the other senses.*

"Mental anguish." *That's anguish in the extreme.*

"Last and final curtain call." *Superseding the first and final?*

"Affix the necessary postage." *The post office will not deliver letters faster with the unnecessary postage.*

"The basic fundamentals." *That's really fundamental.*

"A justice court." *Some dispense other services.*

"He's a human person." *Glad to know!*

"Positive affirmative action." *The negative type never worked.*

(Kissinger): "A hypothetical situation that doesn't exist . . ." *Give me one that exists every time.*

"An unexpected surprise." *And how do you like your surprises?*

"To successfully pass an exam." *Only our best students pass them that way.*

"He kicked his feet." *In contrast to other appendages?*

"A crooked racketeer." *Give me the honest kind.*

"A visual sight." *Like an auditory hearing?*

"Add on." *As opposed to subtract off?*

"From whence." *Whence is enough!*

"You may purchase the property from the seller." *He'd be the logical choice.*

"A perverted sex-offender." *The nonperverted type is not quite as dangerous.*

"Punctured a hole in . . ." *The work, obviously, of a crude puncturer.*

"Orbited around." *Drop around any time.*

"A new innovation." *Enough of those old ones!*

"A new recruit." *Veteran recruits are in short supply.*

"Foot pedal." *Is that like a hand handle?*

"A short three-letter word." *The long kind will never do.*

"Cancel it out." *Anyway, don't include it in.*

"A photographic picture." *Does this differ from a photograph?*

"Therapy treatments." *What's wrong with plain old therapy? Or treatments?*

"First introduction." *Does this differ from an introduction?*

Just Plain Bad English

"The average age was twenty-nine years old."

"Removed out."

"Thank you for joining with us."

"Killed him dead."

"Blood loss was two units of blood."

There is little question that an undercurrent of sarcasm exists (a current that "runs" is a pleonasm) in pleonasties. They should be uttered smilingly and jocularly in the "spoonful of sugar" spirit. Although imperfect, pleonasties constitute a mechanism of reaction unavailable to recipients of the meaningless "Have a nice day" or of discourses heavily laced with "y'know" and "hopefully."

What Did You Call Me? Names and Naming

Names have been with us since those prelapsarian days, but, like dictionaries, their very ubiquity makes them overlooked as subjects of study. Not so for *Verbatim*, which has paid special attention to names both proper and improper. Names on the globe, names in the city, names you'd rather not have, and names to make game of have all been treated here.

Toad Sucks, Akansas

Unraveling the American Place-Name Cover

FRANK R. ABATE

*There is no part of the world where nomenclature
is so rich, poetical, humorous and picturesque
as the United States of America.*

—Robert Louis Stevenson
Across the Plains (1892)

The fascination of American place names—their style and flair and what they reveal about the land and its inhabitants—has captivated writers, scholars, and other observers for more than 150 years. The evaluation of Stevenson, from a collection of essays on his travels across America, is not unusual. Stevenson, a native Scot, had traveled widely through Europe, the United

States, and the South Seas, so he speaks with some experience and perspective. Other notables who have praised American place names include Washington Irving (in an essay written in 1839), Walt Whitman, and Stephen Vincent Benét. The qualities most frequently commented on, perhaps, are originality, uniqueness, and sound. Consider the following categories of American place names, selected from the *Omni Gazetteer of the United States of America*:

Bizarre
Cheesequake, New Jersey
Jot 'Em Down, Texas
Knockemstiff, Ohio
Attaway, South Carolina
Uneedus, Louisiana
Unthanks, Virginia
Toad Suck, Arkansas
Hump Tulips, Washington
Eek, Alaska
Idiotville, Oregon
Who'd A Thought It, Alabama
Zzyzx, California

Indecorous
Sugartit and Beaverlick, Kentucky
Crapo, Maryland
Superior Bottom, West Virginia
Suck Lick Run (stream in West Virginia)
Blue Ball (Arkansas and Ohio)
Pee Pee, Ohio
Shittim Gulch, Washington

Unimaginative
141 U.S. municipalities are named Fairview
   (43 different states).
There are 47 Jackson Townships in Indiana alone.
1,365 streams are named Mill Creek.

Fanciful
Zook Spur, Iowa
Tyewhoppety, Oklahoma
Zu Zu, Tennessee
Tizzle Flats, Virginia
Utsaladdy, Washington

Sic! Sic! Sic!
Smartt, Tennessee
Erratta, Alabama
Embarras River, Illinois

Frontier Americana
Lickskillet, Ohio and Tennessee
Gnaw Bone, Indiana
Turkey Scratch, Arkansas
Dunmovin, California
Rawhide, Mississippi
Cut and Shoot, Texas
Hoot and Holler Crossing, Texas
Horse Thief, Arizona
Jackass Flats, Nevada
Hell and Gone Creek, Oklahoma

American place names reveal the national character, as well as
history and heritage. In addition, significant contributions have

come from many Indian languages and dialects, as well as Spanish, French, and British sources.

It was in the 1920s that serious scholarship on American place names, characterized (unlike most earlier work) by thoroughness, objectivity, and linguistic training, began to be published on a regular basis. Among the scholarly pioneers was George R. Stewart, whose considered reflections are collected in standard works entitled *Names on the Land* (1945, revised 1958 and 1967) and *American Place-Names* (1970). Prof. Allen Walker Read, whose distinguished career now spans seven decades, has contributed solid yet always thoroughly enjoyable papers, and in addition has given us the handy phrase "place-name cover" to describe how place names indeed blanket the country with richness, color, and texture. Other notables in this necessarily brief catalogue of American toponymists include Henry Gannett, working around the turn of the century, who compiled several state gazetteers and a still influential study on the origin of U.S. place names; H. L. Mencken, with several seminal chapters in his *American Language* (1936); and Kelsie Harder, whose *Illustrated Dictionary of Place Names: United States and Canada* (1976) remains the most reliable resource for place-name origins. A full record of work in this field can be found in bibliographies compiled since 1948 under the names Sealock, Seely, and Powell (the latest edition being *Bibliography of Place-Name Literature: United States and Canada, Third Edition,* 1982), supplemented periodically in the pages of *Names,* the quarterly journal of the American Name Society.

Toponymy is remarkable not only for the hundreds of talented contributors who have expanded the scholarship in recent decades, but also because it is not a formal academic discipline, at least not in the United States. There are no departments of toponymy, or even of onomastics that I know of, and no degrees are awarded in these fields. (Whether this is also true of other countries I cannot say. I have read that toponymy, gazetteers, and place-name surveys receive more formal attention in the U.K. and Europe.) American toponymy is carried on by people of all academic disciplines, and from many walks of life. With academia's standard rewards of promotion and tenure not as readily accruing in this work, the study of American place names is by and large in the hands of true lovers of the subject (amateurs in the etymological sense, and dilettantes). What they say and write I have found to be characteristically stimulating and rewarding, not plagued by the turgidity that so often seems to be the norm in scholarly papers.

Place names became an official concern of the U.S. government in 1890. Confusion had reigned over mining claims, land surveys, assignment of post-office names, and exploration reports, and this created havoc and needless expense in bureaucracy, particularly in the government mapping agencies such as the U.S. Geological Survey (USGS), the Army Corps of Engineers, and various other branches of the Departments of Agriculture, Commerce, and Interior. In a move that, from a lexicographic standpoint, is decidedly un-American, the government set up an official board to rule on and standardize the use of place names, both domestic and foreign. The United States Board on Geographic Names was established by an executive order of President Benjamin Harrison in September 1890, and has been active ever since, publishing its decisions and issuing official gazetteers. This may be the only example in which an aspect of the linguistic practice of Americans has been regulated by government fiat.

On the other hand, it is largely because of this unusual intrusion of government that American toponymy has flourished as a field of study. The U.S. Board on Geographic Names has compiled and maintains a massive national database, the Geographic Names Information System (GNIS). This computer file lists more than one million place names of all kinds (plus hundreds of thousands of variant forms): cities and towns, lakes and rivers, mountains and valleys, even facilities such as schools, parks, and cemeteries. The names themselves, along with precise locational data and identification by type, have been painstakingly keyboarded into machine-readable form from the most detailed USGS topographic maps, the so-called 7.5-minute series. Drawn to a scale of 1:24,000, each 7.5-minute map sheet or quadrangle covers an area of 8.6 miles north-to-south by about 7 miles east-to-west (the east-to-west distance varies depending on location, since meridians of longitude radiate out from the poles and are farther apart nearer the equator). At this scale more than 50,000 map sheets are required to completely cover the forty-eight contiguous states. Since it was intended to establish a standard, the GNIS is very regular in format and is compiled and maintained according to carefully prepared procedures. This daunting task is overseen by the USGS, specifically the Branch of Domestic Names, now under the direction of Roger Payne. Less comprehensive government files are also maintained by the Bureau of the Census (listing about 60,000 populated places), and by the National Institute of Standards and Technology, formerly the Bureau of Standards (a compilation, complete with numerical coding, of some 190,000 populated places, locales, and neighborhoods of all sizes).

The work is by no means at an end. Experts, including Mr. Payne, have estimated that there are more than 3,500,000 current place names in the U.S. Consider this figure in light of the fact that the largest English dictionary—now out of print—had 600,000 or so entries, including many obsolete forms. The highest estimates of the size of the English lexicon number far less than the number of place names in the U.S. alone. Were it possible to record and identify all of the current place names (the Place Name

Survey of the United States, under the direction of the American Name Society, is attempting just this), still remaining would be hundreds of thousands of now inactive names, which are of no less importance to historians, genealogists, and the like. Full coverage would also require accurate pronunciations for each name, with sensitivity to local preferences (e.g., MAD-rid, New York, for *Madrid,* BER-lin, Connecticut, for *Berlin,* and PEER, South Dakota, for *Pierre*). It is perhaps understandable that those who undertake the creation of a complete record of American toponymy have chosen to deal with the estimated 3,000,000 named streets and highways across the land as a separate project.

Having had the opportunity to sift through so many American place names in a relatively short span, those of us who edited the *Omni Gazetteer* were particularly struck by the great diversity in American naming practices, and what it suggests about the various eras and cultures that were a part of the settlement of the country. In New England, for example, towns are the primary division of government below the state level. Most of the land area in the six New England states is within town boundaries, and is primarily administered by the town governments. New Englanders, even if they do not live in an urban area, can almost always tell you the name of the town that they live in. As the name *New England* might suggest, many of these town names were transplanted from the British Isles. Bristol, Cambridge, Chester, Durham, Essex, Hartford, Lincoln, Litchfield, Manchester, Marlboro(ugh), Milford, Oxford, Salisbury, Winchester, Windsor, and Woodstock are town names that occur in three or more New England states. Apart from these, names of Indian origin (Kennebunkport, Naugatuck, Scituate), honorifics (Amherst, Franklin), and biblical names (Canaan, Rehoboth, Hebron) account for much of the rest. As one looks elsewhere in the U.S., the preponderance of British borrowings diminishes, and the purely American inventions increase in proportion, as do Indian, Spanish, and French-based names. The well-documented Indian influence is widespread. Spanish names are particularly common in the areas of long-lasting Spanish colonial influence, especially California and the Southwest. French names, of course, are common in the Upper Midwest (where French explorers and missionaries, and French-speaking trappers, left their mark), in states bordering Quebec, and in Louisiana.

The differing forms of administrative divisions in the states is also revealed in naming practices. For example, county government, significant in most of the U.S., is relatively unimportant in New England. In fact, Connecticut and Rhode Island have abolished county government altogether, and in those states the former county boundaries merely furnish a convenient way in which people can refer to a regional group of towns. But as one travels west and south in the U.S., counties are politically vital, and towns, in the New England sense, at least, almost nonexistent. (New England–style "towns" are found to some extent in New York, New Jersey, Pennsylvania, and Wisconsin.) In many rural areas west of the Mississippi, where counties can be as big as New England states and cities are few and far between, people do not associate closely with a city, town, village, or any other such entity below the county level. Mail, of course, comes to a post office that handles rural route delivery, but those who receive such mail may not live in the place with the post office, and hence do not immediately associate with it. When asked where they live, such folks are more likely to say their county, then give a reference point and directions: "Our place is ten miles north of Baxter, off Highway 102, then left two miles on Route 47." So despite more than 200,000 populated place names recorded in the *Omni*

Gazetteer, there are still many areas of the country where the place-name cover is thin. Local informants, we hope, will allow us to correct and expand on the entries compiled so far.

Most of the examples above have been populated places, as these names tend to be more familiar to a broader audience. So we have not examined the bulk of the place-name cover, which is in the form of names for natural features. But perhaps *Verbatim* readers can more readily allow the author the convenience of such specialization when they consider the issue from the viewpoint of a toponymist. As those who work in the field all too soon come to realize, most of the names have yet to be recorded, much less described; the greater burden lies ahead. With time and additional resources we might begin to see the light at the end of the tunnel, perhaps in ten to fifteen years. All the while, of course, just as with all aspects of language, new names are coming into being, others passing out of use, each reflecting a bit of history or culture. Taken together, American place names are a unique primary source, a record of our cultural memory. The publication of that part of the record we do have, however imperfect, will still, we hope, give new impetus to this enlightening, often fascinating study by providing a foundation on which to build.

Unofficial Sectional City Names

FREDERIC G. CASSIDY

Within almost any city or large town we find names that longtime residents know and use regularly, though they are not given on maps or in guidebooks. American cities distinguish subsections name-wise by compass direction, by topography, by occupational, ethnic, and other connections. Some are commonplace, repeated from city to city; other are lively, imaginative, and reveal people's attitudes. I remember a Madison, Wisconsin, bus driver announcing, as we approached the crossing of Park and Regent Streets, "Spaghetti Corners!"—and indeed there were two restaurants and two Italian grocery stores at that intersection.

Some of these nicknames are regionally distinctive. From the field collections of the *Dictionary of American Regional English* (1002 questionnaires completed in fifty states) a large body of responses has been compiled from many kinds of local informants, on which basis one can generalize with reasonable certainty.

Question 1124 was "Names or nicknames for the part of a town where the well-off people live," and the complementary question 1125 was "Names or nicknames for the part of a town where the poorer people, special groups, or foreign groups live." To judge by frequency of responses alone, the chief dividing line in any American town or city is the railroad track—a line that separates residents economically and socially as well as geographically. The well-off people live on *this side* or *the right side of the (railroad) tracks* (61 responses); the poorer people live *on the wrong side* or *across* or *on the other side of the (railroad) tracks* (456 responses). Not only were the tracks mentioned more than seven times as often for the second question as for the first, but there were four times as many variant forms. The nucleus is *the tracks* or *the railroad tracks*; variations come in the preceding words: usually *the wrong side*, or *the other side*, but also *the opposite*, or *south side of the tracks*, as well as *across, below, by, over, beyond, down by, down across*, and *down below the tracks*. The variations themselves are of little importance; the fact that more than half our informants in fifty states used one of these phrases is certainly significant. Social geographers are aware of this, of course; it is interesting to find concurrent evidence from a linguistic survey.

Returning to the first question, no single term for the well-off residential area stood out over all others, but there were 51 responses for *Nob Hill* and its variants. This name became famous in San Francisco and has spread for over a century all over the country—to New York, Pennsylvania, North Carolina, Mississippi, South Dakota, and Arizona in the symbolic sense (not to mention actual borrowings of the name). Nob, an imported English slang abbreviation for *nobility,* suits "the well-off people" and the sense of the question. But what person living *under* the hill could resist turning *nob* into *snob*? Exactly the same number of informants (51) gave us *Snob Hill* and its variants *Snob's Knob, Snob's Alley, Snob's Row, Snob's Slough, Snob's Point,* and *Snubsville.* We have to get our social revenge where and as we can.

As indicative of a probably worldwide pattern of wealthier people building on high ground, the generic *hill* appears in many other names. Among the commoner ones are: *Mortgage Hill* (36 responses), betraying sardonic envy; *Pill Hill* (6 responses) and *Doctor's Row* (3), where rich doctors live; *Society Hill* (4); *Quality Hill* (3); *Millionaire Hill* (2); *Aristocracy Hill* (1); or merely *The Hill* (21 responses). One name puzzlingly breaks the pattern, yet it is certainly genuine since four people from Michigan and Illinois responded with it: *Piety Hill.* It could be ironic, implying that the rich consider their wealth as an earned reward from heaven. Finally, *Sugar Hill* (6 responses) apparently uses the slang sense of sugar as money, and *Yankee Hill* (from Wisconsin) shows the foreign-born settler's awareness that the Easterner came first and got the choice residential ground.

The sardonic force of *mortgage* carries beyond *Mortgage Hill* to a whole series of variants: *Mortgage Row* (15 responses). *Mortgage Lane* (3), *Mortgageville* (2), *Mortgage Heights* (2), *Mortgage*

Ward (2), *Mortgage Manor* (2), and one each of *Mortgage Alley, Flat, Hollow, Knob,* and *Mesa.* No doubt the user of these names consoles himself by knowing *he* won't have to pay that mortgage. (His own is certainly much smaller!)

Millionaire also produces a series of variants besides *hill*: *Millionaire(s) Row* (10 responses); and *Millionaire Avenue, Lane, Ridge,* and *Street* (1 each).

Aristocracy or *Aristocratic Hill* lends itself to punning distortions in *Ritzocrats* (New York), *Roostercrats* (Ohio), and *Aristocrooked* (Pennsylvania)—there's that cynicism again.

An interesting pair are *Striver's Row* and *Struggle Hill*, somewhat on the same order as the *mortgage* names. I read them as suggesting that the striving and struggling are overdone: the namer seems to feel these people are too obvious at getting themselves up in the world.

Next after *hill* the commonest generic is *row* (several examples already given). The most frequent response of this type was *Silk Stocking Row* (29 informants), with its variants *Silk Stocking Avenue* (11), *Silk Stocking District* (6), *Silk Stocking Section* (3), *Silk Stocking Ward* (2), and one each of *Silk Stocking Area, Hill, Neighborhood, Road,* and *Street.* The metaphor is interesting— it refers to women rather than men, and it may be less sardonic than some others. With the replacement more than 30 years ago of silk hose by nylon and their accessibility to women of almost any income level, the *Silk Stocking* names now seem a bit dated. Nevertheless, they must have been widespread and firmly established to have turned up in 54 of our responses.

Another widespread name, *The Gold Coast*, dates in this sense only from 1920 (so says Mathews' *Dictionary of Americanisms*), but we had it in 25 responses, chiefly from the upper Mississippi Valley.

The less common names include *Bank Row* or *Bankers'*

Avenue, and, with a touch of satire, *Big-Shots' Street* or *Town,* *Big-Bug Hill* and *Big-Man's Street.* Three scattered responses for the *Bon Ton Area, Section,* or *Part* of town seem definitely old-fashioned. *Cadillac Alley* shows an interesting clash of connotations. *Cotillion Corner* (from South Carolina) goes back to the antebellum world—perhaps with some nostalgia.

If the better-off people live on high ground, the poorer ones are on low ground, down by the tracks. Railroads were built on low ground for good engineering reasons, but the associated noise, dirt, smells, and low-level damp made their neighborhoods less than ideal for dwelling. However, they were cheaper and usually handy to water, so people who came to build the railroad often stayed. Among common responses were *Shantytown* (55), *Shack Town* (4), *Shanty Row* (2). Railroad tracks often followed river valleys, hence the area names *Down by the River, Over the River, Across the Creek, Across the Ditch*; similarly, the *Other Side of the Bridge, Creek, Railroad,* and *River.* One name recalls a popular song of the 1920s: "Down by the Vinegar Works" (or "Winegar Woiks"). *Lower Town* and *Lowville* bear out the same theme.

Nobody likes slums or can remain unaware of them. Many condemn them directly or indirectly with such names as *Poverty Row* (3), *Poverty Flats, Hill, Park,* and *Peak* (2 each); *Hungry Hill, Hollow,* and *Street* (1 each), *Needmore* and *Lickskillet* (1 each). Of similar type are *Ragtown* (3), *the Jungle* (2), *Scrabble Town, Scuttle Town, Scum Hollow, Rum Row, Battle Row,* and *Brickbat Ridge* (1 each). Others suggest unpleasantness by association with animals, the pig, with proverbial proclivity for mud or dirt, being the favored unfavorite. Variants were *Pig Alley* (3), *Pig Town, Pigsville, Pigtail Alley,* and *Piggy Hollow* (1 each). Then there were *Bedbug Row, Buzzard's Row, Rat Row, Skunk Road,* and *Chinch Hill* (1 each). Though *Dogpatch* was mentioned only once, *Dogtown* was mentioned 6 times. *Cigar-box Row* suggests the flimsiness of the houses; *Tin Can Alley, Blood Alley,* and *Cesspool Heights* are self-explanatory.

Others suggest that these sections are not urban at all but intolerably countrified: *Frogtown* and *Goosetown* (3 responses each), *Gooseville, Coontown,* and *Coon Bottom* (1 each). These refer to animals. *Briar Town* refers to plants, and cheap foods and humble living are suggested by *Hominy Hill, Potato Row, Cabbage Town,* and *Sauerkraut Hill.* Names from backcountry types who are looked down on by city people include *Hillbilly Heights, Hillbilly Section,* and *Conch Town.* I do not know what to make of *Doodleville,* but it is certainly not favorable.

A large number of names simply refer to the foreigners settled in a section together. Though never complimentary, some are at least neutral. To this type, in descending order of frequency, belong *Mexican Town* (6), *Chinatown* (5), *Irish Town* (4), *Dutch Town* (3), *French Town* (3), *German Town* (2), *Russia Town* (2), *Finn Town* (2), *Swede Town* (2), *Swede Alley* (1), *English Town* (1). A number of others are more or less unfavorable: *Polack Town* (4), *Jig Town* (4), *Jew Town* (2), *Wop Town* (2), *Wop Flat, Dago Town,* and *Dago Center* (1 each). One type of name interesting for its form begins with *Little* and then names the nationality or ethnic group: *Little Italy* (15), *Little Mexico* (3), *Little Africa* (2), *Little Canada* (in Massachusetts), *Little Chicago* (in Ohio), *Little Cuba* (in Indiana), *Little Puerto Rico* (in New York), and *Little Tijuana* (in California). These fall somewhere between neutral and unfavorable—they are certainly not strongly unfavorable. And they are a distinctively American type.

The most conspicuously separate or segregated group of people in American cities—no doubt because of their numbers and racial distinctiveness which make them slower to assimilate—are the African Americans. I regret to report it—but it is the fact—that of ethnic nicknames, by far the most frequent response we had was *Niggertown* (34), and after that *Nigger Quarters* and *Section* (4 each) and *Nigger Hill* (3). Avoiding the objectionable word, the next in frequency were *Colored Section* (8), *Colored Town* (5), *Colored Settlement* (2), *Colored Quarters* and *Valley* (1 each). Similarly, *Negro Quarters* and *Section* (2 each) and *Negro Town* (1). Those using the word *black* were: *Black Bottom* (3), *Black Belt* (2), and *Blacktown* (1). The geographic aspects of this are as one would expect: names using the specific *nigger* were concentrated in the South Atlantic and Southeastern states and west to Texas; they diminish as one goes north and west, and we received no responses using this specific from New England, the Northwest, or the West Coast. The occasions for its use there are fewer, and our evidence shows that the term is now avoided by whites who know it is considered insulting by African Americans—except when African Americans use it among themselves, where it may be said in friendly joking without being taken as offensive.

Do any of these nicknames for sections of towns or cities pattern geographically? The answer is definitely *yes*. To mention only the most striking, the *Nob Hill* type, for obvious historical reasons, is strong in California and Oregon; otherwise it was found chiefly in the North and North Midland regions, hardly on the Atlantic Coast or Gulf states. On the other hand, the *Snob Hill* type, of the same frequency, is spread more generally except in the Inner South. The *Mortgage Hill* type is found, in contrast, especially on the Atlantic Coast and in the North, with no instances at all from California or the Southwest. Could this be significant? Don't they know what mortgages are? The *Silk Stocking Row* type is also clearly regional, being concentrated in the Southeast and Mississippi Valley, and hardly found at all in the Pacific states. That it is a rather older term is confirmed by the fact that responses came preponderantly from old informants

(35 old, 18 middle-aged, 3 young). The informants' education may have brought the term to them, as a fairly large proportion were college educated. At any rate, while not obsolescent, the *Silk Stocking* names appear to be somewhat old-fashioned. The *Sugar Hill* type is also quite distinctive but for a different reason: all six informants were from the Atlantic states, and all were black.

In sum, then, nicknames can be real names. They can designate specific or single features such as the original *Nob Hill* in San Francisco; they can also become generalized and, like place-name generics, be applied wherever they seem to fit—like *Snob Hill* and most of the others we have dealt with. They may then attain the status of ordinary words, in which case one might hear a sentence like, "We're developing quite a millionaire's row up there." Then the initial process of place-naming may begin all over with the definite article: "They live in the *East End*" or "on the *North Side*," when both speaker and hearer already know what town or city is being spoken of.

It is also evident that these unofficial names can vary over the country at large both geographically and socially, in distinctive and sometimes significant patterns. Many show the popular imagination at work, with jocular and sometimes grotesque names, names that betray attitudes—amused, derisive, envious, sardonic, rejective. Public opinion expressed through adverse names may even act as a type of social pressure leading to change—not merely by euphemizing the *name* but by stirring public action to remove the conditions that produced the adverse name. In such cases, nicknames given as an emotional safety valve become a lever to produce change.

❧

New Blood in the Namestream

JOHN TITTENSOR

The most respected mechanic in the village of St. Martin d'Ardèche, not far from where I live, is called *Monsieur Salaud*. And in another nearby village the job of mayor is held down by the amiable *Madame Bordel*. Perfectly ordinary-sounding French names—with the sole drawback that *salaud* means 'bastard' and *bordel* means 'brothel'; and all over France these unfortunates have for company the bearers of such names as *Lacrotte* 'turd', *Vachier* 'piss off', *Connard* 'bloody fool', and *Putin* 'whore'—not to mention such real unprintables like *Baize* and *Ducon.*

Having a name in this category is no fun in any language—I speak from bitter personal experience—but at least in most Anglo-Saxon countries, effecting a change poses no great problem. Not so in France, where names are part of the *patrimoine,* the national heritage, and are not to be altered or forsaken lightly: A poet friend had to spend several years and a lot of money to get a missing *s* restored to the official version of his surname, so that now, instead of being *Bâtard* 'mongrel', he's plain old *Bastard* and, what's more, is very happy about it.

But to get back to our *Whores, Brothels,* and so on. Some of them felt strongly enough about their situation to form a pressure group, and now, after a long struggle, the government has caved in: A recent *Journal officiel* lists four pages of people who are to be allowed to change their names—when they can come up with the two thousand-franc fee.

It is not, however, a matter of "you pays your money and you takes your choice." For the *Journal officiel* also provides the alternative names acceptable to the Fifth Republic; and if the *Putins*, for example, do not like *Pertin*, well, hard cheese; they'll just have to stay as they are. While the *Salauds* get a government-guaranteed Hobson's choice: *Saland* is going to remind everybody of that unloved ultra-right general of the Algerian War period and God help anybody called *Asslot* who ever gets the urge to travel in the English-speaking world.

On the credit side two gentlemen called *Hitler* can now safely come out of their bunkers: They'll be known henceforth as *Hiler* and at school their children may enjoy a peace that the fathers (and I, for that matter) never knew.

One imagines that the majority of the *Cocus* 'cuckolds', *Beaunichons* 'nice tits', *Boccons* (unprintable again), and their comrades in suffering are going to take more or less gratefully whatever name the state cedes them. But in doing so they are going to break the heart of Michel Tesnières of the French Onomastic Society. Onomastics is basically the science of worrying about names and Monsieur Tesnières—an appellation, as it happens, regrettably free of all sexual or scatological interest—is much exercised by the fact that three centuries from now 97 percent of all French family names will have vanished, with only 7500 surviving out of the estimated present stock of 250,000.

Up until the seventeenth century you could call yourself anything you liked in France (which makes you wonder what the ancestors of today's *Bastards* and *Turds* were thinking of), but in these more prosaic and regulated times a number of ordinary everyday factors is gradually eroding this part of the *patrimoine*. The French, to the despair of every government since the Revolution of 1789, are notoriously good at not having babies, and even then half the production at any given time are girls, who do not usually pass on their names when they marry. Men are free to pass on their names as much as they like, but some do not marry while others marry and remain childless. Add to this those perverse types who voluntarily renounce such fine family designations as *Cupissol* 'Arsepiss', and the result, according to an anguished M. Tesnières, is that seventy out of every one hundred current surnames disappear in the course of a single generation.

Already the nation is top-heavy, with 25 percent of the population sharing 0.4 percent of the available names. The twelve commonest names now embrace a million people, with the *Martins*—there are already 168,000 of them—heading the list. Maybe when the crunch comes in three hundred years' time, the *Martins*, who by then will in theory be one in twenty of the population, will start demanding the right to call themselves *Brothels* or *Bloody Fools.*

One thing M. Tesnières hasn't reckoned with, though, is the Anglo-Saxon input. The vogue for first names such as *James* (pronounced JEMSS) is still far from its peak, and freedom of movement within the European Economic Community means that English surnames are becoming more and more common here. Already a quick scan of the local phone book reveals the presence of the *Broadbents, Coxes, Cockles, Willings, Whitworths,* and *Crackenthorpes.* Not that the English have a monopoly when it comes to, as it were, injecting new blood into the namestream. The Irish haven't been wasting their time either. Friends in Bordeaux swear by a French plumber called *Patrick McGarvey* and our municipal musical school is overseen by that genial organist—and Frenchman—*Rory Nelson.*

Just a little effort on the part of people with names like this— put *Cox* with *Willing*, for example, and something *has* to happen—could take some of the strain off the neurotically prolific *Martins, Bernards,* and *Petits* and send a welcome ray of sunshine into the gloom-filled halls of the French Onomastic Society. But on second thought, maybe not: M. Tesnières would doubtless see this foreign intrusion as poor compensation for the loss of his homegrown *Whores, Bastards,* and *Hitlers.*

SIC! SIC! SIC!

"THE LOS ALAMOS SCHOOLS SUMMER SCHOOL PROGRAM WILL NOT DISCRIMINATE AGAINST ANY PERSON BECAUSE OF RACE, CREED, NATURAL ORIGIN, SEX, AGE OR HANDICAP."—*Los Alamos Schools Summer School, General Information.* Submitted by Barbara DuBois, Los Alamos.

Onomastica Nervosa

LAURENCE URDANG

Naming the baby? Want to discover the meaning of your given name? There are many books available—some quite good—that provide etymological information about names. It is interesting to note, however, that given names themselves have given rise to denotative and are associated with connotative uses in the language. We are not including words coming from the names of particular people, like *einsteinium, watt, curium, henry,* and other eponyms: We refer here only to first names that have acquired meanings of their own or that, by association, have acquired special connotations. The following list is not exhaustive, but it is a beginning; readers may wish to offer addenda. The label *connotative* is inserted to indicate those words and meanings that come from a source other than the name in the headword but are nonetheless closely associated with it.

Abigail: ladies' maid.
Albert: *Prince Albert,* long-tailed frock coat.

Alexander: cocktail made with cream, crème de cacao, and gin or brandy. Also called **brandy Alexander.**

Bennie: 1. overcoat. Also, jocular, **Benjamin.** 2. (*connotative*) benzedrine; any stimulant. 3. *Benjamin,* benzoin.

Betty: baked dessert, e.g., apple brown betty.

Bill: (*connotative*) invoice.

Cassandra: (*connotative*) bearer of bad prophecy.

Charlie, Charley: 1. *Charlie horse,* leg cramp. 2. *good-time Charlie,* (a) someone intent on the pursuit of enjoyment, usually at the exclusion of more worthwhile activity. (b) a fair-weather friend.

Dagmar(s): torpedolike bumperguard(s) on old Cadillac.

Dottie, Dotty: crazy; daft.

Ernest: (*connotative*) earnest.

Frank: (*connotative*) frank; candid.

George: 1. Also, **real George:** wonderful, marvelous. 2. (*in oaths*) by George!

Guy: 1. any male (or, recently, female). 2. a strengthening support of wire or rope.

Hector: pester.

Jack: 1. any male. 2. lifting device. 3. *Jack-in-the-box,* children's game. 4. *jumping jack,* children's toy. 5. *union jack,* special kind of flag. 6. *Union Jack,* national flag of Britain. 7. *jack off* (from *jerk off*) masturbate.

Jake: okay.

Jane: 1. any female. 2. *plain Jane,* any unattractive female.

Jenny, Jennie: 1. (*connotative*) spinning jenny. 2. (*connotative*) *Genny, Genoa,* large jibsail.

Jerry: (*connotative*) *Jerry-built.*

Jimmy: 1. a burglar's crowbar. 2. (*Australian*) an immigrant.

Joe: 1. any male, esp. in "a good *Joe.*" 2. (Brit. equiv., **Tommy**

Atkins) *GI Joe*, private in the infantry. 3. *Joe Blow* (from the Windy City).

John: 1. prostitute's customer. 2. toilet. 3. *Dear John letter*, a note of farewell to a former lover or spouse. 4. any male. 5. *John Bull*, symbol of Great Britain.

Johnnie, Johnny: 1. *stage-door Johnnie*, someone who loiters about the stage door of a theater, usually a fan or suitor of one of the performers. 2. a child's potty. 3. *johnnycake*, a fried cornmeal cake. 4. *Johnny-come-lately*, last-minute participant. 5. *Johnny-jump-up*, either of two kinds of flower. 6. *Johnny-on-the-spot*, someone who is present and willing to do something. 7. *Johnny Reb*, (a) a Confederate soldier. (b) any southerner.

John Thomas: penis.

Jonah: bad luck.

Jonathan: *Brother Jonathan*, symbol of America.

Judy: any girl (e.g., *This Judy is by no means a rutabaga.* —Damon Runyon).

Larry: call made at the start of a children's game, as in marbles, the first to say it claiming the right to play first.

Laurence: blackish, shimmering reflection seen at the surface of a paved road on a hot summer's day.

Lulu: 1. outstanding example of its kind. 2. perquisite of an elected official.

Magdalene: ("maudlin") silly, tearful sentimentality.

Mary: 1. *Bloody Mary*, cocktail made with tomato juice and vodka. 2. *Virgin Mary*, a Bloody Mary without the vodka. 3. male homosexual.

Mary Jane: marijuana.

Matilda: *Waltz(ing) Matilda (Australian)*, swag or hobo's bundle on a stick.

Mickey, Mick: 1. Irishman. 2. potato, esp. when baked in the coals of an open fire. 3. *take the Mickey out of (Brit.),* ridicule.

Molly: 1. a sleevelike expansion plug for fastening a screw into plaster or plasterboard. 2. *(connotative)* an aquarium fish.

Nancy, Nance: *(Brit.)* pimp or homosexual.

Patsy: sucker; dupe.

Pete: *Sneaky Pete,* cheap wine, as that drunk by derelicts.

Peter: 1. penis. 2. *peter out,* diminish.

Phoebe: bird.

Pierre: *Lucky Pierre,* "always in the middle."

Reuben: sandwich of hot corned beef, sauerkraut, and melted cheese.

Roger: okay; understood.

Sam: *Uncle Sam,* symbol of America.

Simon: 1. *simony,* buying or selling sacred articles. 2. *Simple Simon,* nursery-rhyme character. 3. *Simon sez,* children's game.

Susan: *lazy Susan,* circular tray on a pivot.

Suzie: *Suzie Q,* dance step.

Tom: 1. *(connotative) tomfoolery,* horseplay. 2. *(connotative) tommyrot,* nonsense. 3. *Tommy Atkins,* British GI Joe. 4. *Tom and Jerry,* cocktail; cartoon characters. 5. male of the cat family. 6. *tomcat,* behave like a roué.

Tom, Dick, and Harry: just about anybody.

Veronica: 1. plant. 2. (a) image of Christ on a handkerchief. (b) the handkerchief itself. 3. special kind of pass in bullfighting.

Epistolae

A few more for "Onomastica Nervosa":

Benedict: a newly married man.
Bertha: a kind of cape or deep collar.

Billy: 1. a he-goat. [2. a policeman's club. 3. a poster. 4. *(Australian)* a pot or tin for boiling water over a campfire.—*Editor.*]

Bobby: an English policeman.

Dick: *(slang)*, a penis.

Dolly: a small platform on wheels or rollers.

Jack: 1. *(slang)* money. [2. a he-ass.—*Editor.*]

Jehu: a furious driver.

Jemima: 1. a dove. [2. **Aunt Jemima:** a female Uncle Tom. —*Editor.*]

Jasper: 1. a hick or rube. [2. a variety of quartz.—*Editor.*]

Jock: 1. a jockstrap. 2. an athlete.

Jezebel: a loose woman.

Joey: 1. a clown. [2. *(Australian)* a young kangaroo.—*Editor.*]

Joseph: a chaste man.

Jerry: a chamberpot.

Jenny: 1. a traveling crane. 2. a she-ass.

Charlotte: a kind of pudding.

Charlotte (Russe): a sweet dessert.

Louis: a French gold coin.

Magdalen: a reformed prostitute.

Mary: *(Australian)* an aborigine woman.

Nanny: 1. a she-goat. [2. a children's nurse.—*Editor.*]

Reuben, Rube: a hick or jasper.

Teddy: 1. a one-piece ladies' undergarment consisting of panties and a chemise. 2. a toy bear.

Victor: a winner.

Warren: an area abounding in rabbits.

Xanthippe: a termagant or shrew.

J. BRYAN, III
Richmond, Virginia

Addenda to "Onomastica Nervosa":

(Big) Ben: the clock in the tower of the Houses of Parliament.

(Big) Bertha: a huge railway gun used by the Germans in WWI.

(on the) Fritz: broken; out of order.

George: a generic, like Joe, Mac.

Jerry: *(WWI slang)* a German or Germans collectively.

Judas: 1. a traitor. 2. **Judas tree:** a kind of tree. 3. **Judas Priest:** euphemism for *Jesus Christ.*

Heinie: *(WWI slang)* a German. 2. the behind; the buttocks.

(Tin) Lizzie: 1. Model T Ford. 2. a jalopy.

(Black) Maria: police van for transporting captives.

Mickey (Finn): a knockout drop (especially chloral hydrate, when surreptitiously added to someone's drink).

Moll: a gangster's girl friend.

Ned: euphemism for *hell: to raise Ned.* Also, Hob (from Rob).

Oscar: Academy Award trophy.

Sally (Lunn): *(Brit.)* a sweet teacake.

(Doubting) Thomas: a skeptic.

Timothy: a kind of grass.

Toby: a style of pottery mug or jug.

(Uncle) Tom: a black man who toadies to whites.

ERIC HAMP
University of Chicago

Lots of Englishes

It's about time we all got used to the idea that there are as many Englishes as there are English-speakers. (Although we can thank lucky stars, heavens above, and the other usual thankees that the multitudinous Englishes are as mutually intelligible as they are.) These Englishes from all over the globe—Sussex, Australia, Scotland, and who knows where—make for interesting reading, but even more interesting speaking.

Sussex Speak

BEL BAILEY

Old Sussex dialect is sadly dying out, save in the remoter villages, where the oldest inhabitants still speak it naturally. That is a great pity, as Sussex rustics were once famous for their amusing knack of adapting words to suit their own requirements. For example, a *touch of the old brown crisis* would mean an 'attack of bronchitis' and *I mises* would be Sussex shorthand for 'I surmise or guess'. Typical of the county is still the arbitrary pronunciation of the letters *ee: sheep* is often pronounced as "ship" and *week* as "wick."

The use of the double plural is another old Sussex feature, as in the verse:

> *I saw two ghostesses*
> *Sitting on postesses*
> *Eating their toastesses*
> *And greasing their fistesses*
> *Weren't they beastesses?*

Back in 1904, E. V. Lucas in his *Highways and Byeways in Sussex* noted that the Sussex dialect changed markedly from east to west and that the demarcation line between the two was the lovely Adur Valley—where even the breeds of sheep changed! If one hears the old Sussex dialect at all now, it is usually found in the rural hinterland of the county between Battle (of 1066 fame) and Health-field, or that fine open stretch of country twixt Chichester and Midhurst.

The old West Sussex tendency is to add an extra syllable to monosyllabic words, so *cow* becomes "cayoo," or *fowl* is pronounced "fewoll." In East Sussex respectively these would be "kew" and "fewl." The true "Sussexer" has problems with the letter *h*, so one old traditional dish is the "Plum 'eavy," the *highway* is naturally the " 'ighway," etc. In East Sussex *th* is often pronounced as "d," so that *the, them,* and *that* become "de, dem, and dat." Due to the old Sussex dialect, the village folk could quickly divide all those they met into the sheep and goats: the *homelings* were the natives and the *comelings* those who had come into Sussex from another county.

Frequently heard old expressions include *shennagoo* for 'shall not go', and *drackly* for 'straight away, directly'. High praise is *tidy middling* and *middling* is 'very fair'! *Purdnye* means 'almost'. *Darngurt* is Sussex speak for 'anything very large', as this county is naturally given to emphatic statements. An overdressed woman may be summed up as "looks like a sow saddled" and any impossible task calls forth the comment, "I can't suck flour *and* whistle!" "Leaves back'ards up'ards, it's going to rain" was a favorite saying of the ancient Sussex shepherds. The cowman driving his cows up Steyning High Street would call, "Coup, coup, coup, coom along," as did generations before him.

A scolding woman was said to give her husband "a dish of tongues," and the old Sussex bachelor often gave crisp reasons for staying single: One went on record as saying "Mesel, I ain't no marryin' man, fer I can't see naun in givin' 'arf yer grub away ter get t' other 'arf cooked. I does me own."

Counting words in Sussex were often used by agricultural workers. The sheep were counted in pairs, thus, "One-erum, two-erum, cockerum, shuerum, shitherum, shatherum, Wineberry, Wagtail, Tarydiddle, Den equals twenty."

Many writers have collected gems of Sussex dialect down the years, like Rev. William Parish and another cleric, Rev. Edward Boys Ellman, both before World War I. Parish discovered some amusing differences, as when a Sussex girl cries, "Oh! do adone" she means "Go on," but if she says, "Adone do," she means "Stop at once!"

The ladybird was called *Bishop Barnaby* by Sussex children, as in the old rhyme:

> *Bishop, Bishop Barnaby,*
> *Tell me when my wedding will be,*
> *If it be tomorrow day,*
> *Open your wings and fly away.*

Broom dasher was the traditional Sussex description of a roughly dressed or roughly behaved person, and someone of low intelligence was described as *chuckle-headed,* a term not unfamiliar to Americans. To be *fair clemmed* meant to be 'very hungry, cold, or miserable'. A typical county boast still often expressed is "Sussex won't be druv" and anyone *contrairy* is reckoned to be 'obstinate.' *Darn ma wig* is a humorous expression of surprise. *Frouden* means 'to be afraid' or 'to be "frit" ', whilst 'feeling ill' was once expressed as "I be *gellish ornary* today." *Goistering* was a curious term for 'loud feminine laughter'; a 'bad worker' was called *latchety*: his excuse might well be "Old Laurence has got hold of me today!"

Time and time again the dry Sussex sense of humor breaks through. The sadly defunct Horsham to Steyning railway line was called the *linger and die. My obedience* was a mother's reference to her firstborn child, and a 'ditherer' was called a *messpot. Nineways for Sunday* meant 'a bewildered expression' and is a good example of the originality of thought behind many of the county sayings.

The folklore of the county is particularly rich, and this too gives colorful phrases. *The Miller's glory* refers to the sweeps of the windmill set in the sign of a cross, said to bring luck to anyone in the village getting married. *Shim* means 'a ghost' or just 'a glimpse of someone'. *Pharisees* 'fairies' are also deep in Sussex folklore, while 'something too complex to understand' is called *wigwams for goose's bridles. Long Rope Day* refers to the old Brighton or Hastings custom of skipping for luck on Good Friday. *January butter* is the name for the mud it was thought lucky to bring into the house on one's feet on January first.

Of all the English county dialects, I suspect that Sussex is the richest in its allusions, but I may well be prejudiced in favor of my beloved South Downs. To conclude, here is a snippet of the conversation of an old West Wittering woman, who lived near a scientist:

> . . . such a nice, still man, only he's always losing his recollects. . . . He disremembers everything. Why, the other day he was in a tarrible stodge 'cause he mus' catch the London train, an' prensly there he was back again. He most-in-ginral goos along reading an' a whiffle of wind blew his book an he disremembered what he'd gone for!

SIC! SIC! SIC!

"Albania, a country of two and three-quarters million people about the size of Maryland. . . ." From the *Wall Street Journal,* 6 June 1983. Submitted by Kenneth J. Pulliam, Pfafftown, North Carolina.

Socko Names

GEORGE W. TURNER

How did you sleep?" my son, returning to Australia after eight years in Britain, asked a fellow passenger who had shared his inexpensive hotel in Sydney. "Took a couple of trankos and went right out" was the reply. It was the word *trankos* that brought the flavour of Australia rushing back. It is what Sidney Baker *(The Australian Language)* calls a *hypocorism,* a form ending in *-ie, -y,* or *-ey,* or (especially in Australia) *-o,* to make diminutives or pet forms. In England such forms are associated with children's language *(nursie, potty)*, but such forms are not always or in all languages childish. Latin developing into the modern Romance languages acquired many diminutives, and Russians, Italians, or Swiss Germans, as well as Australians, use diminutives more freely than the English do.

Potentially any word might take an *-ie* or *-o* or be shortened. It is difficult to generalize a separate meaning in Australian English for each of the three possibilities. Perhaps *-ie* is more truly diminutive than *-o*, representing standard English unstressed "little" rather than similarly unstressed "old," so that if there were a word *trankie*, it would be "the little tranquillizer" while *tranko* is "the old tranquillizer," both expressing affection. A possible shortened *trank* would mean much the same, perhaps emphasizing familiarity more than anything else.

In fact *trankie* and *trank* do not to my knowledge exist, and I have encountered *tranko* only in this one instance. But when hypocorisms become established, they sometimes show all these forms (*Com, Commie,* and *Commo* all gain entry to the *Australian Pocket Oxford Dictionary* as colloquial variants of *Communist*). But more often the *-ie* or *-o* form exists alone. *Schoolie* 'teacher', *barbie* 'barbecue', *brekkie* 'breakfast', *greenie* 'large wave', or *trannie* 'transistor radio' appear to have no *-o* variants. Neither does *Pommy* 'Englishman', though the shortened *Pom* is common. Sometimes one or another of two coexistent forms becomes established in a set phrase as *Pommy bastard* but *whingeing Pom* 'English migrant who complains about Australia'.

The existence of one form rather than another appears to be unpredictable, a matter for the particularity of dictionaries rather than the generality of grammar books. A Presbyterian may appear as a *Presbo* or a *Pressie,* not, it seems, a *Presbie* or *Presso.* A member of the Salvation Army may be a *Salvo* or a *Sallie* but not *Salvie* or *Sallo*. Some words have *-o* alone; *arvo* 'afternoon' and *nasho* 'national service, compulsory military training' are examples of this. Again we might take a perfectly good Scottish diminutive *chuckie* 'fowl' and abandon it in favour of the shorter *chook*. Sometimes there are regional variants, as Western Victorian *blockie* and South Australian *blacker* 'occupier of small fruit farm', or *premie* 'premature baby', which I always heard as *prem* in New Zealand.

There is an unpredictable element in pronunciation as well. *Chrissie* 'Christmas' is pronounced with *s* but *possie* '(comfortable) position' with *z*. Similarly *Tassie* 'Tasmania' and *Brissie* 'Brisbane' have pronunciation with *z*. This could suggest that these words are simply formed on the spoken full forms, which are pronounced with *z*, but this would not explain the *z* pronunciation in *Aussie* 'Australia(n)' or *mossie* 'mosquito'.

Besides phonetic and morphological arbitrariness, there is an unpredictable element in the semantics of hypocoristic forms, at least in Australia. A *clippie* is a female bus-conductor but a *connie*, with otherwise the same meaning, need not be female. The *-ie* termination often suggests endearment as in *coldie* 'bottle of cold beer' or *sickie* 'period of sick leave', but it occurs in *blowie* 'blow-fly' (as well as *mossie*). And if it occurs in *sickie*, why not in *compo* '(worker's) compensation'? There may be a phonetic explanation: It would have been difficult to pronounce an *-o* termination in *chewie* 'chewing gum', for instance, and this may explain the formation of *blowie*. Sometimes etymology (and even spelling) determines a form, as in *speedo*, *Abo*, *choco* 'conscript' (from *chocolate soldier*), or *uni* 'university'. Terms like *smoko* 'a break for a cup of tea' and *fleeco* 'one who picks up fleeces in a woolshed' arise from calls such as "Fleece oh!"

Why do manly Australians (for we are talking especially of male language in this) promote diminutives? Perhaps what all hypocoristic forms have in common is an atmosphere of familiarity. They reduce things to size. Violet's father in Arnold Bennett's novel *Imperial Palace* referred to the overpowering hotel of the title as "the pally" in order to maintain his self-respect. So *nasho* and even the rather official *compo* and the early pejorative *reffo* 'refugee' show a desire to acclimatize the unfamiliar, not to be impressed, to cut down tall poppies. But familiarity is also a warm thing and to shorten place names—*Darlo* 'Darlington', *Paddo* 'Paddington' (these two are Sydney suburbs), or the *Gabba* 'Woolloongabba'—makes them sound like home. Perhaps we need hypocorisms in a new country.

Galling Gallicisms of Quebec English

HOWARD RICHLER

The *Oxford Companion to the English Language (OCEL)* is missing an *s* at the end of its title, for it has headings for more than four hundred varieties of our multivaried mother tongue—Australian English, Singapore English, Indian English, Black Vernacular English, etc. Some of the varieties are unfamiliar, like Babu English, "a mode of address and reference in several Indo-Aryan languages, including Hindi, for officials working for rajahs, landlords, etc."

My mother tongue is one of the mutants listed in *OCEL,* and I am constantly being reminded of the peculiarities of my usage.

After giving an American telephone receptionist my phone number, I added, "My local is 222." "Your what?" she retorted. I quickly corrected myself: "My extension is 222." I left a Newfoundland customer perplexed when I told him that I would try to find an item at one of our *filials*, instead of *subsidiaries*. I am guilty of speaking Quebec English.

In Quebec, it is taken for granted that English affects French. One hears expressions like *le snack bar, chequer* (instead of *verifier*), and *un towing* 'a tow truck'. In the business world one encounters a myriad of Anglicisms like *meeting, cash flow, downsize,* and *business* itself. The presence of these borrowings make some Quebecois feel that their language is under threat. More and more, however, the flow is not unidirectional: Most English-speaking monolingual Quebecer will use *metro* for *subway*, *dépanneur* for *convenience store*, and *caisse populaire* instead of *cooperative bank*. The following demonstrates the French influence on Quebecois English:

> The *professor* (teacher) at the *polyvalent* (high school) believed that *scholarity* (education) was being affected by students *consecrating* (devoting) more time to *manifestations* (demonstrations) about the dress code than to their *notes* (grades). During his *conferences* (lectures), their inattention was hurting their *apprenticeship* (learning of the subject matter). He also felt he was getting *collaboration* (cooperation) from his confreres, *Anglophone* (English speakers), *Francophone* (French speakers), and *Allophone* (speakers of neither English nor French) in better serving the *collectivity* (community). He thus had a *rendezvous* (meeting) with the *Director-General* (principal), Monsieur Gendron, and stated that it was a *primordial* (essential) consideration that some teachers be let go before they reached *permanence* (tenure) under the *syndicate* (union)

agreement. Monsieur Gendron wrote back saying that he had requested a *subvention* (grant) in the *annex* (appendix) to his *planification* (policy) budget to the *confessional* (denominational) school board in order that formation *modalities* (training methods) could be created to make teachers more dynamic *animators* (group leaders).

Although terms like *collaboration, rendezvous,* and *annex* might be used in non-Quebec English contexts, they read like inappropriate choices from a synonym dictionary, and *cooperation, meeting,* and *appendix* seem more natural.

The trend towards the Gallicization of English in Quebec coincides with the introduction of pro-French legislation around twenty years ago, and the use of French has gained in prestige as a result, making it more likely for Gallic loanwords to appear in English. Anglophones are speaking French to a greater extent at home and at work, creating a situation in which the French term becomes more familiar than the English. Thus, an Anglophone might use the word *demand* when he means 'ask', *reparations* when he means 'repairs', and *remark* when he means 'notice', because he is constantly employing *demander, réparations,* and *remarquer* when speaking French.

These *faux amis* (false friends), as they are called, are confused both by Anglophones speaking French and Francophones speaking English. They are also among many of the words likely to have their meanings changed in Quebec English. For example, *résumer* does not mean 'to resume' but, as Americans know from their adoption of *résumé* for curriculum vitae, 'to summarize'; and *decevoir* means 'to disappoint', not 'to deceive'. Not many Anglophones in Quebec today use *résumé* and *deceive* in the French sense, but over time I suspect that such usages will increase.

It is often hard to know where English and French begin and end. Franglais includes such classics as *hot-dog steamé* all *dressed,* and a rock music review which declared that a group's appeal was to *male white trash de vieille souche. Vieille souche* is a term that refers to "old stock" Quebecers.

To those who bemoan the loss of the chastity of the French language, all I can say is that the lady never was a virgin: French is essentially mutated Latin corrupted by Arabic, Gaulish, and Germanic, to name a few of the seducers. Even the name of the country, *France,* owes its name (as does *England*) to a Germanic tribe. Language purity is a myth. The reality is that English and French have been borrowing from one another since at least 1066. Ironically, some of the dreaded Anglicisms, like *rosbif* and *club,* were originally Gallicisms that had penetrated English in the eighteenth century.

SIC! SIC! SIC!

"For a month he laid in the berth watching the ships depart through the porthole." From the *Yukon Breed,* by Lee Davis Willoughby. Submitted by Betti Slack, Boulder, Colorado.

English as she is spoke: The new guide of the conversation in Portuguese and English in two parts, by Pedro Caroline (Jose da Fonseca)

MICHAEL GORMAN

We expect then, who the little book (for the care what we wrote him, and for her typographical correction) that may be worth the expectation of the studious persons, and especially of the Youth, at which we dedicate him particularly." With these words, Jose da Fonseca closed his introduction to the most famous and enduring of fractured English phrase books. It was first published in Paris in 1855 and has been republished many times under its original title and, more commonly, under the title *English as she is spoke.* The first American edition of the book ("reprinted verbatim and literatim" in Boston in 1883) contained an introduction by Mark Twain, who wrote that "this celebrated little phrase-book will never die while the English language lasts . . . it is perfect . . . its immortality is secure." Fonseca's sublime ridiculousness is not much read now, yet I am as sure as was Twain that its season will come again and that other generations will rejoice in its unique humor.

There is a great difference between the humor that arises from the simple misuse of language and that which arises from the kind of naive, serious-minded, and, ultimately, inspired assault on its richness typified by Fonseca's phrase book. I once stayed in a Grenoble hotel room which was decorated with the alarming instruction "In case FIRE, avert the boots." I soon realized that it was not my footwear that had to be warded off, but that the message stemmed from a combination of the belief that *avertir* translated as "avert" and the use of a French-English dictionary dating back to the time of the lowly hotel servant known as "the boots." I recalled then my first acquaintance with *English as she is spoke* and, not for the first time, relished the incredible variety of our language and the unconsciously hilarious results caused by its use by less than fluent speakers and writers.

There are classic phrases from other European phrase books. My favorites are the familiar "Stop, the postilion has been struck by lightning!" and the less familiar, but richer in social nuance, "Unhand me Sir, for my husband, who is an Australian, awaits without." Even these gems are single lines from otherwise ordinary works. In the case of Fonseca's book, every page has its memorable lines. He seems to have been incapable of phrasing even the simplest idea without some happy misconjunction of words. The peculiar felicity of his lists, phrases, and conversations came from his rooted belief that he was a master of the English language and had a mission to spread the advantages of that mastery to others.

The book has two main parts. The first consists of lists of words and phrases in Portuguese and English accompanied by their English pronunciations. These lists are found under such headings as "Of the man," "Some wines," and "Drinkings." The second consists of "Familiar dialogues" in English and Portuguese under such headings as "For embarking one's self," "With the gardener," and "With a eating-house keeper." The book is rounded out by various small appendices, of which my very favorite (and the most sublimely Fonsecaian) is the section headed "Idiotisms and proverbs." Any one of these idiotisms is perfect in itself, but they can be divided into the hilariously loony and the cryptic. Examples of the first are:

> *The walls have hearsay*
> *According to thy purse rule thy mouth*
> *Big head, little sens*
> *He is beggar as a church rat*

The wisdom of these last phrases is not obscured by the peculiarity of their expression. On the other hand, it takes a very wise head to tease the meaning out of:

> *Nothing some money, nothing of Swiss*
> *He steep as a marmot*
> *Take the moon with the teeth*
> *Cat scalded fear the cold water*
> *Which like Bertram, love hir dog*
> *He turns as a weath turcocl*

However, before one can move on to a mastery of English idiotisms, it is necessary to learn more basic words and phrases. For example, consider the "Properties of the body," among which one finds:

Drowsiness, Yawn, Contortion, Lustiness, Sneesing, Belch, Watching

Armed with these basic concepts, one can then proceed to the "Defects of the body," such as:

A blind, A hump, A left handed, A squint-eyed, The scurf

Knowing the body, its properties and defects, one can begin to think about more concrete matters, such as food and drink. For this one needs "For the table":

Some plates, The bottle, Some knifes, Some groceries, Some crumb

and "Eatings," such as:

Some boiled meat, Some fritters, A stewed fruit, Some jelly broth, Some wigs, A chitterling sausages, Some dainty dishes, A litl mine, Hog fat

With such a repast one would have such "Drinkings" as:

Some brandy, Some orgeat, Champaign wine, Some paltry wine

I should pause here to note that Fonseca had a number of singular theories about English. These theories were more or less what one would expect of a man who thought that *Chinaman* was a trade; they included the ideas that *a* and *an* were masculine and feminine articles, respectively, and that *some* was a plural article, as in "some garlics." He also appears to have believed *it* to be the masculine third-person singular pronoun.

To return to his lists, we find the "Quadruped's beasts" such as:

Shi ass, Dragon, Young rabbit, A mule and "Fishes and shell fishes,"

such as:

Some fritters, a stewed fruit, some jelly broths, some wigs . . .

Bleak, Calamary, Muscles, Hedge-hog, A sorte of fish, Torpedo

If one were fortunate enough to catch any of these quadruped's beasts or fishes, one would no doubt cook them with "Seasonings":

Some wing, Some pinions, Some hog'slard or "Pot-herbs,"

such as:

Some succory, Some cabbages, Some corianders

When one's appetite and thirst are satisfied, there are such games to play as:

Gleek, The billiard table, Carousal, Pile, Even or non even.

One of the most useful features of Fonseca's phrase book is the phonetic transcription of English pronunciation given next to the English words and phrases. It is my private conviction that these pronunciations formed the basis for the unique accent used by the late Peter Sellers in his characterization of Inspector Clouseau in the *Pink Panther* series of films. Take, for example, Fonseca's pronunciation for one of his most creative Englishisms, the eatable *Some wigs.* The phonetic equivalent is "Seume uigues." In those letters one can read the very essence of Clouseau, as one can in the phonetic transcription of *Gun-powder,* "Guenepau'-der."

The "studious Portuguese and brazilian Youth" to whom Fonseca addressed his great work will, no doubt, have spent many studious hours learning the words and phrases in the first part before approaching the second part with understandable trepidation, for the second part was to build on their acquaintance with the English conversation. Understandably, the author introduced them gently. The first dialogue "For to wish the good morning" contains such staples of conversation as:

—Good morning, sir, how do you do today?
—Very well, I thank you
—To much oblige to you
—He is very well
—I am very delight of it. Were is it?
—He is in country
—Give a seat to the gentilman

—It is not necessary, it must go to make a visit hard by
—You are too in haste

Perhaps one wishes to make a morning visit:

—Is your master at home? Is it up?
—No sir, he sleep yet
—I go make that he get up
—How is it, you are in bed yet?
—Yesterday at evening, I was to bed so late that I may not rising me soon that morning
—Well! what have you done after the supper?
—We have sung, danced, laugh, and played
—What game?
—To the picket
—I am no astonished if you get up so late
—Adieu, my deer, I leave you. If can to see you at six clock to the hotel from————, we swill dine together

A strong personality emerges from these dialogues. It is that of an inquisitive, fussy, but congenial and clubbable soul, a sort of Portuguese Pepys delighting in gossip and food and wine and company. For instance, "With a hair dresser":

—Master hair dresser, you are very lazy. If you not come sooner, I shall leave you to
—Shave-me
—Your razors are them well?
—Comb-me quickly; don't put me so much pomatum.
—What tell me? all hairs dresser are newsmonger

One can see all his qualities in "For to ask some news":

—Is it true what is told of master M——?
—I have heard that he hurt mortally
—I shall be sowow of it, because he is a honestman
—Which have wounden him?
—Two knaves who have attacked him
—Do know it why?
—The noise run that is by to have given a box on the ear to a
    of them
—I believe it not
—Are you too many amused to the ball last night?
—Plenty much, and Madame L——has call for me your news

and in "For to dine":

—Sit down here by me. Do you like soup?
—Gentilman, will you some beans?
—Peter, uncork a Porto wine bottle
—Sir, what will you to?
—A pullet's wing
—I trouble you to give me a pear
—This seems me mellow
—Taste us rather that liquor, it is good for the stomach
—I am too much obliged to you, is done

Fonseca's studious youth were not to be contented with a mastery of English. Other European languages were of concern to them:

—How is the french? Are you too learned now?
—No too much, I know almost nothing

—They tell howeuver that you speak very well
—These which tell it they mistake one's
—Not apprehend you, the french language is not difficult

No matter how difficult these languages might be to acquire, a man with a command of foreign tongues was a man to be envied:

—How is that gentilman who you did speak by and by?
—Is a German
—I did not think him Englishman
—He is of the Saxony side speak the french very well
—Tough he is German, he speak so much well italyan, Spanish and english, that among the Italyans they think him Italyan, he speak the french as the Frenches himselves. The Spanishesmen believe him Spanishing, and the Englises, Englisman.
—It is difficult to enjoy well so much several languages

Even the linguistic paragon discussed in the previous dialogue could well be at a loss for words when presented with an unsatisfactory horse by a rascally servant. Not so the Fonseca of "For to ride a horse":

Here is a horse who have a bad looks. Give me another; I will not that. He not sall know to march, he is pursy, he is foundered. Don't you are ashamed to give me a jade as like? he is undshoed, he is with nails up, it want lead to the farrier. He go limp, he is disable, he is blind. That saddle shall hurt me. The stirrups are too long, very shorts. Stretch out the stirrups, shorten the stirrups. The saddles girths are roted, what bat bridle? Give me my whip. Fasten the cloak-bag and my cloak

Having disposed of the thoroughly chastened servant and the blind horse, one could journey forth into the country to do "The fishing":

—That pond it seems me many multiplied of fishes. Let us amuse rather to the fishing
—Here, there is a wand and some hooks
—Silence! there is a superb perch! Give me quick the rod. Ah! there is, it is a lamprey
—You mistake you, it is a frog! dip again it in the water
—Perhaps I will do better to fish with the leap
—Try it! I desire that you may be more happy and more skilful who acertain fisher, what have fished all day without to can take nothing

If the disappointments of the fishing are too much to take or if one were unfortunate enough to fall in the water while dipping a frog, it could become necessary "For to swim":

—Sir, do you row well?
—He swim as a fish
—I swim on the cork. It is dangerous to row with bladders, becauses its put to break
—I row upon the belly on the back and between two waters: I know also to plunge
—I am not so dexterous that you
—Nothing is more easy than to swim; it do not what don't to be afraid of
—Tel undress us
—The weather it is cloudy it lighten, I think we go to have storm
—Go out of the water quickly

But life cannot be entirely devoted to pleasure. The sordid realities of life can impel even this devotee of food and fun to have dealings "With a banker":

—I have the honour to present you a ex change letter draw on you and endorsed to my order
—I can't to accept it seeng that I have not nor the advice neither funds of the drawer
—It is not yet happened it is at usance
—I know again the signature and the flourish of my correspondent; I will accept him to the day of the falling comprehend there the days of grace, if at there to that occasion I shall received theirs orders

No doubt baffled by this reply, the client resorts to a simpler monetary request:

—Would you have so good as to give me some England money by they louis?
—With too much pleasure

There are many other examples of how to manage the commerce and pleasures of the world and, if, by any remote chance, these should fail the aspiring English speaker, he or she can reflect on higher matters expressed so well in familiar idiotisms. For example, who could fail to find solace and wisdom in the saying "After the paunch comes the dance"?

Fonseca's book ends, with perfect appropriateness, with an absolutely useless index. However, it would do him an injustice to close on such a negative note. Much more suitable as an epitome of his friendly philosophy and love of language and learning is this passage from "With a bookseller":

—But why, you and another book seller, you does not to imprint some good works?

—Ther is a reason for that, it is that you cannot sell its. The
actual liking of the public is depraved they does not read
who for to amuse one's self ant but to instruct one's

—But the letter's men who cultivate the arts and sciences they
can't to pass without the books

—A little learneds are happies enough for to may to satisfy
their fancies on the literature

Amen to that, speaking as one happy learner whose fancies
have been satisfied often by this marvelous book.

Dictionaries and Their Makers

Dictionaries, as objects, are ubiquitous. Dictionaries as subjects of investigation are not. *Verbatim* has published many wonderful articles explaining just what goes into the dictionary sausage, which, thank goodness, is more fascinating than off-putting. Dictionaries and the men and women who make them deserve more recognition, if not more scrutiny, and the consumers of dictionaries could only benefit from learning more about what makes a good dictionary—and who makes a good dictionary.

Sexual Intercourse in American College Dictionaries

SIDNEY I. LANDAU

The *American Heritage Dictionary (AHD)* published in 1969 became the first general American dictionary to include *fuck. Webster's New World, Second College Edition (WNW)*, published in 1970, stubbornly omitted it, and while one may sympathize with the practical argument that its inclusion might hurt sales to schools ([it would be] "unwise" [to suffer] "the risk [of] keeping this dictionary out of the hands of some students"), the editor also argues that words of this sort are "so well known as to require no explanation." This is disingenuous, since on those grounds thousands of other words could also be omitted, and more importantly, it is quite at variance with confident assertions about the scientific detachment of the "trained lexicographer," who disregards "the crotchets and prejudices of individuals"— everyone's, that is, except his own. In 1973, the *Merriam-Webster's New Collegiate, Eighth Edition (MW8)* was published; the editors, having observed that the heavens had not fallen, included *fuck.*

As the ensuing discussion will show, the tabooness of *fuck* exists not so much in the supposedly coarse contexts in which it is used—pace D. H. Lawrence and other liberated lovers—as in the essential meaning which every modern man and woman professes to find entirely wholesome: "sexual intercourse."

AHD defines *fuck* as "*Vulgar Slang:* To have sexual intercourse with," *sexual intercourse* as "Coitus, especially between humans," and *coitus* as "Sexual intercourse between two human beings." This is a circular definition, which is no definition at all.

It is also illogical, for if coitus by definition includes two humans, how can it be "especially" between humans? It is obvious that even though *AHD* enters *sexual intercourse,* its decision—let us be charitable—not to define it suggests that it is regarded as self-defining. But there is no question that the phrase is a lexical unit worthy of definition: It is the only widely accepted, nonvulgar way to refer to the act essential to many forms of life, and it is fair to say that among humans there is more interest in it, more is written about it, and still more imagined about it than any other subject.

AHD has four definitions of *sexual*: "1. Pertaining to, affecting, or characteristic of sex, the sexes, or the sex organs and their functions. 2. Having a sex or sexual organs. 3. Implying or symbolizing erotic desires or activity. 4. Pertaining to or designating reproduction involving the union of male and female gametes." *Intercourse* is defined as "1. Interchange between persons or groups. 2. Coitus," *copulate* as "to engage in coitus," which is defined, you'll recall, as "sexual intercourse . . . ," which is defined as "coitus." It is odd to find a dictionary that is fearless about *fuck* but squeamish about *sexual intercourse.* It is by now obvious that such blatant circularity can hardly be an oversight, and the wistful hope that *sexual intercourse* is self-explanatory simply won't do: It could refer to a discussion about sex or to any close physical embrace, neither of which conforms to the widely understood meaning of the term.

MW8's treatment is not much better. It defines *sexual intercourse* as "sexual connection esp. between humans: coitus: copulation," but there is no entry for *sexual connection,* and the presumption of self-explanation is no more valid for this phrase than for *sexual intercourse.* The only sense of *connection* in *MW8* that applies to the sense in which it is used in "sexual connection" is "the state of being connected." Thus *sexual connection* means "the state of being sexually connected," and could apply to any sexual contact, such as fellatio, cunnilingus, or anal intercourse. *MW8* defines *intercourse* as "coitus; copulation," and *coitus* as "the natural conveying of semen to the female reproductive tract, *broadly:* sexual intercourse." Although this definition avoids the outright circularity of *AHD*'s treatment, it still does not define *sexual intercourse. Copulate* is defined as "to engage in sexual intercourse," which is defined as "sexual connection," which is not defined; *coitus* and *copulate* lead right back to *sexual intercourse.* One does get the impression that the editors are not saying all they know about this subject. And this in the much publicized climate of sexual liberation that is supposed to characterize the '70s.

WNW pretends that the whole subject of sexual contact does not exist. It has no entry in place for *sexual intercourse,* though it defines *coitus* with nervous succinctness as "sexual intercourse." *Copulate* is "to have sexual intercourse." At *intercourse* we are witness to the fullest flowering of *WNW*'s recognition of the act of creation: "the sexual joining of two individuals; coitus; copulation: in full, sexual intercourse."

One could more easily excuse such inadequate treatment of a term of immense importance and broad currency if it were in accord with the treatment given other terms. Here is *AHD* on *transformer*: "A device used to transfer electric energy, usually that of an alternating current, from one circuit to another; especially, a pair of multiply wound, inductively coupled wire coils that effect such a transfer with a change in voltage, current, phase, or other electric characteristic. See step-down transformer, step-up transformer." (The same dictionary needed but four words to define *sexual intercourse*!) Here is *WNW* on *triangulation*: "*Surveying, Navigation* the process of determining the distance between points on the earth's surface, or the relative positions of points, by dividing up a large area into a series of connected triangles, measuring a base line between two points, and then locating a third point by computing both the size of the angles made by lines from this point to each end of the base line and the lengths of these lines." Here is *MW8* on *toxin*: "a colloidal proteinaceous poisonous substance that is a specific product of the metabolic activities of a living organism and is usu. very unstable, notably toxic when introduced into the tissues, and typically capable of inducing the formation of antibodies on injection." We should all learn things we'd never dreamt of if we were told half so much about *sexual intercourse*.

A word about the pre–*AHD* books. The *Funk and Wagnalls Standard/College* (first edition, 1963) has no entry for *sexual intercourse* and defines *intercourse* as "sexual connection; coitus." It has no entry for *sexual connection*, and *coitus* is listed as a variant of *coition*, which is defined as "sexual intercourse." *Copulation* is defined as "sexual intercourse; coition." The *Random House Dictionary, College Edition* (1968) (*RHD*) is the only college dictionary that actually defines *sexual intercourse*: "genital contact, esp. the insertion of the penis into the vagina followed by ejaculation; coitus; copulation." *RHD* defines *coitus* as "the act of sexual intercourse, esp. between human beings," and *copulation* as "sexual union or intercourse." *Intercourse* is "sexual relations or a sexual coupling, esp. coitus." *RHD*'s treatment of sexual terms is almost as slight as that of the other books, but at least circularity has been avoided.

There are clearly certain advantages to avoiding the whole issue. One doesn't have to worry about whether homosexual contact, for example, is "sexual intercourse," and if it is, how to arrange the definition to allow for the possibility of this and other variations while still specifying the heterosexual act as the usual meaning of the term. And one may be permitted to speculate whether pleasure (not to mention appetite) ought to be included as a powerful incentive associated with the sexual act, certainly among humans and plausibly among other animals as well. Precision can indeed be dangerous, but dictionaries have not been reluctant to be precise about other subjects, and perhaps the time has come for them to make the attempt about this one.

Epistola

Judging from the quality of Sidney I. Landau's review ["*Sexual Intercourse* in American College Dictionaries," *Verbatim* I, 1], this letter should be addressed to Mr. Urdung and the address should be Peyton Place.

I contracted to get a publication for word lovers. Instead, we get a shocking, sophisticated, non-functional complaint about unsatisfactory definitions of "fuck."

So I am asking you to fuck off. Do not send us any more of your letters. Return our money immediately.

MARTIN FINCUN
Fincun Court Reporters
Cleveland, Ohio

SIC! SIC! SIC!
"We treated between 70 and 71 people." Mary Zeigler, assistant director of nursing at Coshocton County Memorial Hospital, quoted in the *Columbus Dispatch,* 27 March 1983. Submitted by Dorothy Brauson, Columbus, Ohio.

How Big Is Your Dictionary?

ROBERT ILSON

Britain and North America are not only literate, but "dictionarate." In Britain, the dictionary's "success is shown by the fact that more than 90 percent of households possess at least one, making the dictionary far more popular than cookery books (about 70 percent) and indeed significantly more widespread than the Bible (which was to be found in 80 percent of households in England in 1983, according to the Bible Society)." In North America, "It was established some years ago that there are more dictionaries than television sets . . ." (Preface, *American Heritage Illustrated Encyclopedic Dictionary,* 1987).

So you, dear reader, probably own a dictionary. But how big is it? Let us consider two recent British dictionaries. The *Collins Cobuild English Language Dictionary* of 1987 (*Cobuild*) boasts xxiv plus 1703 pages. The *Collins English Dictionary* of 1986 (*CED*) has xxvii plus 1771. Looking at these figures, or at the books themselves, one would assume that the two dictionaries are of roughly the same size. And in one sense they are. But between *water* and *watt* there are 54 main entries in *Cobuild* and 148 in *CED*. They share such entries as *water biscuit* and *waterworks.* But in addition *CED* alone enters *water measurer* ("a bug"), *Watford* ("a town north of London"), etc. On the other hand, the shared main entry for *watershed* has 23 words in *CED* but 93 in *Cobuild.* And the word *waterless* is a main entry in *Cobuild,* explained in 20 words, whereas in *CED* it is naught but a so-called "undefined runon"—merely mentioned, but not explained explicitly, as a sub-entry at *water.* So *CED* enters more items than *Cobuild,* but devotes less space to explaining them. And that is probably as it should be. *CED* is intended for the adult native speaker of English, whose main concern is with understanding a large number of unfamiliar items (including proper names) encountered in reading and listening. *Cobuild* is intended for the foreign learner of English, whose dual concern is with understanding and using the core vocabulary of English, and who, having achieved that aim, can "graduate" to a dictionary for native speakers—like *CED*.

More generally, the size of a dictionary is a function of two variables: the number of items entered (its "macrostructure"), and the amount of information given about them (its "microstructure"). In Charles McGregor's words, a dictionary that says "a lot about a little" and one that says "a little about a lot" can end up roughly the same size. *Cobuild* and *CED* are far from being such polar opposites, but they exemplify this general point.

In measuring dictionaries, how far can we rely on the dictionaries' own estimates of their size? Let us consider the dust-jacket blurbs of *Cobuild*, *CED*, and two other native-speaker dictionaries: the British *Longman Dictionary of the English Language* of 1984 *(Longman)* and the American *Merriam-Webster's Ninth New Collegiate Dictionary* of 1983 *(W9)*. Here is what they *say*:

Cobuild: over 70,000 references
CED: 170,000 references
Longman: Over 225,000 definitions and more than 90,000 headwords
W9: Almost 160,000 entries and 200,000 definitions

Both *Longman* and *W9* estimate their macrostructure (headwords/entries) and their microstructure (definitions). But what of *Cobuild* and *CED*? What do they mean by *references*? In *CED* the relevant definition of reference seems to be "a book or passage referred to," or perhaps "a mention or allusion"; in *Cobuild*, "something such as a number or name that tells you where you can obtain the information that you want, for example from a book, list, or map. . . ." We are none the wiser. It is only from an article *about CED* that we learn it has "171,000 entries," which suggests that Collins means by *references* what Merriam-Webster means by *entries*. But *CED* and *Cobuild* certainly do not say so!

And what about *Longman*'s headwords? Their relevant definition of *headword* is "a word or term placed at the beginning (e.g. of a chapter or an entry in a dictionary)." Does that mean that the number of headwords equals the number of entries? And that therefore *Longman*'s macrostructure (number of *entries*) is much smaller than that of *W9* or *CED*? We need to look more closely at the meaning of *entry*.

For *entry* our four dictionaries have this to say in their relevant definitions:

Cobuild: a short article about someone or something in a dictionary or encyclopedia, . . .

CED: an item recorded, as in a diary, dictionary, or account.

Longman: a dictionary headword [!], often together with its definition.

W9: "4b . . . (3): HEADWORD (4): a headword with its definition or identification (5): VOCABULARY ENTRY"

W9's relevant definition of *headword* does not even mention dictionaries: "a word or term placed at the beginning (as of a chapter or an entry in an encyclopedia)." But its definition of *vocabulary entry* is about dictionaries only:

a word (as the noun *book*), hyphened or open compound (as the verb *book-match* or the noun *book review*), word element (as the affix *pro-*), abbreviation (as *agt*), verbalized symbol (as

Na), or term (as *man in the street*) entered alphabetically in a dictionary for the purpose of definition or identification or expressly included as an inflected form (as the noun *mice* or the verb *saw*) or as a derived form (as the noun *godlessness* or the adverb *globally*) or related phrase (as *one for the book*) run on at its base word and usu. set in a type (as boldface) readily distinguishable from that of the lightface running text which defines, explains, or identifies the entry

If we can sort out all the details here—no mean task—it emerges that *W9*'s *vocabulary entries* include both what I earlier called *main entries* (like *watershed*) and what I called *subentries* (like *waterless* in *CED*). But it appears that *Longman*'s *headwords* are only those that are, or introduce, main entries. So we still have no way of knowing whether *Longman*'s macrostructure is smaller or larger than *W9*'s! Nor do our troubles end here. For in its Explanatory Notes (p. 12), *W9* not only calls our attention "to the definition of *vocabulary entry* in this book," but also introduces us to a wholly new notion, that of *dictionary entry*:

> The term *dictionary entry* includes all vocabulary entries as well as all boldface entries in the separate sections of the back matter headed "Abbreviations and Symbols for Chemical Elements," "Foreign Words and Phrases," "Biographical Names," "Geographical Names," and "Colleges and Universities."

No sooner have we assumed that *W9*'s macrostructure of "Almost 160,000 entries" means *vocabulary entries,* than we must face the possibility that it includes such other dictionary entries as *Harvard U., McGill U.,* and *Abilene Christian U.* Have they been counted in? We simply do not know. But, as a British journalist might say, we should be told. For *W9*'s exemplary precision in telling us what vocabulary entries and dictionary entries are is offset by its vagueness about which type of entry its PR–wallahs have counted for their blurb.

Furthermore, our gratitude to *Longman* and *W9* for saying something about the size of their microstructures is offset by our sorrowful recognition of how little they say. Counting definitions is a start. But a definition can range from a single-word synonym (*entry 4b(3)*: HEADWORD) to the 117 words of *W9*'s definition of *vocabulary entry*—and beyond! And the microstructure of dictionaries includes more than just definitions: It can embrace examples, illustrations, synonym essays, usage essays, etymologies, and all sorts of other information. Everyone talks nowadays about making dictionaries user-friendlier. How about making their publicity buyer-friendlier as well?

Aux armes, citoyens! Let us strive to get dictionary publishers to cry their wares in ways that allow us to compare them. But, *citoyens,* let us not forget that the value of a dictionary resideth not in size alone. The best dictionary for *me* is the one that gives about the word or phrase that puzzles *me* the information *I* need at the moment *I* need it. People have different reference needs at different times. The standardization of the way dictionaries estimate how much they contain need not, and should not, entail the standardization of what they contain.

Eccentricity in English Lexicography

ELMER SUDERMAN

From the beginning of English lexicography the craft has been serious, often pedantic. The first dictionary in the form in which we know them today, Robert Cawdrey's *A Table Alphabeticall of Hard Usuall English Words,* published in 1604, is solemn and brief, defining about 2,500 words. Cawdrey evidently didn't think of either *lexicography* or *lexicographer* as hard words, for he defines neither. But then, since the *OED* has as its first citation for *lexicographer* as 1658 and for *lexicography* as 1680, one could hardly expect him to define a word which was not yet in wide use.

He must, however, have had some indication that such a word would come into the language because *lethargie,* which would have come just before *lexicographer,* is defined as "a drowsie and forgetfull disease," and *leuell,* meaning "right and straight," would immediately have followed. I'm sure Cawdrey didn't deliberately omit *lexicography,* because he knew that the disease which makes us drowsy and forgetful is common to both lexicographers and the rest of us in the use of words and that we often assume that dictionaries are *leuell,* that is, "right and straight," or correct and authoritative. A good example of our right and straight attitude is evident in John Wesley, if he was indeed the author of the *Complete English Dictionary Explaining Most of those Hard Words which are Found in the Best English Writers* (1753), who assures us that his dictionary, "by a Lover of Good English and Common Sense," is both right and straight. It is, he thinks, "the best English dictionary in the world." Henry

Cockeram's *English Dictionarie,* published 130 years earlier (1623) makes a similar claim: "What any before me in this kind have begun, I have not only fully finished but thoroughly perfected." Lexicographers were not modest, either in the seventeenth or eighteenth century; they were very sure that they were right.

And they were serious. They were interested in a practical, correct, definitive, and usable tool where the reader would be able to find, in Cawdrey's self-assured words, "the true writing, and understanding of hard, usuall English wordes, borrowed from the Hebrew, Greeke, Latine, or French, Etc. With the interpretation thereof by plaine English words, gathered for the benefit & help of Ladies, Gentlewomen, or any other unskilfull persons. Whereby they may the more easilie and better understand many hard English wordes, which they shall heare or read in Scriptures, Sermons, or elsewhere, and also be made able to use the same aptly themselves."

So much for Cawdrey's title page, or a part of it. It is not brief, but the definitions are. Some are defined in one, two, or three words. *Literature* is "learning." *Lumber* is defined, correctly enough for that time, as "old stuffe," *malidie* as "disease," *mutation* as "change," a *baud* as a "whore," and *driblets* as "small debts." His two-liners are limited mostly to words like *libertine* ("loose in religion, one that thinks he may doe what he liketh"), *luxurious* ("riotous, and excessive in pleasure and wantonesse"). *Theology* is "diuinitie, the science of liuing blessedly for euer," and a *hipocrite* is "such a one as in his outward apparrell, countenaunce, and behauior, pretendeth to be another man, then he is indeede, or a deceiuer."

Cawdrey's method is not much different from that exhibited by the early American dictionaries. Cawdrey describes an *abricot* as "a kind of fruit" which, though it fails to distinguish it from other fruits, is nevertheless not much different from Noah Webster's definition in his *A Compendious Dictionary of the English Language* (1806) in which *apricot* is defined as "a fine kind of stone fruit." Webster further defined *literature* as "learning, reading, skill in letters or books," and *grammar,* which Cawdrey doesn't define at all, as "the science of writing correctly." Cawdrey does make us smile now and then, particularly when he spells *progresse* as *grogresse* and *vicinitie* as *virinitie*; but such misprints were not deliberate or intended to be humorous or entertain the reader.

Early lexicographers were often capricious. What seems far-fetched and therefore titillates us today was not so then. Thomas Blont in *Glossographia or a Dictionary Interpreting All Such Hard Words whether Hebrew, Greek, Latin, Italian, Spanish, French, Teutonich, Belgick, British, or Saxon as are now Used in our Refined English Tongue* (London, 1656) had no intention of being ridiculous in defining *Hony-Moon* as "applied to those married persons that love well at first and decline in affection afterwards. It is hony now, but it will change as the moon." Blont further describes, quite seriously, a ventriloquist as "one that has an evil spirit speaking in his belly, or one that by use and practice can speak, as it were, out of his belly not moving his lips."

Edward Phillips's humor is not deliberate but based on ignorance. In the *New World of English Words* (London, 1658) he locates California in the New World, which is correct enough. It is, he says, "a very large part of Northern America," but he isn't certain whether it is a continent or an island.

At least one lexicographer was deliberately idiosyncratic in his definitions. That lexicographer, of course, is Samuel Johnson. He did not refrain from allowing his wry humor to intrude even in the definition of his craft. A lexicographer, he wrote in *A Dictionary of the English Language* (1775), is "a writer of dictionaries." So also had every other lexicographer who had defined the word before him. So also is it defined today. But Johnson did not stop there, but added: "a harmless drudge, that busies himself in tracing the original, and detailing the signification of words." So he defined his craft in the first edition and so the definition remained in the five editions which were published in his lifetime. Johnson was aware, as no other lexicographer before or after him has been, that the writer of dictionaries must enjoy words and can, without harm to the definition, intrude his own opinions and prejudices. Unfortunately, most lexicographers cannot distinguish their prejudices from what they consider the final word on the subject.

Johnson was even more eccentric in other definitions. *Oats,* he said, is "a grain, which in England is generally given to horses but in Scotland supports the people." A *stockjobber,* he wrote, is "a low wretch who gets money by buying and selling shares in the funds." Many would agree that the definition is still apt. Nor was Johnson afraid of words which until recently have not appeared in even the most authoritative dictionaries. He simply defines the noun *fart* as "Wind from behind," and turns to Suckling to illustrate the word:

> *Love is the fart*
> *of every heart;*
> *It pains a man when 'tis kept close;*
> *And others doth offend, when 'tis let loose.*

For the verb he is satisfied with the definition "To break wind from behind." To illustrate the meaning of the word from a reputable source he quotes Swift:

As when a gun discharge,
Although the bore be ne'er so large
Before the flame from muzzle burst,
Just at the breech it flashes first;
So from my lord his passion broke,
He farted first, and then he spoke.

I personally regret and am even a little surprised that Johnson does not include the definition of *fizzle* as "a silent fart" when used as a noun and "to break wind backwards with little noise" when used as a verb. These definitions appear both in Phillips's the *New World of English Words* (1658) and later in John Kersey's *New English Dictionary,* published in 1772. *Fizzle* retains that definition in the *OED*, which gives citations as early as 1532 and as late as 1848. Webster's *Third New International* retains the definitions as well, although the bluntness is somewhat dulled. I have often wondered why, if there is a word to describe a silent fart, there isn't also a word for a silent fart which smells, a silent one which doesn't, a loud one which smells, and a loud one which doesn't. Such discriminations would, don't you suppose, improve the precision of the English language.

Lexicographers do, then, at least on occasion, allow their eccentricities to enter into their definitions. And others do at times have their fun at the expense of the lexicographer and of the dictionary. At least they give the lexicographers work to do. We are accustomed to calling any dictionary "a Webster's," having gone so far as to enter into a lengthy court case in which the court decided that the word had, at least in the United States, become a generic term for any dictionary. In the nineteenth century an English dictionary in America was often labeled as a *Richardanary*, often simplified to a *Richard* or even a *Dick*. The only reference to this usage that I have been able to find was in John S. Farmer, *Americanisms—Old and New,* privately printed by Thomas Poulter and Sons in London in 1889.

Farmer is one of the most readable of all dictionaries. I would willingly take him along for a week on the proverbial desert island. He pays attention to American slang as well as to more colorful American definitions. While I was unable to find any definition in *Farmer* as delightful as Captain Francis Grose's definition of a vainglorious or ostentatious man as "one who pisses more than he drinks," Farmer has collected a number of rather eccentric words and definitions.

My favorite, I think, is *sockdolager,* which he defines as "a heavy blow, a conclusive argument; a winding-up, a general 'finisher.' " He traces the etymology to a corruption of *doxology,* "and hence the signal of dismissal." He gives other etymologies, probably more correct, but to my mind not nearly as delightful as its connection with *doxology.*

Farmer points out, moreover, that early settlers in America called all fruits *apples*; that a *back house* is a privy; that at Harvard "to have no bowels" is to be poor, destitute, or without means and adds that the expression is of scriptural derivation, "the word being used in a somewhat similar sense in the Bible" (I wish he had given some examples); and that a *peacemaker* is a Texas term for a revolver. President Reagan's label for the MX as the "peacekeeper missile," is, of course, in the same euphemistic tradition. On the other hand, in the nineteenth century a *Quaker* was either a member of the Society of Friends or a cannon made of wood, placed in the porthole of a vessel in order to deceive the enemy. Farmer defined *pimple* as "the head"; *Pork and Beans* as "the American national dish"; *prayer bones* as the "knees"; *to have prunes in the voice* as "speaking huskily, the cause being emotion"; *Ready John* as money; *rosebud* as a "young unmarried woman"; and *slim* as "one of indifferent stand in the community, either as regards social position, morals, or politics." A *tooting tub* is a pejorative term for a church organ, and *to worry* is to take a drink.

Neither Noah Webster, who published the first American dictionary in 1806 and in 1828 the first unabridged, nor Joseph A. Worcester, whose *Universal and Critical Dictionary of the English Language* (1848) was Webster's chief competition, included many interesting definitions, although both seemed to be afraid of the word *leg* as too vulgar, even for use in a dictionary. *Limb* was the preferred word, although Webster does speak of the *leg* of a table. The prejudice of the lexicographers echoes the prejudices of the people in general. *Pants, trousers, breeches* were often replaced by variants, many of them introduced by Charles Dickens. Farmer and Henley in their *Dictionary of Slang and Colloquial English* (London: 1912) list such words as *ineffables, inexpressibles, unthinkables, unutterables, unwhisperables*, etc. The "etc." at the end is theirs: They must have been tired of looking for euphemisms for *trousers* and *pants*. After all, *pants* and *trousers* don't sound so bad to us now, and probably didn't offend everyone even in the late nineteenth century.

But the dictionary does more than define words authoritatively and eccentrically. It also furnishes us with fascinating though now discredited information. Noah Webster, in his 1806 edition, informs us that the world was created in 4004 B.C. but fails to give the hour, set by Bishop Usher at 9:00 A.M. Enoch was translated into heaven in 3013 B.C., and the great flood swept away all but Noah's ark in 2348 B.C. A year later, in 2347 B.C., Babel was built and the languages of the world came into being. Webster doesn't tell us what the original language was, however. In 2328 B.C. Noah migrated eastward and founded the Chinese monarchy. Joseph died in Egypt in 1635 B.C., and Moses was born in 1571 B.C. One hundred and fifty-two years after Moses wrote the Pentateuch (1452 B.C.; he died the same year), the first Olympic games were held. All this, and more, Webster told his readers.

Even more practical information comes from Cockerham's *English Dictionary* (1623), the first lexicon to use the word *dictionary* in its title. He warns his readers that the *Hiena* is, like the wolf, a "subtile" beast that can counterfeit the voice of a man and will at night call shepherds out of their houses and kill them. On a more cheerful note he advises his readers that the dung of a lizard is good to take away spots in the eye.

The Reverend Thomas Cooper's *Thesaurus* (1565), the first great classical dictionary, would have been published five years earlier had not his wife, fearing that too much lexicography would kill her husband, burned the first manuscript. . . . And I had best quit before my wife burns my manuscript.

SIC! SIC! SIC!
"Slow Down . . . Children Playing Sleeping Drunks on Road." From a road sign in Newnes, Australia, in the *National Enquirer*, 5 October 1982. Submitted by Fairfax Stephenson, Seal Beach, California.

The Seating of Zotz

WALTER C. KIDNEY

Read widely and you end up with a magnificent but not totally useful vocabulary. For my part, I find no application for such words as:

gumphion: death's-head banner displayed at funerals;
ergastulum: house of correction for Roman slaves;
dob-dob: member of the hoodlum element in a lamasery;
verbunkos: dance performed to persuade people to enlist in
   the Hungarian army.

What a waste. And I regret missing any chance to drop into my conversation the months of the Maya year, just for their Dunsanian sound. The Maya had eighteen twenty-day months, plus five or six official days of bad luck. The year began with *Pop,* which fell between the *Nameless Days* and *Uo. Uo* fell between *Pop* and *Zip,* and so on. Even more Dunsanian, suggesting a play for grades six to eight, was *The Seating of Zotz,* the correct name for what otherwise would have been *Twenty Zip.*

Some fifteen years ago I worked on a job ideal for collecting such glittering trash, the *Random House Dictionary* project. Much of my time was spent in technology, and my working day was a shower bath of *bruzzes, brobs, froofs, snaths, downrights, chime hoops, larry cars, equation kidneys, cullin stones, crizzle glazes, glost fires, muffle furnaces, blue billy, sugar of lead, butter of arsenic,* and *Victoria Green Mother Liquor.* The sea yielded *futtock shrouds, euphroes, baggywrinkles,* and *paravane skegs.* Lists of standard paint colors included *Cream Dream, Pewke,* and *U.S. Army Pansy.* My Japanese sword mounts won satirical attention from John Ciardi. Heraldry was mine too, a whole private language. I learned not to use *or* "gold" in definition examples because my colleagues would always fire them back with penciled "Or what?" 's. But I did enter the various ways of describing a disk. Depending on the tincture, a disk is a *bezant, plate, torteau, hurt, gulp, guze, ogress, pellet, gunstone,* or *fountain.* Crosses can be—among other things—*crosslet, potent, avellan, moline, paty, formy, fitchy,* or *paty or formy fitchy at the*

foot. An *escutcheon semé of cross-crosslets* is *crusily*, and if the cross-crosslets are *fitchy* it is *crusily fitchy*. An escutcheon is sometimes divided by *dancetty, urdy, undy, embattled,* or *embattled grady* lines, and can be *barry, bendy, paly, barry-bendy, paly-bendy, paly-wavy, lozengy, chequy,* etc. The sun is in its *splendor,* the moon is in her *complement* or *detriment,* the pelican is in her *piety,* the lion is *gardant passant* and *ducally gorged,* and royalty is represented by *opinci, yales,* and *enfields,* one of which has *swivel-mounted horns.* How the Scottish dragon with flames issuing from *both* ends is blazoned I never did discover.

Meanwhile a friend in biology was encountering the *sarcastic fringehead,* the *confused flour beetle,* and the *free-living flat-worm.*

Some of these things did get into the dictionary, but in most cases there was nothing to do but pause, admire, and dismiss them gently.

Armchair Linguistics

Armchair linguistics is a fascinating pastime. It requires no messy fieldwork, no tree diagrams, and no tape recorders. All you need is a comfortable chair, quiet time for some evidence-gathering in the recesses of your own Sprachgefühl, and perhaps a pencil and pad of paper. Hot or cold drinks are optional. Sending your findings in to *Verbatim*—it's for the advancement of science, after all!—is not.

Self-Referring Words

ALEXANDER J. POLLOCK

Self-referring sentences, notably the paradoxical "This sentence is false," are sufficiently familiar. But the notion of self-referring *words* was new, at least for me, when it occurred to me the other day while I was waiting for an elevator. Self-referring words denote or describe themselves—for example, the word *word* is itself a word, and the word *useful* is itself useful.

I was already intrigued by these words by the time we were riding up on the elevator. Other readers of *Verbatim* may wish to participate in answering three questions which self-referring words raise:

1. How many of them are there?
2. Can we formulate general principles about them?
3. How widely are the categories "self-referring" and "nonself-referring" applicable?

Having posed the questions, any logophile of spirit must attempt answers.

It is obvious that the vast majority of words are not self-referring. My current list follows:

1. Nouns

THE WORD:	IS ITSELF A:
a. *word*	word
b. *term*	term
c. *noun*	noun
d. *substantive*	substantive
e. *symbol*	symbol
f. *sign*	sign

2. Adjectives

THE WORD:	IS ITSELF:
a. *useful*	useful
b. *English*	English
c. *français* (etc.)	français (etc.)

d. *acceptable*   acceptable
e. *unobjectionable*   unobjectionable
f. *intelligible*   intelligible
g. *meaningful*   meaningful
h. *understandable*   understandable
i. *thinkable*   thinkable
j. *sesquipedalian*   sesquipedalian
k. *ordinary*   ordinary
l. *analyzable*   analyzable
m. *inflected*   inflected
n. *polysyllabic*   polysyllabic
o. *definable*   definable
p. *expressible*   expressible
q. *printable*   printable
r. *writable*   writable
s. *pronounceable*   pronounceable
t. *speakable*   speakable
u. *utterable*   utterable
v. *learnable*   learnable
w. *teachable*   teachable

I have so far three principles:

1. Only nouns and adjectives can be self-referring. This is because words themselves are objects in the cultural world; thus they can only be referred to by names or descriptions of objects, i.e., by nouns or adjectives.

2. Self-referring nouns are always grammatical or linguistic terms applicable to nouns. This appears to be the only way for a noun to name itself.

3. Self-referring adjectives have a wider range of meaning than self-referring nouns, because they can express many aspects of

words (than which nothing has more aspects). The self-referring adjectives listed above bring out, respectively, that words are:

    a. practical

    b–c. in some language or other (This class of self-referring adjectives is represented in each language I am familiar with by one word—namely the adjective which describes words, including itself, as being in that language. As an aside, I wonder if, of the few thousand languages there are, any is so unself-conscious as not to have a word for itself, as one language among many?)

    d–e. socio-cultural

    f–i. cognitive

    j–k. stylistic

    l–n. structured

    o. semantic

    p–u. variously expressible

    v–w. pedagogical

My question here is whether, in principle, every noun and adjective can be unambiguously classed as either self-referring or nonself-referring.

It is clear that there might be disagreements about the classification of given words, for reasons such as:

1. Different senses of the same word—for example, *sign* in the sense of 'an indication of meaning' is self-referring; in the sense of 'an inscribed board used for advertising' it is not.

2. Differences in taste or opinion—some people might think *interesting* interesting and *euphonious* euphonious; other people might not.

3. Differences in theory—some people might speculate that

words in some sense exist or are things, thus making *existing* and *thing* self-referring; others' speculations might reach opposite conclusions.

Such disagreements are not objections in principle, however. In principle, we can sort out the senses of words, and settle or at least understand and handle differences of opinion, taste, and theory. But is there a word which cannot in principle be assigned to one of our two categories?

It seems to me there is one: the word *nonself-referring*. If *nonself-referring* is nonself-referring, it obviously describes itself and thus must be self-referring. If, on the other hand, *nonself-referring* is self-referring, then it must describe itself and be nonself-referring. So the self-referring word can lead us to paradox equally as well as the self-referring sentence.

Doubtless, as journal articles say, further research of this intriguing subject is needed. And the inviting field of the self-referring phrase lies all untrodden before us.

Epistola

As a mathematician, I found A. J. Pollock's article "Self-Referring Words" an interesting example of rediscovery. The fact that the concept of "nonself-referring" can lead to paradox has been familiar to some mathematicians and logicians since, roughly, the beginning of the [twentieth] century. It is a pleasure to find the paradoxical nature of the concept recognized in a linguistic setting.

Various logicians, among them preeminently Bertrand Russell, noted that the antinomies of logic tended to contain the concept that Mr. Pollock calls "nonself-referring," and which in mathematics is usually called "impredicable," as contrasted with "predicable." (Perhaps a more accurate pair of terms would be *self-impredicable* and *self-predicable*.)

Some apparent paradoxes can be resolved. That of the Spanish barber, e.g., (who, you may remember, shaved everyone in his town except those who shaved themselves) can be settled by denying the possible existence of such a person. Similarly, when Gonseth (1933) suggested the difficulty facing a librarian who wished to compile a bibliography of all bibliographies which did not list themselves, we can counter by saying that such a task cannot be carried out.

But other paradoxes cannot be so resolved, since part of the paradox shows the existence of the "product" in question. In Russell's terminology, the question whether the word *impredicable* is predicable or, alternatively, is impredicable (after all, it ought to be one or the other, right?) is a genuine antinomy: we cannot simply deny the existence of the word.

Research into this type of question—the subject being generally called metamathematics—continues apace. Not too long ago, Gödel showed (roughly speaking) that within any discipline of logic or mathematics, theorems could be validly formulated which could not conceivably be proven true or proven false. The prototypical such theorem is the famous "This theorem cannot be proven true," which poses obvious difficulties to someone trying to prove or disprove it. The theorem quoted is simply a formalization of the similar "This sentence is false," which opens Mr. Pollock's article. Gödel's work is taken as demonstrating that mathematics is intrinsically "incomplete" in that questions may be posed which cannot be answered.

There is a related question: Is mathematics consistent? That is, having proven some theorem, say, Theorem X, are we sure that the antithesis of Theorem X, say, Theorem anti-X, cannot be proven? It would be unfortunate if we could deduce both X and anti-X from valid argument. But there is now reason to believe that a proof of consistency cannot be achieved—not simply that we do not know one at the moment, but that one cannot conceivably exist. As someone said, "We know God exists, for mathematics is consistent; but we know the Devil exists, for we cannot prove that consistency."

ALAN A. GROMETSTEIN
Stoneham, Massachusetts

Nullspeak: A Question of Rotating Strawberry Madonnas

STEVE BONNER

Some linguists concern themselves with the evolution of languages over time. Others prefer to study language as it is used at a fixed point. I suggest we pause for a moment to consider language as it will never be used. Ever. This involves the deliberate construction of phrases that could never, under any circumstances, be construed to have any meaning whatsoever. Consider the expression:

rotating strawberry madonna

I submit that no human being has ever uttered this phrase. More important, I suspect that no one ever will. I am unable to construct a scenario in which a speaker would find it necessary to use this construct. Note that the important criterion here is that the phrase not only be absurd, but thoroughly unusable. I'm

Rotating Strawberry Madonna

not sure what it would mean for a madonna to be "strawberry," and I certainly see no advantage in having one that rotates. Here are a few more:

glorious B-flat noodles
carbonated burlap gentleman
forgetful elbow soda
mighty duckie snacks

concealed explorer fondue
feathery professor moments
angry tuba gravy

The more memorable expressions of this form have some properties in common. For example, they must conjure up imagery. They must deal with familiar, everyday objects in order for any absurdity to peek through. Thus, even though a *glorious B-flat cyclotron* may never be devised, the expression doesn't warm the heart quite like the noodles, simply because our daily experience with cyclotrons may not, a priori, preclude the possibility of their being either glorious or tuned in the key of B-flat.

But why do we insist that our expressions be absurd? Aside from the sheer frivolity of it all, we should note that every memorable passage that we have ever read has used a (perhaps slightly) absurd—or at least creative—use of images. P. G. Wodehouse writes:

Bashford Braddock removed his opera hat, squashed it flat, popped it out again and replaced it on his head.

He seemed disappointed that he could not play a tune on it.

This nervous tic of Bashford's leaves us with a whimsical mental superposition of a man's garment and an orchestral instrument. Braddock may be persuaded to provide us with a:

polyphonic garment rendition

The effective use of metaphor in literature requires that the quantities under consideration be normally separate entities. It does us no good to liken two things which are understood to be equivalent from the outset. Indeed, the entire creative process itself is nothing more than a deliberate synthesis of opposing, or even contradictory, notions.

Having rationalized as to why we engage in such nonsense, we may now proceed with reckless abandon:

> *naughty symphonic potatoes*
> *accelerating tweed mailman*

I suppose, as in the case of the *garment rendition,* we could try to produce a situation in which we would be compelled to discuss the *accelerating tweed mailman.* But to engage in such an endeavor would be to miss the point. The mental picture we get exists independently of the specific situation, and any attempt at producing a world in which the mailman might live would only serve to distract.

If we can devise useless phrases, why not useless words as well? For example, how about the word *geoslavic*? In morphology, it seems not at all unreasonable. But I challenge the reader to place it in context—any context. Here are a few others:

> *agrinasal*
> *micromatrimony*
> *hexayummy*
> *rotunditron*

An object might be describable as "yummy," but the addition of the prefix *hexa-* just doesn't seem to add anything. (This is not, of course, to say that Madison Avenue won't use it anyway.)

One might describe "words" such as *geoslavic* as "semantic fragments." After all, we are adjoining chunks of words—roots, prefixes, and suffixes—to obtain new words that convey rather curious, hybrid notions of (perhaps) dubious usefulness. One might draw an analogy between this and genetic engineering.

Components of words selected at random and spliced together may, if done correctly, produce a new, living thing, which takes on a personality all its own. Thus, even though I've never seen a *rotunditron*, I have already begun to form a mental picture of one.

How does this process differ from that used in Lewis Carroll's "Jabberwocky"? When Carroll informs us that it was *brillig*, and that *the slithy toves did gyre and gimble in the wabe*, we (somehow) have an idea of what he is talking about. Such is the power of suggestion. This is, of course, precisely why "Jabberwocky" has always been so very entertaining. But unlike our semantic fragments, Carroll is playing with phonology, not semantics. *Slithy* sounds as though it ought to mean something. Our fragments operate on semantic units. *Agri-*and *nasal* are both firmly implanted in the Indo-European lexicon, and are both used in a variety of useful ways (and now in a way that is not at all useful).

I can't help but wonder whether a technical journal somewhere has already coined the word *geoslavic*, perhaps in reference to Polish lignite deposits, or some such thing. I sincerely hope not.

SIC! SIC! SIC!

"Signs mark the growth—from bustling neighborhood 'botanicas' selling cult supplies to headless chickens left in church pews." From the *Houston Post*, 9 June 1984, p. 11G. Submitted by Betty Dillingham, Houston, Texas.

Polysemania, Semantic Taint, and Related Conditions

JOHN ELLISON KAHN

pol•y•se•ma•nia *n* [POLYSEMY + MANIA; syncope of *polysemimania*: compare *mineralogy*] (1985): an abnormal awareness of possible ambiguity; an uncontrollable tendency to bring to mind the inappropriate or unintended sense of a word in any context.

A traveling companion looks up from her book—a collection of science fiction stories—and says, "It's a dead giveaway, this one: The lead character's name is Hilda . . . don't you see?—Hitler." A word- and hormone-intoxicated friend during my adolescence ("I wonder who that friend could be"—Ogden Nash) constantly trades tenuous *double entendres* with his fellow schoolboys ("There's something I want to put to that Gloria." "Yes, it's time you got something straight between the two of you.") to the point where ordinary conversation becomes impossible (*hor*mone! *con*versation! be*comes*!) In its extreme form, the overingenious poet or crossword puzzler is afflicted by a hysterical muteness, having arrived at the mad (and obvious) intuition that almost any utterance is susceptible of a faulty interpretation. (And the microbiologist ended by starving himself, knowing what he knew, and unable to trust the purity of any food offered to him.)

Like neurosis, polysemania afflicts us all to some degree; the occasional registering of an unintended pun might almost be taken as a proof, or at least a condition, of our semantic competence (just as various mild neuroses are the lot, and the proof, of our Western humanness, Freud suggested). But only those whose neuroses are fairly disabling need be thought of as neurotics, and only those whose powers of communication and comprehension are seriously impaired by polysemy need be regarded as polysemaniacs. (In both conditions, the problem, of course, is deciding on the cut-off point.)

Polysemania is not new. Hamlet and Othello were victims of it in their way. Pathological punsters have no doubt always plagued polite society, and willful verbal misunderstandings have always ruined human relationships. The history of linguistic taboo even reveals a mild kind of mass polysemania: the discontinuation of *ādl*, 'illness' in Old English (to be replaced by the euphemism *disease*), through a clash with *adela* 'dirt', was not the work of some individual polysemaniac; similarly, the twentieth-century decline, noted by Bloomfield, in the use of *cock* in American English to refer to a male chicken points to a nationwide awareness of and embarrassment at the awkward dual meaning of the word.

Polysemania does, however, seem to be more widespread today than in former times. There are several reasons for this. Perhaps there is, for a start, simply more polysemy about of the relevant kind: New metaphorical senses, through the process of "radiation," are continually accumulating. And there is perhaps more semantic sensitivity, too (which is not to deny that there is also greater insensitivity nowadays than formerly). The fashion for self-scrutiny and self-improvement perhaps prompts middle-class speakers to reflect more carefully on the words they use and hear. The media have taken to showing a greater interest in language than in the past: The newspaper columns of William Safire or Philip Howard, for instance, or the various series of BBC radio programs on language—examining current usage and monitoring abuses—have sharpened the lay educated public's linguistic alertness. Finally, modern philosophical, linguistic, and literary methods of analysis (as these have filtered into secondary and higher education) encourage an intense concentration on individual words—their several kinds of ambiguity, the amount of scrutiny they seem to demand.

But you cannot encourage a sensitivity to words without risking a hypersensitivity. The overingenious readings of Empson and occasionally of Leavis stem partly from a semantic overloading of the words in a text—the attribution of a twentieth-century meaning, for instance, to a word in a seventeenth-century poem. More of this in a moment. Overheated word-consciousness is a particularly favorable environment for various other linguistic conditions: polysemy proper, connotation, "semantic taint," "idio-connotation," and so on.

Connotation seems to gain strength in the hothouse of a word-conscious mind. The honorific/pejorative associations of a word tend to intensify. This is true of both universal connotations (*stingy* = bad; *thrifty* = good) and optional connotations (*parsimonious* = good or bad, according to the context, or to your own feelings about the word and the world; similarly *conservative, genteel, muckraker*: you may regard these terms favorably or unfavorably, but the chances are that your regard is a fairly strongly felt one).

It is true, too, of "idio-connotation"—the unique set of associations that a word has for an individual user—its semantic fingerprint, so to speak. Proust's place-names provide a standard example. An example of my own: In my family, a common term of endearment is *Petunia* (based on *pet?*), and I cannot hear the word *petunia* "purely," even when it is spoken by a florist. One last example: When I was eight or nine, I read the following definition on a sweet wrapper: "A damsel is a little plum." (The joke, such as it is, had to be explained to me by my father.) To this day, I cannot divest the word *damson* or the word *plum* of a slightly saucy overtone.

The modern word-conscious mind is a good breeding-ground too for "suggestibles," as they have been called. The word *fatuous* has a suggestible: *fat.* Polysemaniacs cannot read or hear the word *fatuous* without conjuring up some image or other of fatness, possibly a paunchy wise-guy at a party. Near-homonymy generates and sustains obvious suggestibles for such words as *titter* and *hoary*, and even farfetched "idio-suggestibles": *pith*, for instance (as a result of a joke about lisping); or *prognathous* for *prognosis*.

When a word acquires a distinctive coloring in any of these various ways, it can be said to suffer "semantic taint." (This does not imply deterioration—witness *petunia*—though the taint usually does take that form.) The words *appeasement* and *pacification,* in the wake of Munich and Cambodia, have acquired distinctly unfavorable connotations. It would be a very ignorant or a very audacious speaker who used *appeasement* in a quite neutral and literal way today. *Appeasement* and even *pacification* have probably gone further than just acquiring new connotations and have acquired new denotations too. It is in fact polysemy that is the major cause of semantic taint. *Gay* and *queer* are more clear-cut examples. Their relatively recently acquired denotations have strongly tainted, though not quite yet fully tabooed out of existence the use of the words in their earlier senses. No up-to-date language-user could unselfconsciously speak or write the words *gay* and *queer* in their old acceptations. Not so much through fear of being misunderstood as through fear of raising an inappropriate laugh. Traditionalists may continue in defiance to parade the word *gay* forthrightly in its older sense (though attested in British underworld slang as long ago as 1935, *gay* in the sense of 'homosexual' became widely established only in the late 1960s and early 70s), but in their decrying of the new sense and its "annexation" of the word they are in effect admitting its firm hold. Or consider the modern use of *pathetic* in British English, 'inadequate, feeble, useless', which is now almost certainly more frequent than the older sense of 'arousing sympathy; pitiful'. It would be unwise, in Britain at least, to write of "the prima ballerina's pathetic performance in *Swan Lake*" if what you are intending is a eulogy.

Though the turnover of the primary meanings of words is greater today than in past times, it remains a turnover of dominance rather than of existence. A primary sense may be overshadowed and subordinated, but it is likely to persist for a long time. *Surprise* in the sense of 'to see or attack unexpectedly; to catch unawares' survives, though the more modern sense of 'to astonish, shock, or amaze' had probably gained the ascendancy as long ago as the early eighteenth century. (Similarly, *jealous, intercourse, luxuriously.*) Not that all dethroned senses survive, of course; the displaced senses of *disease* and *crafty*, for instance, have died out, but that was the work of generations if not centuries. (Similarly, *obsequious, silly, admirable, undertaker, edify, quaint, quick, curious, sad, lewd, cunning, shrewd.*)

The "survival" of a sense is a tricky notion, however. A dislodged sense may survive merely in people's passive rather than active vocabularies. Educated speakers would understand (though not without being distracted) the phrase "friendly intercourse between the nations," but they would be unlikely to initiate it in ordinary conversation. Some words, even though "tainted," do remain in the active repertoire, since there is no convenient synonym. *Balls*, to take the most obvious example. Circumlocution is sometimes possible: "I'll meet you at the courts, and get some tennis balls on the way." But not consistently: You cannot repeatedly complain that "Our tennis balls keep disappearing"; at some point you have to speak simply of "our balls." The middlingly sensitive man will after a time stop noticing the notional ambiguity; the polysemaniac will be pulled up short every time and have to grit his teeth and wait for the distraction to fade.

What remedy? "Try not to think of an elephant" goes the children's joke. Try likewise not to be distracted: for the poly-semaniac, prurient puns never lose their gloss, their incapacitating distractiveness. Further examples: *diaphragm, come, fairy, grope, hole, period, piles, pill, prick, screw, stool, streak, tart, tool*—all tainted, all indispensable.

To a greater or lesser degree, many tainted terms are dispensed with nowadays. In some cases, the loss is a small one, since the word in its old or unprovocative sense may be old-fashioned any-way and easily substitutable: *bondage, curse* ("'The curse is come upon me,' cried / The lady of Shalott"), *ejaculate, erection, gay* and *intercourse* again, *make love* ("Emma found, on being es-corted and followed into the second carriage by Mr. Elton, that the door was to be lawfully shut on them, and that they were to have a tête-à-tête drive . . . scarcely had they passed the sweep-gate and joined the other carriage, than she found her subject cut up—her hand seized—her attention demanded, and Mr. Elton actually making violent love to her"), *lover, motion, prophylactic, seduce* (though A. L. Rowse, just a few years ago, wrote in the *TLS* of "the half-wild cat I am engaged in seducing at present.")

With other shunned expressions, however, the loss is clearly an impoverishment. It would be very risky in British English to use *back passage* in its literal sense. The following sentence, from the *Yearbook of the British Pirandello Society*, 1981, is almost certain to elicit a snigger: "Also, in the finale, the audience see the aunt, Lena, touching La Demente for the first time, but it's behind the pane, in the back passage." So too with *pick up, jerk off* ("She watched Rena back the yellow Mini into the main stream of traffic and jerk off to the right. Then she let out a low sigh."—A. N. Wilson, *The Healing Art*), and so on.

Note that semantic taint is not always sexual or scatological in origin. Taint can be transmitted by political associations *(fellow traveler, solidarity, comrade)*, modern history *(holocaust, Watergate, Lebanon)*, sociology *(chauvinist, WASP, certifiable)*, entertainment *(python, Tom Jones)*, science *(transplant, plastic—* "God's plastic arm"), or mockery or puristic disapproval (vogue words and modern clichés such as *ongoing situation, adrenalin,* and *parameter*, and "misuses" such as *aggravate, hopefully, psychological moment,* and *viable*).

How disabling is semantic taint, really? The fact is, it seldom generates fully paralyzing polysemania. Empsonians do manage to continue reading, even after undertaking their exhaustive analyses of single words within a poem or play. Perhaps some natural immune-system comes into operation to counteract semantic taint. When the commonest linguistic microorganisms—*make, thing, pull, blow, rear*—acquire bawdy meanings, then some filter or antibody must be at work if linguistic life and sanity are to be preserved. Or rather, some controlling mechanism: the virus is not destroyed but kept in check. It is as though one goes through life with a mild fever. One copes. One accepts one's hopelessly anachronistic readings of old texts, but puts them to one side: "A man who exposes himself when he is intoxicated, has not the art of getting drunk" (Boswell, quoting Johnson).

> *I have heard that hysterical women say*
> *They are sick of the palette and fiddle-bow,*
> *Of poets that are always gay...*

All things fall and are built again,
And those that build them again are gay.

—W. B. Yeats, "Lapis Lazuli"

You did not come.
And marching Time drew on, and wore me numb.

—Thomas Hardy, "A Broken Appointment"

The modern senses of *gay* and *come* must not be allowed to affect one's final reading of such lines, even though they will almost inevitably enter one's consciousness and impinge on one's first reading.

A few corollaries and qualifications:

First, alongside semantic taint, there seems to be a reverse process, though it is quite rare. In certain contexts in certain dialects, the words *bugger* and *shit,* for instance, may undergo decontamination, as it were: "He's an energetic little bugger, that youngster of yours"; "Hey shit, man, look at that car move!" More subtly, terms originating as metaphors may through frequent use come to lose their metaphorical feel: Just as *abysmal* no longer evokes the idea of an abyss, so perhaps *virgin snow* no longer evokes the idea of a virgin.

Second, British and American English differ in semantic taint. Some expressions that are tainted for North Americans—*rubber,* notably—are free of taint for most British speakers. And vice versa: *back passage* (again), *bog, on the job, sod, spanking, stuff.* (Compare the differing standard interpretations of *to knock up* or *to keep your pecker up* in British English and American English.)

Third, some words seem to remain surprisingly resistant to taint. In *conversation,* for example, it is the centuries-old sexual association rather than the standard sense that has been subordinated. (Contrast *intercourse.*) So too with *know.* More recent stalwarts include *fruit, hump, nuts, purge, skin,* and *aides.* Or so it seems to me. But this might just be my idio-connotation, or lack of it. A proper survey is needed to ascertain the truth of the matter here.

Fourth—accordingly—research is necessary. A few pointers, then, by way of conclusion, for some adventurous doctoral student in search of a dissertation: Try to draw up a comparative service list of various tainted words decade by decade this century; to what extent has *come,* for instance, declined in recent years, and been replaced by *arrive* where appropriate?; trace the fluctuations in popularity of such given names as *Lou, John, Adolph* (and *Hilda?*) over the years; devise tests (along the lines of the *Measurement of Meaning* by Osgood et al.) for measuring semantic taint, and propose ways of incorporating the results of such tests into standard English dictionaries; compare the twenty-seven stylistic values—*poetic, facetious, laudatory, vulgar*, and so on—used in A. S. Hornby's *Oxford Advanced Learner's Dictionary of Current English.*

Two examples, finally, of the kind of material that might be used in testing a subject's "distraction-index" in the course of such research: Try assessing in yourself the "purity" of your response to the humor of the following joke, and to the datedness (or simple badness) of the lines of poetry:

"How can you put up a sign saying 'Beware of the Dog'?— that dog of yours doesn't even have any teeth left . . ."
   "That's true, but if he ever gets his jaws around your ankle, he can give you a really nasty suck."

Her beauty smooth'd earth's furrow'd face!
She gave me tokens three:—
A look, a word of her winsome mouth,
And a wild raspberry.

—Francis Thompson, "Daisy"

SIC! SIC! SIC!

"Now for 24 hours a day, I can sleep, swim and be completely active!" An ad for hair replacement, from the *New York Times*, 19 August 1984. Submitted by Rosemary Darmstadt, Glendale, New York.

Tosspots and Wraprascals

ANDREW E. NORMAN

One of the English language's most colorful and expressive techniques for forming nouns seems to have passed out of fashion over the last century or two. As defined by Professor Leon Lipson of Yale Law School, who introduced me to this word category in 1973, such nouns are composed of a transitive verb followed by its direct object and denote the implicit subject of the verb. I call them "tosspots."

Even the most straightforward, practical "tosspots" bristle with energy and imagery in comparison with commoner types of composite nouns—*breakwater, scarecrow, pickpocket, shearwater* (a bird that flies swiftly and smoothly a few inches above the surface of the sea). A *toothpick* has its primary purpose built into its name, but it is just as likely to be stuck into a canapé, whereas a *picktooth* springs into action as one utters the word. A *flycatcher* 'bird' knows its job and will do it when it has to, but a *catchfly* 'plant' vibrates with lethal greed. A *circuitbreaker* is obviously designed to perform its function, but can one rely on it? A *break-circuit* will do what it says, no doubt about it. A *screwdriver* promises results but neither tells how it will put the screw in place nor offers to remove it if necessary, while a *turnscrew* tells its whole story.

These qualities of energy, imagery, and succinctness make "tosspots" ideal for invective, frequently with a humorous twist. Here are some particularly rich categories:

Troublemakers: *scapegrace* 'wild and unprincipled', *rakehell* 'lewd and dissolute', *scarebabe* (*-bairn* in Scotland), *drawblood*, *flingbrand*, *blowcoal*, *makebate* (as in 'debate'), *stirpassion* and *stirstrife* (why the wildflower *loosestrife* is accused of this propensity I know not), *spitfire* and *shitefire* (though not *strikefire*, which is high-proof gin). *Fusspot* may be read either as 'potfusser' or as 'pot of fuss'; similarly, *fuss-budget*. Such ambiguities are the spice of "tosspot" hunting.

Criminals: *cutthroat, cutpurse, suckpurse* (extortionist), *burngrange* (a rural specialist; Absalom ignited Joab's fields just to attract his attention), *drawlatch, pickpocket,* and *picklock* (which is also a tool, and if one could find a *pick-wick* nowadays those Zippo lighters would last forever). *Stretch-halter* and *stretch-hemp* (and *stretch-neck*, for which the *OED* cites only Conan Doyle's *White Company*) clearly signify wishful thinking by the speaker, but a *stretchrope* is only a bellringer, and *Stretchlegs* is a personification of Death. Frustration of justice is implied by *scapegallows, slipgibbet,* and *sliphalter*. A *lickhalter* is just a knavish wag.

Flatterers and toadies: *scrapeshoe, clawback,* and *scratch-book, suckfist, pickthank(s), lickspittle* (also *-spit*) and, possibly, *flatter-cap*, though perhaps only when he is gushing over millinery.

Parasites: *lickladle, -box, -dish, -platter, -trencher,* and *-spigot* (not to be confused with a *suckspigot*, who comes later).

Contempt for extremes seems to be inherent in the form. If one bends over backwards to avoid such epithets as *spend-, slip-* or *slidethrift, spillgood,* or *scattergood,* one incurs hostile mutters of *sparethrift* or *saregood, scrapepelf* or *scrape-good, pinchfist* or *skinflint* (also *flay-* or *fleaflint*), *pinchgut* (usually reserved for a ship's purser), *scrapescall* or *pinch-, scrape-, spare-, scratch-* or surprisingly, *sharepenny* (*share* = 'shear'). But a *lickpenny* is something that costs too much (as in "Law is a *lickpenny*, Mr. Tyrrell," in Scott's *St. Ronan's*). And *catchpennies* are cheap goods priced for quick sale.

Join your friends in a drink or two, and if you're not a *tosspot* or *blowpot*, you're a *suckpint, suckspigot, suckbottle,* or *blowbottle*. Abstain, and you're a *drink-water* (not a *catch-water* nor yet a *spurnwater*, which are both kinds of ship's scuppers).

Heap a second helping on your plate and provoke a chorus of *stretchgut, fillbelly, lickfingers, flapsauce,* or *stopsauce*. Make a mess, and you're a *spillbread*. A *spurncow*, however, is neither a dieter nor a vegetarian but a cattleherder (as in *cowpoke; spurn* = 'spur'). And a *fillpot* is neither a glutton nor a sot: the *OED* gives it, along with *filldike* and *fillknag*, as an epithet for the weatherful month of February.

Truly the "tosspot" is harsh on flattercaps and short on flattery. It makes our most dedicated healer a *sawbones*, Heifetz or Menuhin a *scrapeguts*. It gives us *killjoy* and *spoilsport* (a *stopgamble* is not a *spoilsport* but the act of one, just as *lickfoot* is the act of a *lickspit*). It ridicules the *tattletale* or *telltale* (which can also be a piece of cloth or yarn tied to rigging to indicate apparent wind direction) and the *rattletrap* or *claptrap*, to which I should

Smell fungus

like to add the *wagjaw*. It exposes the shirking *scrimshank*, who presumably preserves his legs from unnecessary exertion. A *suck-egg* may be either an avaricious person or a weasel, or just a young person. A *cracktryst* cannot be relied on, a *lackwit* should not be listened to, and a *choplogic* should be avoided altogether. *Smell-fungus* was Sterne's pseudonym for Smollett; it was later used by such writers as Washington Irving and Frances Trollope for grumbling *findfaults* in general.

Not every "tosspot" 's connotation is derogatory, of course. *Burnewin* is not a *wagjaw* but a blacksmith (*win* = 'wind'). A butcher is a *killbuck* or *killcalf*. A *chafewax* sealed the Lord Chancellor's documents until the post was abolished in 1852. *Screw* better expresses prisoners' attitudes toward their guards than the literal and neutral *turnkey*. Nor is the *daredevil* inherently evil, though less than unalloyed admiration is implied in *tossplume*, *dashbuckler* or *swashbuckler*. (Note that *buckler* = 'shield'. The corruptly back-formed verb *swashbuckle* suggests that Errol Flynn buckled a swash.) Simple respect is so ill at ease in the "tosspot" form that I have found only two examples, both obsolete: *shunthank(s)* and *speaktruth*.

As for "tosspots" that exclusively denote women, all I have found accuse them of immoral behavior: *flingdust* and *flingstink*, and the milder *shaketail* and *wagtail* (which is also the name of a bird that performs the gesture in a less suggestive manner).

Rounding out the human "tosspots" are three interesting foreigners. A *catchpoll* or *-pole* was originally a *chasepoll*, a borrowed French witticism equating a tax collector's pursuit of his prey with a farmer's pursuit of his chickens, *poules*. Also from the French comes *fainéant* for 'do-nothing', though there appears to have been some false etymology at work in this case—the original was *faignant*, a simple present participle. Finally, *shunfield* (battlefield, that is) is attributed to Hobbes, who coined it to translate *phugoptolemos* in the *Odyssey*. (A *shunpike* is not a person but a free road that parallels a toll road.)

There is a cluster of "tosspots" beginning with *make-*, some of which do or can refer to persons, but their backs are often broken by hyphens, and a first-class "tosspot" retains a hyphen only to clarify pronunciation (e.g. *drop-piss*, *stretch-halter*). In one or more of the *OED*, *Webster's Second* and the *Random House Dictionary*, I have found *make-ado, -belief, -faith, -fire, -fray, -game, -king, -law, -mirth, -peace, -shame, -sport, -talk,* and -way. Makeweight is not given a hyphen, whereas make-work and make-rime are; what ties them together is that they do only what they are said to do—any secondary function forfeits the name. In contrast, makeshifts perform innumerable functions.

Several plants and animals, in addition to those already mentioned, have earned "tosspot" names for various reasons, usually strikingly apparent and often quite whimsical. Several varieties of grass are called dropseed, but only stangury is drop-piss. I have never grown stonecrop; now that I know it as prickmadam I am tempted to try. Breakstone and break-bones are straight translations of saxifrage and ossifrage (or perhaps the other way round?). Among the birds may be observed the scaredevil (a swift) and the dipears (I wonder; I have never seen a bird's ears), and the nicely contrasting cases of the turnstone (which does) and the killdeer (which doesn't but says it does). The whippoorwill would merit special status among "tosspots" because of its tucked-in adjective if one could be sure it was falsely boasting of its own obsessive sadism rather than odiously begging somebody else to do it or even, perhaps, reporting a crime. There are two fish, the suckstone (remora) and the jumprock (another sucker, native to the southeastern U.S.), and a worm, the lockdor. Spincop is a pleasant name for the spider, though perhaps inferior to "webster" (see Michael Innes's The Spider Strikes). The only quadruped I have found besides the suckegg (weasel) is the Indian elephant in the elegant, if hyphenated, role of carry-castle.

The "tosspot" is heavily indebted to mariners. In addition to the birds, fish, and objects noted above, it has given us dread-naught (or -nought) for a formidable ship of war; stop-water, a makeshift devised when proper caulking is impossible; cutwater, which is not only a bird but the bow of a ship, or a rope or cable in front of it, or a construction on the upstream side of a bridge; and *halyard,* the rope that hauls up a sail—sails having been attached to *yardarms* when ships were square-rigged.

The rest of my collection are scattered all over the language. After a hearty *breakfast,* one may seize one's *carryall, holdall,* or *catchall* and board a *jerkwater,* which was a train that stopped frequently to do just that, consequently becoming an adjective for towns so benighted that no train could be expected to stop there for any other purpose. *Lacklustre* is strictly an adjective in the United States, but it is acceptable as a noun for such a condition in England, where *stick-jaw* is gummy candy, a *spitfrog* is a small sword and a *lockspit* is a trench no wider than the tool it is dug with, used to mark ('lock') the turf ('spit') either to assert a legal claim or to guide the diggers. *Breakneck* is also usually met as an adjective, but as a noun it means either a fall of that kind or a place likely to produce one. A *drawstop* on an organ does what it claims. And a *scarefly* is either a device or an epithet for Jupiter or Beelzebub, according to the *OED.*

Any "tosspot" hunter is sure to chase up blind alleys. Among those that have deceived me: *tipstaff* (he may do it, but his title comes from the metal tip on his staff), *quitclaim* (surprisingly, *claim* is the verb; *quit* = 'quits' or 'even'), *bobtail* and *bangtail* (*bob* and *bang* = 'crop', and these are just bobbed examples of humdrum past participle formations), and *lockjaw* (not conclusively eliminated, but 'locked jaw' is given as an alternative form).

There are more than enough pleasant surprises, however, to keep one's spirits high. Deep from the subconscious suddenly leaps *stickum*! A stray puzzle supplies *wraprascal,* a voluminous cloak that could conceal a sword or bludgeon—and leaves one wondering whether a *crossword* does what it says or merely tells the solver to do it.

This is a serious problem in the world of games. *Spoilfive* is legitimate, I think, for it is the rules that do the spoiling if a specified sequence of cards does not appear. In the twentieth century sport of *crinklefender*, too, I am persuaded that the game, not the player, is the subject of the verb. I fear the reverse is true in *leapfrog, shove-ha'penny, drawgloves,* and *blowpoint* (a relative of darts). The names of these games are really directions to the players, like 'pick-up-sticks' and 'capture the flag.' Nor is *sweepstakes* a "tosspot," because the race does not sweep the stakes, the winner does (or used to, before changing social mores added shares for second, third, and fourth).

Perhaps the best thing to do with "tosspots" is to make up new ones. The champion is undoubtedly James Thurber, who enriched his beloved language with some twenty-four in one short article called "Do You Want to Make Something Out of It?" (included in *Thurber Country* and *Alarums and Diversions*). His contributions range from the *grabcheck* (a big spender, a generous fellow) to the *tossgraver* (an eloper . . . a *grablass*) and the *smackwindow* (the common June bug, or *bangsash*). It was here that Thurber introduced the unforgettable "*kissgranny*. (1) A man who seeks the company of older women, especially older women with money . . . (2) An over-affectionate old woman, a *hugmoppet,* a *bunnytalker*" and "*pressgrain*. A man who tries to make whiskey in his own cellar; hence, a secret drinker, a *hidebottle,* a *sneakslug*." What makes Thurber's achievement even more remarkable is that he was not consciously coining "tosspots"; he was losing sleep trying to think of words with specific letter combinations such as *abc* and *sgr* to use in the game of Superghosts.

Surely we need more "tosspots" to strengthen and enliven our language, though not as much as we need more Thurbers. But unearthing old "tosspots" is still rewarding. My latest find is the mysterious *flexpeng*; not only can the *OED* give no derivation, it is not even sure it means 'a gudgeon'.

And the rule against hyphens must not be taken too seriously. It might stop us from giving adequate thought to the question of *shut-eye*: who or what is the subject of the verb? Above all, it would deprive us of Professor Lipson's doubly unique—negative and imperative—discovery: the *forget-me-not*.

Quasi Malediction: The Case of Linguistic Malentendu

D. G. KEHL

One of the anecdotes to come out of Bernard Malamud's twelve years of teaching at Oregon State recounts how the yet-unpublished novelist concluded his first class by leaning over the lectern and saying, "It has been brought to my attention that many of you people here today are practicing celibacy. I have nothing against this practice and will not penalize you for it." When a few nervous giggles issued from the back of the room, Malamud pointed his finger at the gigglers and said, "I have documents in my possession which show that each one of you back there matriculated within the last two weeks. One as recently as this morning." It is rumored that when the session ended with the sound of more nervous laughter, most of the class stole forth to consult dictionaries or roommates.

When the same linguistic ploy was used a year later, allegedly by Claude Pepper's opponent in the 1950 senatorial election in Florida, the provincial rural listeners either had no dictionaries and roommates or felt no need to consult either. The remarks,

which had a considerably more devastating effect, were as follows: "Are you aware that Claude Pepper is known all over
Washington as a shameless extrovert? Not only that, but this man
is reliably reported to practice nepotism with his sister-in-law,
and he has a sister who was once a thespian in wicked New York.
Worst of all, it is an established fact that Mr. Pepper before his
marriage habitually practiced celibacy" (*Time,* 25 April 1983,
p. 29). Pepper was soundly defeated by 67,000 votes.

These two anecdotes illustrate what might be called quasi malediction—fancy but unfamiliar, sinister- or risque-sounding
words somewhere between paronomasia and malapropism. Like
the pun and double-entendre, quasi malediction is based on similarity of sound between two words with vastly different meanings, but, unlike the pun, it is less a play on words than a
confusion between words: linguistic *malentendu.* Like the malapropism, quasi malediction involves similarity in sound between
words, but, unlike the malapropism, it is not used incorrectly,
nor does it express an untruth. Rather, the confusion results from
a kind of linguistic short-circuiting through phonetic association.

If it seems hard to believe that the example Malamud used in
1949 would work effectively on today's more sophisticated fresh-
men, here is a suggested update: "It has come to my attention
that many of you are openly practicing altruism. Furthermore, I
know for a fact that there are numerous thespians on campus and
a great deal of unabashed homogeneity. As if that weren't incredible enough, there are openly acknowledged philatelists, Sa-
turnians, and practitioners of Satyagraha! To those of you
tittering in the back, let me say that I have seen students on this
campus openly defenestrating and can assert unequivocally that
you people have been masticating up to three and four times a
day—and even doing it openly in groups."

It would not be hard to imagine Senator Sludgebottom,

reactionary member of the state legislature's Appropriations Committee, speaking in opposition to the proposed budget for State U. "I wonder if you, my esteemed colleagues, and the morally upright taxpayers of this state, realize what is going on at State U., supported by our tax dollars! On a recent visit to the campus, I saw students openly festinating on the malls, conjugating in the halls, and even lucubrating in library stalls till all hours of the night! Altruistic professors are teaching things like syntactics, synonymy, syncretism, and synergism. And, incredible as it may seem, professors make a habit of examining students' theses! Furthermore, I have documented proof that several have openly advocated polysyndeton! One of the custodians told me that he has found used phylacteries around the campus. English professors actually teach their students to conjugate, even providing demonstrations, and talk about copulative verbs and genitive case, about rising action, climax, and falling action! Because of such a paradisaic atmosphere, which spawns lustration and plenipotent activity among students, tax monies are now being expended on such things as CLEP examinations and herpetology! If we don't put our foot down now, next thing we know the administration will be dispensing phylacteries in the Student Union!"

Unlike the punster, who relies on his audience's awareness of the two words' denotations, the user of quasi malediction relies on his audience's ignorance of the denotation and confusion over connotation through phonetic association. Unlike Mrs. Malaprop and her kin, who confuse the denotation of two words and substitute one for the other on the basis of connotative confusion, the user of quasi malediction, fully aware of both, chooses an erudite but pejorative-sounding word, intending the false connotation to short-circuit the correct denotation.

One of the few belletrists to make use of quasi malediction in fiction is Peter De Vries. Perhaps his favorite example, at least the most often recurring (appearing in four of his twenty novels) is this one: "I have just found out my husband is heterosexual" (*The Tents of Wickedness* [Boston: Little, Brown, and Co., 1977], p. 223). Another version occurs in *Madder Music,* when a character announces at a fashion-show luncheon hosted by his wife, "Hi. I'm a closet heterosexual" (*Madder Music* [Boston: Little, Brown, and Co., 1977], p. 196).

In De Vries's *Through the Fields of Clover* there is this interchange:

> "He's a famous philatelist."
>
> "I suppose the theater is full of those. . . . Well in that case I suppose a girl is safe from him at least. . . . Has he ever undergone treatment for it?"
>
> "It's hopeless. He's up all night with the things. Some rare specimens in his collection."
>
> "I can imagine. Can you tell me something about his background? Where is he from?"
>
> "Walla Walla. His father was the town podiatrist."
>
> "Then it runs in the family. My, this sort of thing is on the increase" (*Through the Fields of Clover* [New York: Popular Library, 1961], pp. 42–43).

When Cotton, the confused character, finally gets it all straight—or thinks she does—someone tells her that So-and-so is a well-known pederast, and she says, "Tell me, does he have a large practice?"—an example of true malediction unrecognized. Later in the same novel, another character says to Cotton, "You're still interested in monads." Cotton's mother, Mrs. Marvel, replies, "Well, intellectual often goes with high-sexed" (Ibid., p. 170).

Another example occurring in two of De Vries's novels uses *charisma* as quasi malediction: "They tell me you have charisma. You certainly don't look well. Are you taking anything for it?" (*Madder Music*, p. 193. See also *Mrs. Wallop* [New York: Popular Library, 1970], p. 76).

Then there is the woman who fed her husband oysters "because she'd heard they were good for virility—thinking that was something to be cured" (*Mrs. Wallop*, p. 113); the woman who thinks *afro* is short for *afrodisiac*, having something to do "with colored people being so highly sexed" (*The Glory of the Hummingbird* [New York: Popular Library, 1974], p. 103); the character who thinks *exhibitors* are "preverts" (*Madder Music*, p. 74); the character who thinks a penal colony is a place where male chauvinists should be incarcerated (*I Hear America Swinging* [New York: Popular Library, 1977], p. 149); and the character who says, "I seemed to have an animus—I didn't know what that meant, but it sounded dirty" (*Reuben, Reuben* [New York: Popular Library, 1964], p. 16).

Quasi malediction is innocent language which *sounds dirty*. Sometimes the connotative short-circuiting is completely unintentional on the part of the speaker or writer. Any English teacher who has attempted to teach Emily Dickinson's poem "There Is No Frigate Like a Book" to a class of undergraduates has been introduced to the effect of unintentional quasi malediction in the classroom! The same nervous giggles can be heard when one uses such innocuous words as *fructifying, frigorific, feckless, scrutable*, and *copulative verb*.

Examples of quasi malediction with anatomical associations are: *Regina/reginal, Künstlerroman, cochlea, cochinal, cockchafer, cockshy, cocksure, penal* and *penology, titillate, titivate, tit for tat, asinine*, and *assonance*. Associations with bodily functions and scatology (a word sometimes confused with *eschatology*, thus rendering the latter, in those cases, quasi malediction) have produced such examples as: *crapulence/crapulous, shittah, piscine, pisiform, piscatology, epistemology, fasces, infarct/infarction,* and *mensuration.* Sensitive speakers will be wary of talking about *seminal influences, Pithecanthropus Erectus, cunning lingua franca,* and in the case of Catholic theology, *ejaculatory prayers.*

When words are used with full reliance on the audience's knowledge of denotations and awareness of, with no confusion over, the connotations, the result is a form of paronomasia. For example, the movie *E.T.* used a pun on *Uranus.* Similarly, such titles as Jerzy Kosinski's *Cockpit* and Mickey Spillane's *Erector Set* are double entendres, whereas Robert Coover's *Pricksongs and Descants* could validly be called an example of quasi malediction—if for no other reason than the fact that relatively few would be acquainted with those forms of medieval music.

Humorless readers of C. S. Lewis might summarily dismiss as unintentional quasi malediction what is more likely an effective double entendre. In his Preface to *The Screwtape Letters*, Lewis, discussing the depiction of angels in visual art, refers to "the frigid houris of a teatable paradise." Both adjectives can be read as effective puns: the beautiful, black-eyed, seductive, Persian nymphs are not only stiff and formal but also sexually cold, just as the "paradise" is characterized not only by an atmosphere of people sitting at tea but also by a profusion of ample, abundant, and available teats! Such a reading hardly conflicts with the attitudes of a writer who argued eloquently in *The Four Loves* for humor in the bedroom!

More than most linguistic modes, such as paronomasia and malapropism, quasi malediction has diametric force. On one hand it can be used perniciously for propagandistic manipulation and even character assassination—the linguistic form of guilt by association—but on the other hand it can be used beneficially in the cause of Thalia: to create effective humor. Perhaps more widespread knowledge of the mode will decrease manipulation and increase and enhance the humor.

Slang, Jargon, and Other Limited-Range Vocabulary

Slang is a sexy topic; it is reported by the newspapers and lambasted by the educators, so you know it's fun. Jargon is more often criticized, usually by those who understand that the same words which ostensibly promise you knowledge can serve instead to exclude you from it. Slang and jargon are all about belonging, whether it's to a prison gang, the circus, or the tiddlywinks team. Once you know the lingo, you're much more than halfway in.

Lingua Collegiensis circa 1850

CHARLES LAFAYETTE TODD

Reading through my bound copy of *Verbatim*, volumes III and IV, I ran across a piece by Sterling Eisiminger of Clemson University entitled "College Slang 1975." As a collector of such arcane items during my years as a professor of speech at Hamilton College in Clinton, New York, I was frequently called upon by several older colleagues on our joint faculty-student "Sin Committee," known officially as a "Student Activities" committee, to translate some of the words and phrases that came so trippingly off the tongue of our student members. For example, I recall a case in which a roomie of a young gaper who had caused some damage at an Eastern women's college (Skidmore) tried to explain his friend's behavior. "Well," he announced, "we rolled off on the Skids that weekend, and Joe got stuck with a turkey. As a result he got snoggered, started to flail and caused some demo." I translated this along these lines: 'This obstreperous young fraternity pledge drove to Skidmore for a weekend mixer, found himself paired off with an unattractive date, drank too much and demolished some furniture.' According to Eisiminger, Clemsonites are familiar with *gapers* and *turkeys*—though I am not certain they are aware of *flailing* and *demo*.

All of this brings to mind one of my more cherished books, *A Collection of College Words and Customs,* published by Benjamin Homer Hall while a senior at Harvard, in 1851. Hall, who was apparently acing his courses in Latin, Greek, and Rhetoric, got bored, as so often happens to over-achieving seniors, and purchased "two quires of note paper" which he proceeded to fill with "a strange medley, an olla podrida, of student peculiarities" he had picked up from his fellow students and through occasional visits to other New England colleges. Arranging these linguistic peculiarities in alphabetical order, adding notes as to their meanings and possible origins, he sent off his collection to a Cambridge publisher, John Bartlett. Fearful that Harvard's formidable president, Jared Sparks, might look askance at his publication, he used a pseudonym; but somehow Sparks discovered the young author's name, and, to Hall's amazement, called him into his office and presented him with a three-volume set of *The History of Harvard College* with some complimentary remarks on his "scholarly achievement." Shortly after his graduation, Hall went to work in earnest, canvassing student magazine and newspaper editors in thirty-four other colleges throughout the country. The response was obviously enthusiastic, for in 1856 Bartlett published a "Revised and Enlarged Edition" of 506 pages, bearing the name B. H. Hall. It was replete with an index and a list of all of the contributing colleges. Save for a history of Eastern Vermont, it was the only book by Hall ever published; he spent most of his career as editor of the Troy, New York, *Whig*, and died in 1892.

Reading through Hall's collection of mid-nineteenth-century (and earlier) college slang, one is struck by the unchanging pre-occupations of college students: passing and failing tests, currying professorial favors, labeling the peculiarities of their peers, complaining about college food and other conveniences (or lack of same), cheating when necessary, and trying to survive four long years without being rusticated ('sent home for a few weeks to think it over'), or being ruthlessly expelled. About the only aspects of college life that Hall fails to dwell upon are terms applied to that rare commodity on college campuses, females (who, as Elizabeth Cady Stanton's father pontificated, "suffered from a defect of sex") and the consumption of "ardent spirits," which was kept very much under wraps at the time except by Eliphalet Nott, the president of Union College in Schenectady, New York, who constantly warned his students against the "spontaneous combustion" which might result if one smoked while drinking. Incidentally, I was pleased to discover that Hamilton College produced sixteen entries, edging out Columbia and Dartmouth but outclassed by Harvard, Yale, Bowdoin, and Union.

One of the main obsessions of college students in those days was the ubiquitous privy, and, on this subject, Hall certainly got around. His first entry is *bogs*, emanating from England's Cambridge University. At Harvard it becomes a *mingo*, derived, he says from the Latin, *mingere*, "a structure estimated at less than 2000 pounds avoirdupois which could easily be burned down." (Of course, we know better: *mingere* is Latin for 'urinate.') He cites the *Williams College Monthly Miscellany* as lamenting the "incineration of the Lem—may it rise from its ashes like the Phoenix." At Hamilton College it was called the *Joe*, named, says Hall, for president Joseph Penny, who was often careless about having the equipment "purified" at appropriate intervals. When the campus Joes gave out, Hamilton students sometimes hired horse-drawn carts and took off down the Hill, where they liberated local privies in Clinton and burned them on campus during ceremonial occasions. It was called *burning the Joe* and, says Hall, "the derivation is obvious." Union College called it the *Burt*, named after the "architect of the sacred latrinae at the institution." At Wesleyan it became a *minor*, reflecting, Hall assumes, its "spatial inadequacies." Today's students are much less inventive, referring to their sanitized facilities simply as the *John*, or the *can*.

As for one's peers, few of the terms used to delineate them were flattering, although Princeton referred to those who were very pleasant and agreeable as *bucks*, usually well *groomed*, or *diked out*. Opposites at Dartmouth were called *gonuses*, defined by the author as "uncouth or stupid fellows." Overly pious and sententious lads were referred to at Washington College in Pennsylvania as *donkeys* or *lapars*. Nearby Jefferson College transformed the latter into *long ears*. When donkeys, etc., became too vociferous in their attempts to reform their peers at Harvard they were told to *ferg*, or as students would say today, *cool it*. Cheating or attempts to do so produced such words as *gamming* (University of Vermont), *chawing* (Dartmouth), or *gassing* (Williams).

The ancient art of currying favor with a professor, now known almost universally by even the more refined students as *brown-nosing, ass-kissing,* or *sucking up,* was treated more gingerly by Hall's contemporaries and produced a multitude of strange words such as *cahooling* (University of North Carolina), *coaxing* (Yale), *fishing* (Harvard), and *bauming* (Hamilton). Hall provides no explanation for the Hamilton term, though one suspects it derived from the name of a student who was adept in such matters. With regard to failing a crucial test, the author produces a fine medley of appropriate terms such as to *Barney,* to *dead,* and to *burst* (all from Harvard). Princeton students referred to a complete failure as a *blue fizzle*; Middlebury lads *balled up,* while Yalies simply *flummuxed.* In most Southern colleges, says Hall, the word is *cork.* Incidentally, Yale flummuxers were known as students of the science of *Flunkology.* Walking out on a professor who arrived late to class also came in for its share of descriptive words. Students at Hamilton and other Eastern colleges *bolted.* Bowdoin boys, however, simply staged an *adjournment.* During the 1880s one entire Hamilton class staged a mighty bolt from the entire College, and there is a stone marker on campus bearing a carved bolt in memory of a class that never enjoyed a commencement exercise.

B. H. Hall's prodigious research produced many other student linguistic peculiarities too numerous to mention here, though I can't resist adding to his *olla podrida* the word *fat,* which at Princeton meant a letter containing money from home—one of the more glorious events in the life of college students throughout the ages.

Slayer Slang

MICHAEL ADAMS

Buffy the Vampire Slayer (BTVS), a recent teen television hit, coins slang terms and phrases in nearly every episode, many of them formed in the usual ways, some of them at the crest of new formative tendencies, and some of them interesting, not only lexically, but morphosyntactically. The show incorporates familiar slang, too; the familiar and newly coined "slayer slang" together compose a particularly vivid snapshot of current American teen slang. Examination of mainstream and cult magazines, fan books, and websites, however, suggests that slayer slang, far from being ephemeral vocabulary, steadily intrudes on everyday speech and may be here to stay.

Joss Whedon, a versatile screenwriter whose credits include *Alien: Resurrection, Toy Story,* and *Speed,* introduced Buffy the Vampire Slayer in the eponymous feature film (1992). He subsequently adapted the story for the small screen. The series premiered on March 10, 1997, and this year completed its third season. Its fairly large following, the largest of any show on the U.S. WB (Warner Brothers) network, consists of teens and twenty-somethings who share a taste for Anne Rice novels and cinema on the cusp of the fantastic. Fans of the show have proved extraordinarily dedicated to it: They support a *Buffy* industry that already produces the obligatory T-shirts, posters, trading cards, jewelry, and shot glasses and has generated a dozen novelizations, a quarterly magazine, five or so books about the show, and dozens of articles in dozens of magazines. In December 1998 there were 1,816 websites worldwide devoted to *Buffy,* most of them located in the United States, but including sites in Canada, Australia, Great Britain, Germany, France, and Singapore. "*BTVS:* Slayer Central," a site chosen at random, registered over 25,000 hits in 1998, and no wonder: that site has received the Buffy Index Award, the Graveyard Award, *BTVS* Land's Award, the Nosferatu Award, and the Buffy Award for Outstanding Sites, among others. Homage for Buffy is more frequent, more sincere, and more competitive than most of us can imagine easily.

The series opens with a formulaic introduction to vampire slayers, of which Buffy is only the most recent: "As long as there have been demons, there has been the Slayer. One girl in all the world, a Chosen One, born with the strength and skill to hunt vampires and other deadly creatures ... to stop the spread of their evil. When one Slayer dies, the next is called and trained by the Watcher." Buffy is a reluctant slayer: Vampires interfere with her cheerleading career and her social life. After burning her Los Angeles high school to the ground during a prom in order to kill the vampires who attempted to turn the event into a blood-fest, Buffy Summers moved to Sunnydale, California. Unable to escape her destiny as the Slayer, however, she encounters her new Watcher, Rupert Giles, who poses as Sunnydale High School's librarian. Sunnydale, we discover in the first episode, is located on a Hellmouth, and vampires roam the streets freely, bent on nothing less than the destruction of this world. Though her identity should be secret, a few friends know Buffy as the Slayer and assist her: Willow Rosenberg, her best friend, is a brilliant computer nerd who once loved her childhood friend Xander Harris; Xander is clever enough, too, though an underachiever, has a crush on Buffy, but has always loved Willow; Cordelia Chase is rich, popular, acid-tongued, and unaccountably in love with her boyfriend, Xander; Oz, incidentally a werewolf, is usually just Willow's boyfriend and plays guitar in a band; and Buffy falls in love with Angel, a reformed vampire who turns bad again, and whom Buffy is forced to kill at the end of the second season. By twists of plot too convoluted to rehearse here, a rival slayer named Faith appears in the third season, a high school drop-out, horny, leathered, and tattooed. They are all average kids, in average relationships, battling the forces of adolescent evil, personified, in a sense, by vampires, demons, and monsters; they are also particularly adept speakers of American English, especially of slang.

Of course, the show employs plenty of familiar slang, some recorded in dictionaries and some not. The oldest item, *five-by-five,* Faith may have gleaned from the *Random House Historical Dictionary of American Slang,* where it appears, in the sense Faith employs, in a single quotation from 1983: "How are you?" Buffy asks Faith, to which she responds, "Five-by-five." "I'll interpret that as good," glosses Buffy in turn, and very near the dictionary's 'perfect, fine'. If Faith's Goth-chick slang veers towards the obscure, other characters favor the teen mainstream: "Don't worry, I can *deal,*" Buffy assures her companions; "So, you're not *down* with Angel," she acknowledges of Spike, Angel's rival among Sunnydale vampires; "That's the sound she makes when she's speechless with *geeker* joy," Xander explains of Willow; "Don't forget, you're supposed to be a *girly girl,* like the rest of us," Willow reminds Buffy. "Great," says Willow, "I'll give Xander a call. What's his number? Oh, yeah, one-eight-hundred-I'm dating a *skanky ho*"; "You just *went*

O. J. on your girlfriend," Buffy remarks to one unfortunate; "My egg *went postal* on me," she explains after a monster hatches from it. Buffy, just like any real American teen, develops crushes on *hotties,* but if the love is unrequited, the situation is, *like, totally heinous.* Buffy, far from abject, *chills.* Maybe she'll stay at home on Saturday and *veg* rather than indulge the boy's unromantic *riff.* If the *hottie* in question asks her out again, she might see an *upside* and be *good to go,* or she might ask herself, *"What's up with that?"* refuse him sarcastically with archaic, and therefore insincere, slang, like "Wow, you're a *dish,"* and then *bail. Whatever,* you get the idea.

But the show does more than merely capture current teen slang; rather, it is endlessly, if unevenly, inventive. Thus Buffy, only tentatively supporting the romance budding between Xander and Cordelia, assures them, "I'm glad that you guys are getting along, *almost really."* Vampires, apparently cast into fashion Limbo on the day they become undead, are often marked by their unstylish wardrobes. "Look at his jacket," says Buffy of one them. "It's dated?" asks Giles, to which Buffy responds, "It's *carbon-dated."* When Cordelia dumps him, Xander asks a young, not awfully proficient witch to cast a love spell on Cordelia; when it backfires and affects everyone *but* Cordelia, he muses to Giles, "Every woman in Sunnydale wants to make me her *cuddle-monkey."*

Most of us are lucky if we're carefree, but the Slayer thinks in grander terms: "I don't have a destiny," she retorts, when reminded of her cosmic role. "I'm *destiny-free."* When bitten by his infant nephew, Oz is shocked to learn that he belongs to a family of werewolves: "It's not every day you find out you're a werewolf," he explains, "That's fairly *freaksome."* In spite of the lunar cycle, Oz's popularity, his social position, is intact, but not everyone in high school is so lucky, as Cordelia, ever alert on such matters, points out: "Doesn't Owen realize he's *hitting a major backspace* by hanging out with that loser?" Teens map their own linguistic territory, as opposed to their parents', with slang, and sometimes "improve" earlier slang to stake their own generation's claim. Cordelia complains to a petulant Buffy, "Whatever is causing the Joan Collins *'tude,* deal with it. Embrace the pain, spank your *inner moppet,* whatever, but get over it." Cordelia's coinage puts her divorced parents' pop-psychological jargon in its place.

With vampire slaying and other important teen responsibilities imminent, Buffy and her cohort are forced "to do *round robin*" which, as Willow glosses, is "where everybody calls everybody else's mom and tells them they're staying at everybody's house." Slang for Sunnydale teens, as for teens worldwide, serves as a transgressive code. Fun abounds for average teenagers, who *round robin* to party in the Sunnydale graveyard, but, as the Slayer who inevitably saves them from rising vampires ruminates, "It's all *mootville* for me." Instead, she's forced to play miniature golf with her mother's boyfriend; when she cheats and the boyfriend, actually a robot who makes people like him by lacing baked goods with pleasant sedatives, overreacts, she admits, "Yeah, I kicked my ball in, *put me in jail,* but he totally *wigged.*" Man or robot, the prospect of a boyfriend for mom unsettles her: "You know how dispiriting it is for me to even contemplate you grownups having *smoochies,*" a sentiment echoed in the hearts and minds, at least, of teen viewers everywhere.

Lest the show seem "cleaner" than other adolescent TV, sex comes up frequently, especially regarding Buffy's relationship with Angel. Angel, though a vampire, had regained his soul, but when he and Buffy have sexual relations, her first, he finally experiences true happiness, the trigger that fires his soul back to Hell. Given the plot on its own terms, and the way in which the story metaphorically represents one take on adolescent sexual experiment (whatever boys say before sex, they're monsters afterwards, sex kills, etc.), the show's references to sex are, for the most part, predictably innocent. Unlike the other characters, however, Faith is sexually active, her sexual language potent and notably absent from the dictionary record: "Bet you and Scott have been up here *kicking the gear stick*," she remarks to Buffy as they hunt vampires on Lovers' Lane; unable to leave the subject alone, she asks, "Do you ever catch kids *doing the diddy* out here?" Faith's sexual references aren't always euphemistic and lighthearted, however. At her earthiest, she grunts: "I mean, I'm sorry, it's just, all this sweating nightly, side-by-side action, and you never put in for a little after-hours *unh*?" Sometimes she is even racier, but careful of the FCC: "Tell me that if you don't get in a good slaying, after a while, you just start itching for some *vamp* to show up so you can give him a good *unh.*"

It is difficult to imagine the value of such terms to the show, embedded as they are in a rich and dynamic context, context that resists excerption. Meaning, then, is sometimes difficult to isolate, but not the sociolinguistic importance of slayer slang: Every major character in the show coins or derives terms to reflect subtly his or her social and psychological experience. The result is clever, precise, and expressive, as the language of adults, slang or other, naturally cannot be. Neither Buffy nor any of her associates is, as Oz denominates a particularly dim bulb, "a master of the *single entendre*," and the show's continual use of slang, not to mention its running commentary on the English language, successfully dignifies teen language and the range of teen experience for which it speaks.

Evidence already quoted proves that the English language often occupies the writers' minds, and thus it often occupies the characters' minds, as well. *Buffy the Vampire Slayer* is an especially language-conscious television show. The characters are backhanded definers ("Man, that's like, I don't know, that's moxie, or something"), bemused grammarians (in one episode, Willow struggles to determine whether one should say "slayed" or "slew"), amateur etymologists (" 'The whole nine yards'— what does it mean? This is going to bother me all day"), or self-conscious stylists ("Again, so many words. Couldn't we just say, 'We be in trouble? . . . Gone.' Notice the economy of phrasing: 'Gone.' Simple, direct"), whatever the situation demands. "Apparently Buffy has decided that what's wrong with the English language is all those pesky words," Xander remarks in one episode. But the problem may not be the absolute number of words so much as the plethora of inadequately expressive ones. As the show continually demonstrates, teens dissatisfied with the language they inherit can invent a language in which the words are not pesky, but relevant.

While much of the show's slang reproduces the current teen lexicon (good fortune for slang lexicographers, who comb the media for words generally spoken, and then only recently), *Buffy the Vampire Slayer* not only invents slang, but intends to do so. As Sarah Michelle Gellar, the actress who plays Buffy, explained to *Rolling Stone* (2 April 1998), "Let me tell you how un-Buffy I am . . . For the first episode, I come in and yell, 'What's the *sitch*?' I did not know what '*sitch*' meant. I still have to ask Joss [Whedon], 'What does this mean?' because I don't speak the lingo. I think he makes it up half the time." "The slang? I make it all up," says Whedon cheerfully, though Gellar's estimate is more accurate. Once America's busiest teen, Gellar nonetheless surely knows plenty of slang, and her ignorance of Whedon's lingo is one indication of its novelty. Viewers recognize and appreciate the show's characteristic innovation: While playing the Buffy the Vampire Slayer Drinking Game (for which the official shot glasses come in handy), viewers are invited to drink whenever Buffy utters a "Buffy-ism," though we are told that this category "Does not include CBS's (Cute Buffy Sayings) like: 'Goodbye stakes, hello flying fatalities.' " According to the rules, CBS's deserve two sips, where Buffy-isms warrant only one, but the game neatly distinguishes the show's linguistics from its poetics.

SIC! SIC! SIC!

"If you are seated in an exit row and you cannot read this card, or cannot see well enough to follow these instructions, please tell a crew member." From an emergency instruction card on United Airlines planes. Submitted by
J. Robert Orpen, Jr., Chicago.

Of Eating Rubber and Sno-Cones

GERALD ESKENAZI

I guess I had been hanging around locker rooms too long. Some years ago, I was sitting quietly with my son Michael at a World Series game. Suddenly, I jumped up when one of the Mets hit a line drive. I yelled, "It's a tweener!" My boy thought that was hysterical. *Tweener* does sound silly, I'll admit. Almost risqué, in fact. But I explained that a tweener is a line-drive hit between the outfielders. It is part of the rich lexicon of inside-sports expressions—that is, those used by the athletes themselves, and of which "civilians" are rarely aware.

The world of sports abounds with these descriptive, and often clever and funny, words and phrases. In more than thirty years of covering sports, from the frozen ropes of football to the shake-

and-bakes of basketball, I have delighted in a well-turned phrase by athletes. They employ a sense of humor in describing what they do and the perils and joys of their job.

Hockey brought me my first inside look—or listen. I learned of a *snow-thrower*. No, it is not something one hauls out of the garage after a winter storm. A snow-thrower is a 'sissy,' a 'skater who throws snow when he screeches to a halt and the ice shavings fly.' Presumably, he has stopped short of having contact, of *mucking it up.* Some might call it prudent, but not hard-nosed hockey players.

To a fan, a goalie on the receiving end is being bombarded with a flurry of shots, but to the hockey player, the goalie is *eating rubber.* Actually, it is an expression that made sense at one time. The goalie's mask came to prominence only in the 1970s. Before then, a barefaced goalie literally "ate rubber." He lost a few teeth, and the referee would hold up the game while the goalie went to the trainer's room and "took twenty"—the number of stitches he needed to repair his face. Even the face mask, which is mandated by the rules these days, was looked at as de-masculinizing the game. When Jacques (Jake the Snake) Plante, the great—and safety-conscious—Montreal Canadiens' goalie of the 1960s, donned one the first time, a fan yelled, "Hey, Plante, Halloween's over!"

Athletes generally laugh at danger or pressure, and their language reflects that approach. When a pitcher is taken out of the game, he is miffed because the manager *took the rock out of my hands.* That is an unusually insensitive description of a ball—*rock,* as if it were nothing more than something one might pick up in field of dreams.

A lovelier phrase, I think, is *painting the black.* This also harkens to a time when the grass was green and the beveled edge of home plate was black. The black portion served to offset the white plate, making it easier for an umpire to call a runner out or determine balls and strikes: It was not supposed to be part of the plate. But umpires allowed pitchers that outer limit. The *black* these days is virtually buried in the home-plate dirt, not visible to the fans. Indeed, the pitcher cannot even see it. Yet a pitcher who is *painting the black* is getting his ball on the edge, nipping the corners, so to speak. His control is impeccable.

My favorite baseball expression is a *sno-cone*, because it is the most aptly descriptive. When a fielder leaps or dives for a ball— just barely gets it to stay in his glove, but most of it is sticking out—that is a *sno-cone*.

Other expressions need no translation for a ballplayer, although they certainly are arcane to the fan in the stands. When a spectator sees a mischievous curve ball, the player sees an *Uncle Charlie*, a *yellow hammer*, or a *yakker*. There is probably an African American slang component to some of the newer expressions; certainly, *Uncle Charlie* seems to be a takeoff on *Mr. Charlie*, 'the man, or boss, or someone or something to be respected.' While the TV announcer is getting excited about the home-run the hitter has just stroked out of the park, the batter is probably thinking, "I took the pitcher *downtown.*" *Downtown* likely is another word with a black source, suggesting a good time or at least some movement as a baseball.

Carl Yastrzemski, the Hall of Famer with the Red Sox, never boasted. But in a book we collaborated on he told me he was proud of his ability to avoid being frightened by *chin music*, a 'pitch aimed at the head.'

And there certainly are some fellows with a strong arm—a *good hose*, they would say—who can *bring it* and create harmonics with their fast ball rippling the air. Of course, their fast balls are *heaters.* The trickier pitchers, though, *turn the ball over*: their pitches reach the batter with a slight reverse curve, something known to the public as a *screwball.*

I am sure there are other crossover words, but *tweener* is one that is good enough to play two sports. In football a *tweener* is a 'person whose size complicates life for the coach': Is the player big enough for the defensive line or is he outsized for linebacker? He is a *tweener.*

A familiar football expression in the coaches' meeting rooms is *red zone,* referring not to the off-limits hot-spot these big fellows seek out in the wee hours but to the area between the opponents' twenty-yard line and the goal line—the zone one should be able to score from. A good quarterback can get one in. Some do it by throwing a *frozen rope*—a 'tight spiral that zips toward the receiver on a straight line.' And when that goal line is finally crossed, the scorer might even celebrate by trying to *roll six*— 'spin the ball on end, like a top, in the end zone'.

Unlike athletes in other sports, boxers do not have time to stage a demonstration after a good move. They have to wait until the match is over. Their workmanlike approach to the so-called "sweet science" is indicated by the phrase *riding the elevator,* meaning that a fighter is multidimensional and doing a classic job: He is attacking the body as well as the head.

Amateur boxers wear tank shirts, the pros do not. So when a fighter turns pro, his manager proudly says, *"He took off the vest."* And if the fighter becomes good, cuffing around an opponent, stinging him and raising purple welts and a bloody nose, he will have performed a *paint job.*

Basketball, the newest sport, has many expressions only a few years old. The record book may list the top rebounder with a banal number, but to his peers he is *climbing glass.* A fan marvels at a clever guard's ability to dribble: *"He's got a good handle"* is the way his teammates describe it. An announcer might describe someone's "playing time," but when the game is over players talk about their *minutes:* the more, the better. If one *shoots a brick* too often, though, he will have fewer minutes. *Shooting a brick* is 'bouncing the ball off the backboard' rather than swirling it right into the net.

I have whimsical creations of my own. I have often wondered if in Montreal, where the Expos play, they say, *"Où sont les sno-cones d'antan?"*

Fanguage

GREG COSTIKYAN

In the 1930s, writers of letters to the science fiction pulp magazines began to meet each other and form clubs and groups of science fiction fans. Many of these groups became quite tightly knit, and science fiction fandom became a genuine subculture all its own. Today, that subculture continues and grows; while some fans are only occasional fans, others see fandom as the core of their life. They work as necessary to bring in the green, but most of their interest and activity is involved in the production of fanzines, the attendance of conventions, and the like. Over the years, fandom has developed a jargon and idiom of its own, which has been partially co-opted by other "fannish" groups such as Trekkies, wargamers, Rocky Horror freaks, and Creative Anachronists.

Although the word *fan* is in general usage outside fandom, for

fen (plural of *fan*) it has a specific meaning. A *fan* is 'a member of that community known as *fandom*'. *Mundane* is the opposite of *fannish*; while one's *fannish persona* is *Yang the Nauseating*, founder of the Dark Horde, one's *mundane persona* may be *Robert Asprin*. In noun form, a *mundane* is 'a nonfan'. A *trufan* is 'a true-blue, dyed-in-the-wool fan'; a *fringefan* is 'one whose main interest in fandom lies elsewhere than in science fiction'—examples are Trekkies and wargamers. A *neofan* is 'one making a debut into fandom'; a *BNF (Big Name Fan)* is 'the opposite of an *LNF (Little Known Fan)*', and I'm aware the acronym doesn't work. A *pro* (usually preceded by the adjective *filthy*, as in *filthy pro*) is 'a professional science fiction writer'; a *one-time pro* is 'a writer who has had only one story published' (and is stereotypically thirsty for the supposed glories of professional status).

BNFs spend most of their time drinking *bheer* (anything is more fannish if an *h* is inserted before its first vowel; *Ghod* is another example). They also *smof* a lot. *Smof* is an acronym for *secret master of fandom* and was originally coined to describe those who had grandiose dreams of "taking over fandom"; I have no idea how the noun was transmuted to a verb.

Much of the fannish vocabulary deals with printing and the publication of *fanzines*. *Fanzine* is one of the few fannish words that has passed into general use; as originally coined, it meant 'any fannish publication which was published for *egoboo* "a boost to the ego" and not profit'. As it is used in the mundane world, it means 'any magazine that enthusiastically supports a famous figure'. Thus, screen magazines are, according to Bill Safire, *fanzines*; according to fans, they are definitely mundane magazines and anything but fanzines. Fans preserve the distinction between mimeo and ditto, which has been lost in general usage. Mimeography is what produces the black printing of army orders or cheap political flyers; ditto reproduction produces the purple printing used on high school tests and the like. In the mundane world, both processes are now known as "mimeography."

Another term used in relation to publishing is *corflu,* a contraction for the *correction fluid* used for mimeograph stencils. Bad liquor is sometimes likened to "strained corflu"; according to fannish tradition, it is possible to make a potable alcoholic drink by straining *corflu,* although I have yet to meet anyone who actually claims to have done so. *Fanac* is a contraction for 'fannish activity' and includes attending conventions, contributing to fanzines, and the like. A *loc* is a letter of comment; a *poc* is a postcard of comment. Many fanzines are available only to those who write locs or articles or send other fanzines in trade; despite the fact that many fen are objectivists or libertarians, fen have a traditional horror of filthy lucre and will generally ignore monetary considerations where fellow fen are concerned. *Nexish* means 'next issue,' and *lastish* means 'last issue'.

Conventions are also an area for which many fannish terms have been developed. A convention is a *con,* a term having no relation to confidence men; most conventions have names like *WorldCon, PhilCon, DenVention,* and the like. A *relaxicon* has few programming items and is mostly 'a fannish get-together'. A *GOH* is 'the Guest of Honor at the convention'. A *con party* is 'a party at a convention run either by the committee running the convention or by another committee which is bidding to run the World Science Fiction Convention at some point in the future'. A *dead dog party* is 'a party after the end of the con, where everybody lies around like the aforenamed animal'. Fannish songs are *filksongs,* and a group of people singing such are *filks-inging.* (The term probably originated as a typographical error.) The *hucksters' room* is 'the convention area where dealers in books and science fiction paraphernalia are renting tables where they may vend their wares'.

Fans often swear by *Ghu, Jones, Crom, Cthulhu,* and the *Great Ghod Gestetner.* A fan who drops out of fandom is said to have *gafiated* (*gafia* being an acronym for 'get away from it all'). In diplomacy fandom, 'one who drops out of the hobby without returning subscription money to his subscribers' is a *burn out* and has *rotated* (an acronym for 'run off to Argentina'). The abbreviation for *science fiction* is *sf* (usually spelled with lowercase letters) and *never* "sci fi." "Sci fi" is a term used to describe bad Hollywood science fiction movies, trashy science fiction novels, and bad science fiction written by mundane writers. (Jacqueline Susann's *Yargo* is sci fi.) ST is the abbreviation for *Star Trek* (usually spelled with capitals); *Trekkies* are 'starstruck ST fans who run around in Starfleet uniforms, wearing plastic Spock ears', while *Trekkers* are 'more serious Star Trek fen'. To a *trufan*, however, all ST *fen* are *Trekkies*, and probably moronic scum.

Crottled greeps are 'a fannish food'; there is a difference of opinion as to whether crottled greeps taste like nectar or something more earthly. In any case, the usual response to an inquiry as to the nature of crottled greeps is "If you do not enjoy them, do not order them." I am informed by educated opinion that Szechwan sea slugs taste very much like crottled greeps.

A *faan* (pronounced FAYAN) is 'an overly enthusiastic fan', and needs to gain some fannish savoir faire. A *slan* is 'a fannish superman' (the term derives from A. E. Van Vogt's novel of the same name); "He's a slan" is the fannish equivalent of "He's a helluva guy."

In closing, may your pigs prosper; Live Long and Prosper; Nuke the Whales; *Elen Sila Lumenn Omentielvo*; and *la, la, Cthulhu, R'lyeh Ftagn Nyarlathotep.*

SIC! SIC! SIC!

"PULL TO RIGHT WHEN FLASHING" Road sign on highway outside Detroit. Submitted by Mary M. Tius, Portland, Maine, who reports that no light is visible in the vicinity of the sign.

Winking Words

PHILIP MICHAEL COHEN

Twenty years ago, a group of Cambridge students decided to establish a sport where they could excel, the traditional ones being tiresomely full of experts. When they chose tiddlywinks

and began standardising rules and equipment, they surely had no idea that it would become nationally prominent (with the aid of the *Goon Show* players and Prince Charles) and even take root across the Atlantic. There is now a small but enthusiastic community of U.S. winkers, concentrated at Eastern colleges but with colonies elsewhere.

This form of tiddlywinks offers great scope for strategy as well as physical skill, but even the most serious winkers retain a light-hearted attitude toward the game. This is particularly clear in the vocabulary. The two basic actions of the game are called *squidging* (shooting a wink with a special oversized wink, or *squidger*) and *squopping* (covering a wink with another, thereby paralyzing it).

While HYTHNLBTWOC was beating Zoo at the 1974 North American Championships, I was collecting vocabulary. The list which follows does not seem to have changed much since.

birthday or **Christmas present** an unexpected stroke of good fortune, such as bad shot by an opponent.

bomb a long-distance shot used to break up a pile of winks. Also *v.i.* and *v.t.*

boondock to shoot (a wink) far from the scene of action or off the mat. Incidentally, winkers who graduate and move away from the centers of activity are said to be "boondocked."

Bristol an effective gromp (q.v.), developed at Bristol U., in which the squidger is held perpendicular to the pile and parallel to the line of flight.

butt to knock (a wink) on or off a pile by shooting another wink at it on a low trajectory. Also **kick.**

click off to remove a wink from another with a shot that ends by just touching (clicking against) the wink below, not moving it.

constipated said of a position in which one has winks, but because they are squopping other winks, they are tied down and useless. (Free = unsquopped.)

dance (of a wink) to wobble around on another wink, the rim of the pot, or the mat.

drunken wink a wink that behaves unpredictably or bizarrely.

eat to squop; especially, to squop thoroughly, completely covering the lower wink. Also, sometimes, **chomp.**

Goode shot a shot used when one has a wink touching, but not on an unwanted pile. The wink is pressed hard into the mat and when released, goes through the pile, thoroughly scattering it.

gromp to move a pile as a whole onto another wink or pile. Also *v.i.* and *n.* Also **trundle**—an Ottawaism.

lunch to pot an opponent's wink to gain strategic advantage; to trounce, especially in "get lunched."

nurdle to shoot (a wink) too close to the pot to be pottable or otherwise useful. Obsolete in England, where it originated in the early '60s.

perversion any winks variation, such as Winks Tennis.

Petrie piddle desquopping a wink by squeezing it out from underneath a pile.

piddle to make microscopic adjustments in a pile, usually to walk it off a friendly wink.

shot an exclamation of commendation for a good shot. *Antonym:* **unlucky.** A Briticism, with some currency in America.

sub or **submarine** *v.t.* or *v.i.* To shoot a wink (usually one's own) under another. In England called an **autosquop** or **ULU.** (The latter, pronounced YOO-loo, is said to refer to an unfortunate habit of the University of London Union team.)

SIC! SIC! SIC!

"Through the use of ultrasound, University of Washington researcher . . . studies women who develop high blood pressure during pregnancy with the assistance of AHA-WA funds." From *Heartlines,* a Washington affiliate newsletter of the American Heart Association, vol. 6, no. 2, 1988.

Clown Talk

THOMAS H. MIDDLETON

Ron Jarvis, a friend of mine who is not only an actor and a professional clown, but a man with a keen appreciation of words, shared several hours, a couple of six-packs, and a trove of circus talk with me recently. I'm glad I had the presence of mind to find a tape recorder and get him to back up to where he'd begun and then keep going with a fascinating discussion about circuses and particularly about circusese. Most professions have their own jargons. Some are tedious and some infuriating to the

outsider; and some are rich and colorful. The circus's jargon, not at all surprisingly, is rich and colorful.

It didn't come as a great surprise that circus people call the area inside the big top or other circus enclosure "the hippo-drome." One of the dictionary definitions of *hippodrome* is "cir-cus." Within the hippodrome is the *hippodrome track*. To assist in the mechanics of preparing the circus show, the hippodrome track is divided into the *front track* and the *back track*. Since the hippodrome track is round, the designations of back and front tracks are arbitrary. These are the equivalent of *downstage* and *upstage* in a proscenium-arch theater. Without this convention, it would be next to impossible to direct the circus show. Each ring in a circus usually has its track. European circuses are generally one-ring. The three-ring circus was, not surprisingly, an American innovation, America being the home of "More is Better."

I asked Ron if he knew the origin of the expression *the big top,* a colorful but not entirely predictable term for an enormous tent. He said that in the old days, there were several tents in the regular circus setup. There was the big one, containing the hippodrome, and there were the smaller tents that contained the menagerie, the freak shows, the "balley girls," and the other attractions on the periphery of the main show. These tents lined the midway. The midway is a thing of the past. It was a passage everyone had to go through in order to get to the big top. It offered enticements to lure cash from the crowd before they got to the main show. The big tent was called *the big top* to distinguish it from these smaller tents. OK, you [say], but how come *big top* instead of *big tent*? The smaller tents were never called *little tops.* Good question.

Now let's move on to those balley girls, also sometimes called *cootch dancers* or *cooch dancers* or *kooch dancers* or *kootch dancers,* so named because they danced the *hootchy-kootchy. Balley* is my own spelling. Ron thought it was probably *bally,* but I prefer *balley,* because *balley* makes it fairly clear that the *all* in there rhymes not with *all, ball,* and *fall,* but with the *all* in *alley.* "Lots of these words weren't meant to be spelled, anyway," says Ron, which puts us in a whole new mode of thought, bringing up a vast and complex host of questions in etymology and linguistics. Mencken, in his discussions of circusese, spells it *bally,* but I assert my right to *balley.*

Clowns are called *Joeys,* after Joseph Grimaldi (1779–1837), a great English clown and pantomimist.

The great American contribution to clownhood is "the tramp." That tramp face was created during the Great Depression, when hoboes rode the rails. If you're old enough to have done much traveling on a train drawn by a coal-fired steam locomotive, you'll remember the taste and smell and feel of the soot that permeated even the fanciest passenger cars, and you'll have little trouble imagining the look of a hobo who had ridden the rails without benefit of closeable windows. Their faces were blackened by the soot, and when they disembarked, they'd wipe their eyes and their mouths, and that's how tramp clowns were born, with their faces blackened except for the clean areas around the eyes and the mouth.

Clowns, as a rule, are used as a distraction in the circus. A very few clowns have developed as circus stars, but clowns are, for the most part, sent in in a version of the Stephen Sondheim send-in-the-clowns sense, though their routines are more often employed in covering a shift of paraphernalia than in distracting the crowd's attention from a tragedy. Where, in the theater, a curtain is drawn or the lights are doused, in the hippodrome the clowns are sent in.

A newcomer to the circus is called a *first-of-May* because the circus season starts on the first of May. "He's a first-of-May Joey" means he's a brand-new clown—wet behind the ears. A veteran of the circus, on the other hand, is a *thirty-miler* or a *forty-miler*, from the distance normally traveled between towns in the old-time circus. Incidentally, you'll be pegged as a first-of-May if you don't call the calliope a cally-ope.

A clown's shower bag is called a *douche bag*. If you're like me, your first thought is that *douche bag* must be a joke. A moment's reflection, however, in the light of the international composition of the circus, and you remember that the French *douche* and the German *Dusche* both mean 'shower', so the clown's *douche bag* almost certainly came from the French and German clowns, and I should think the spelling comes from the English *douche,* which, in turn, comes from the French.

We all know that *Hey, Rube!* is the circus cry for help, shouted when there's trouble. Ron told me about when he was with Barnum and Bailey, playing Denver—"all these Hungarian clowns, and we're sitting in a bar with all these local cowboys hanging around, and the cowboys hear the accents and figure the Commies have landed. No shit, I heard more 'Hey Rube!' calls in Denver than anywhere. I did a lot of hiding under tables."

A few more terms:

blow-off the finish of a clown's routine. Sort of a visual punch line.

bull any elephant, male or female

bull-hook what the elephant-handler uses to control the bulls of both sexes

cherry pie extra work taken on to supplement income. (Ron did laundry for the trapeze artists, acrobats, etc.)

clown alley quarters where the clowns dress and make up before the show

dukey ticket. (Spelled "dukey," I suppose, because it probably came from a mispronunciation of *ducat,* but it's probably one of those words that were never meant to be spelled)

flukum cotton candy

mud greasepaint

redlight to toss a cheat, thief, or other bad character off a moving train. (What is now called, I think, "piggyback loading," meaning 'putting cars and trucks on freight train flatcars', used to be called "circus loading," because the first wagons to be loaded on flatcars were circus wagons and trucks)

working the house strategic sales of popcorn, peanuts, and other salted goodies to work up a thirst before the soda pop is offered. (The big top has "sidewalls," which can be raised to let in cool air when the weather is stifling. Soda-pop concessionaires have been known to tie the sidewalls down using Gordian knots)

We recorded several others, but by that time, the six-packs had progressed to harder stuff, and some of our words are not entirely clear on my tape, so rest content with these samples, at least for now.

Mantic Mania

ROBERT DEVEREUX

Since the dawn of recorded history, and probably even before then, man has been curious about the future and has explored countless ways to penetrate its mysteries. Most frequently he has looked to the heavens and the movement of the heavenly bodies, thus giving rise to the "science" of astrology (as well as to its lesser known sister "science," genethlialogy). Despite its preeminence and antiquity, however, astrology has never had a monopoly on man's mantic efforts. Other paths of inquiry have led to the practice of, for example, *cleromancy, sciomancy, crystallomancy, alphitomancy,* and *spodomancy,* to name only a few.

Investigation reveals, in fact, that at one time or another, man has indulged in a great variety of different types of divination that involved an equal number of objects, or methods, or both. The objects and methods used seem most impractical to the modern pragmatic and scientific-oriented mind as a means of forecasting the future. Yet, each has been used as a basis for a pythonic system practiced sufficiently in time or geographic area that some anthropologist, historian, or lexicographer has felt obliged to confer on it a distinctive name or, perhaps more accurately, to record the distinctive term used for such system.

The names of divination systems comprise in English a relatively large and distinctive group of words ending in *-mancy*, a combining form meaning 'divination'. But since nothing in the English language is ever without exceptions, two cautionary observations are in order. First, not all words ending in *-mancy* are names of divination systems; *aldermancy* and *psychomancy* are good examples. Secondly, there are a number of divination systems whose names end in something other than *-mancy*. *Astrology* and *genethlialogy* have already been mentioned. Others include, for example, *chirognomy, chiroscopy, haruspicy* (or *haruspication*), *hieroscopy, horoscopy, keraunoscopy, omoplatoscopy, orniscopy,* and *palmistry.*

Another aspect of mantic terminology that perhaps merits mentioning is that it includes a considerable number of synonyms. For example, *chiromancy, chirognomy, chirosophy,* and *palmistry* are all words to describe the same mantic system. Other sets of synonyms include, in addition to the aforementioned *haruspicy* and *haruspication; caloptromancy* and *enoptromancy; spodomancy* and *tephramancy* (or *tephromancy); alectryomancy* and *alectoromancy; astromancy* and *sideromancy; crystallomancy* and *gastromancy; hieromancy* and *hieroscopy; necromancy* and *sciomancy; ornithomancy* and *orniscopy;* and *scapulimancy* and *omoplatoscopy.* The other side of the coin is represented by *gastromancy,* which is not only a synonym for *crystallomancy* but also the term for divination by ventriloquism.

Since readers of *Verbatim* can reasonably be assumed to have more than ordinary interest in words, they are invited to test their knowledge of mantic terminology by matching up the following list of names of twenty mantic systems with the companion list of the objects/methods used therefor. Answers will be found below.

Name of System	Thing Analyzed/Observed or Mode of Divination
1. *alectryomancy*	1. livers of sacrificial animals
2. *anthropomancy*	2. arrows drawn at random from a quiver or other holder
3. *axinomancy*	3. clouds
4. *belomancy*	4. rooster selecting grains of food placed on letters of the alphabet
5. *capnomancy*	5. dreams
6. *halomancy*	6. entrails of sacrificed victims
7. *haruspicy*	7. feces
8. *hepatoscopy*	8. fingernails or claws
9. *lecanomancy*	9. fire or forms appearing in fire
10. *myomancy*	10. flight or other characteristics of birds
11. *nephelomancy*	11. human entrails
12. *oneiromancy*	12. lines or passages of a book
13. *onychomancy*	13. movement supposedly toward a guilty person or piece of agate or jet placed upon a heated ax-head
14. *ornithomancy*	14. movements of mice

15. *pedomancy*	15. salt
16. *pyromancy*	16. shoulder blades, usually blotched or cracked by fire
17. *scapulimancy*	17. smoke, when victims sacrificed by fire
18. *scatomancy*	18. soles of the feet
19. *sideromancy*	19. straws burning on hot iron
20. *stichomancy*	20. water in a basin

1. (4) 2. (11) 3. (13) 4. (2) 5. (17) 6. (15) 7. (6) 8. (1) 9. (20) 10. (14) 11. (3) 12. (5) 13. (8) 14. (10) 15. (18) 16. (9) 17. (16) 18. (7) 19. (19) 20. (12)

Identity and Language in the SM Scene

M. A. BUCHANAN

For the past seven years, I have been studying the process of identity formation among SM/radical-sex practitioners living in and around New York City, in preparation for my doctoral thesis in cultural anthropology. Among the first things that I noticed when I started doing my research was the importance of language in the definition of what people in my subject group did, how they thought about it, and how they saw themselves in relation both to other differently pleasured people (swingers, clothing fetishists) and the "normal" world. I also found that problems arose between practitioners and nonpractitioners at the

intersections of language: that because the SM world has co-opted so many ordinary words and phrases, these became almost unintelligible to outsiders.

I have two favorite examples of this. The first involved an informant of mine who was asked to give a speech on SM to an organization of "vanilla" (nonkinky) men. My informant was Chinese American (I'll call him John) and one of the leaders of a very prominent SM organization here in New York. The group had been trying to promote itself as being open to people of color, so when John was asked to give a talk to a local group of Asian and Pacific Rim gay men, he jumped at the chance. John went to the meeting in his finest *leathers* and wore the colors of his organization.[1]

After doing the usual *SM 101* lecture and emphasizing that he was considered a leader in his community,[2] he opened the floor to questions. There were none. He was rather disappointed. He could tell that his audience was being more polite to this strange guest than anything else. Finally when the meeting was over, a Chinese American couple approached him. They said that they had enjoyed his talk, and were surprised that *leathermen* were inclusive.[3] They had always thought that SM was something that only weird white men did.[4] Still, they said, they didn't think that they could ever try kinky sex. They preferred their own quiet sex life the way it was. Out of curiosity at this complacent couple, John asked them what they enjoyed the most about their sex lives. "Well, what we really like is choking each other. None of that wild stuff for us."[5]

The second story is about a women's SM organization that was looking to increase its numbers. The group knew that there were many women in the city who were doing SM in private. Some of these women even turned up in the local sex clubs, but they never came to any of the events of the women's groups. Finally the membership committee decided to make up a flyer that could be used as an ad in the local gay paper and distributed at clubs. Unfortunately they kept having problems with the wording. If they said "masters and slaves welcome," there were women of color who wouldn't attend meetings because the terms were considered offensive. If they said "dominants and submissives welcome," the switches[6] and undecided might not come, because they'd feel excluded. If they said "butches and femmes welcome," straight women and androgynous lesbians might not come, because the terms implied a particular lesbian-oriented dichotomy. Finally the committee decided to put "all women welcome" on the flyer, which led to the crisis about the transgender male-to-female who wanted to join (but that's another article).

In both stories the essential problem was the real or anticipated misunderstanding of SM language. Language acts as the markers for the parameters of thought. What may and may not be contemplated by members of a society is encoded in the language used by its members.[7] When the language of one group collides with or is appropriated by another, something gets lost in the translation that at least one group doesn't see as necessary.

SM practitioners often see themselves as crossing an invisible boundary into a parallel universe, SM Land. They refer to the time "outside of the Scene" as "real life," as though what they do inside the scene is less real or more ephemeral and shadowy than the grind of going to the supermarket. Yet the ideal for many people is to become "hardcore," "lifestyle," or "24/7" to live, eat, and drink SM all the time, or at least to incorporate it into their daily lives. Doing so, however, requires a heightened ability to translate one's secret language to the world outside, so that vanilla neighbors, coworkers (if any), and strangers will tolerate one's presence even if they find one's living choices unacceptable. If one cannot or will not go completely hardcore, then one has at least to mask oneself with the aura of plausible deniability, even to the point of denying one's proclivities to oneself.

The terms *D/S* and *B&D* are perfect examples. *D/S* stands for *dominance and submission,* which sounds a tad less scary than *SM*. The term was popularized and probably invented by heterosexuals in SM chatrooms, where the majority of visitors are nice, middle-class people with houses in the suburbs. The term is consciously used as a way of distancing practitioners from the implications and stigma of SM, even though the terms are exact synonyms for each other. *B&D,* or *bondage and discipline,* is said by practitioners to be a milder version of SM, less violent than that nasty stuff, although somehow the "nasty stuff" never quite gets defined. Perhaps it's because, again, *B&D* and *SM* are actually one and the same, with *B&D* having slightly more emphasis on roleplay. The desire to mask one's participation in one's own personal theater of cruelty seems to be almost as strong as a desire to create one in the first place.

But the desire to mask oneself does not merely arise from shame over one's own behavior. As I said before, one has the neighbors to think about. And the police: A local organization had a talk a few years ago on the subject "daddies and their little girls." The meeting was attended by a variety of people, including two of the most obviously on-duty undercover cops the world has ever seen. They were probably the only ones in the room who were horrified to see three women in their thirties and forties talking about the joys of dressing in bobby socks and going to the park with their older lovers. The terminology of "ageplay" had apparently not found its way to the captain of the local vice squad, who would have done well to buy a copy of *Sensuous Magic,* by Pat Califia, and saved himself and his officers the trouble of a tedious (to them) meeting.

In a few cases, SM organizations have actually had sit-downs with the police to explain what all the mysterious terms on their flyers and in their books mean, and they have been successful in removing the constabulary's unwarranted fears of illegal behaviors. They have even written glossaries of both well-recognized and little-used terms for newcomers, so that their world might be a bit more comprehensible. I leave you with a few terms and their translations:

Body Modification—altering the surface of the body, whether temporarily or permanently. In other words, tattooing, branding, scarification, permanent piercing, corsetry. Earrings and a bustier would be considered body modification.

Collar—a length of chain, leather, or other adornment placed around the neck to indicate that a person is in service to another. This may be worn for the evening or for a longer period.

Forced crossdressing—what it's called when a man brings a bag full of women's clothing that he's bought for himself to a dominatrix and pretends that he doesn't want to wear them.

Flagging—indicating one's preference as a top or a bottom and what type of activities one likes by wearing keys, jewelry, or bandannas on one side of your body or the other. Left means top or dominant; right means bottom or submissive.

Houseboy—a bottom whose duties include cleaning, waiting on guests, answering the door, laundry, cooking, and any other household duties the top may assign. The bottom may or may may not live with the top, and this may or may not be a sexual relationship. Although I have heard rumors that there are female house servants, I have never run across one. For some reason, only men seem to like doing chores as a sexual outlet.

Negotiation—the exchange of information on SM preferences and limits, and the decision of whether or not to play between two or more prospective partners. The SM equivalent of dating.

Property—a bottom, who by the nature of the relationship is owned or controlled, either partially or completely by the dominant. Often there is a written contract that spells out the terms of the relationship.

Role-reversal—what some practitioners call it when a man gives up sexual and other types of control to his (always) female dominant. Naturally, role-reversal is only a temporary state of things.

Wrapping—the accidental delivery of a whipstroke that causes the tips to land on the side of the body as opposed to the front or the back. Wrapping is considered to be bad because it can leave marks and be quite painful.

*Other Languages
(Just the Good Parts)*

Studying other languages is, for most of us, hard work. We stumble along, stuttering and mumbling, trying to elide the syllables we're unsure of, wishing that our parents had had the foresight to have learned another language well enough to serve it to us with our mother's milk. *Reading* about other languages, on the other hand, is easy, edifying, leaves you with a full, satisfied feeling, and requires no messy conjugating. Herewith, then, are some of the good parts of Welsh, Latin American Spanish, Japanese, and Hocus Pocus.

Instant Welsh

MICHEL VERCAMBRE

I broke imaginary eggs on the rim of a nonexistent frying pan and made sizzling noises. I pretended to fill tumblers of ice-cold milk and to drink them with apparent delight. I beat the air with my arms and clucked like a hen and mooed deep and long. But the features of the old, old woman who had opened the door of the farmhouse half way up the mountain and who had answered my polite request for a few eggs and some milk with a steady flow of Welsh remained blank. As blank as mine had been when she had been speaking Welsh. My miming must have been wanting as I got neither egg nor milk. But the humiliating thing was that I, relatively bilingual and with a smattering of a few other languages, have been able to make myself understood in most parts of western Europe, but was thoroughly checkmated not sixty miles as the crow flies from Manchester. . . . I decided to learn Welsh forthwith, there and then, without more ado.

Of course, it was not going to be plain sailing. I knew that. We—my wife, our three children, and I—had been invited to spend ten blissful days in an idyllic white cottage in the middle of a field near a couple of lakes in the depth of Caernarvonshire. The nearest village was a couple of valleys away; our neighbors were sheep and lambs. It was definitely known that a road mender did sleep in a one-room cabin near the abandoned slate quarry. These were perhaps not the best conditions in which to learn the Welsh language, but what I lacked in amenities I thought I would make up in "ambiance" for there we would be for ten days, practically incommunicado.

My only tutor was one of those paper napkins on which are

printed some hundred brightly colored pictures of objects and things in common use, such as bread, cheese, house, sea, sun, chair, etc., with the Welsh name above and the English underneath. You know the sort of thing. Very useful in its way, no doubt, but rather limiting to someone of scholarly disposition.

It was then that Chance took a hand. Would you believe that I found in the rafters of our host's cottage a dusty Welsh-English Dictionary compiled by W. Richards, L.L.D., in 1890? . . . It was like reaching that peak in Darien. A whole new world was about to be revealed to me. And into this unknown land, this strangely melodious language, with its roots dating back to the time when the world was young, I set forth, with my paper napkin and my pocket dictionary compiled in 1890.

As I read on, picking out a word here and a phrase there, the personality of Dr. Richards began to appear. The aims of a lexicographer, these days, is undoubtedly to be as objective and exact as possible when dealing with concepts as intangible as the meanings of words. Dr. Johnson himself was roundly criticized for letting his prejudices interfere with his definitions. We do not go to a dictionary for opinions or for subjective judgment, and the more remote the personality of the compiler, the better. Dr. Richards obviously entertained a different idea of his mission.

His interests quickly became clear. That he was a theologian there can be little doubt, and anyone would have been able with the help of his dictionary to plough through a sermon on predestination or a debate on the difference between transubstantiation and consubstantiation. This in a *pocket* dictionary, you understand. Dr. Richards must also have been interested in demonology, witchcraft, familiars, rhabdomancy. (You wish to know the Welsh for *rhabdomancy*? Well, another time, perhaps.) Then there was Dr. Richard's interest in diseases. Far from simply giving us the Welsh for *rheumatism,* he goes into details of the symptoms, and I will spare you a five-line description of the scabs in a case of *blue jaundice*. If you should catch blue jaundice in Wales, I strongly advise you to have Dr. Richards's dictionary at hand. (Incidentally, since *jaundice* means the 'yellow disease,' how can it be blue? But let it pass.)

Dr. Richards never stops astonishing us. You would think that the word *bye-laws* was not one which in a pocket dictionary would be given much space. But wrong you would be. Dr. Richards gives us a minitreatise on the application of bye-laws in Scotland in the fourteenth century, which is not particularly useful if you are lost in a fog and, on knocking at the door of an isolated Welsh cottage, you are faced by an aged gentleman who has no English.

I fear that Dr. Richards did not have us in mind when he set to work, for he omitted to include such words as *tomato, bathroom, cutlet, cauliflower,* and *railway station.* Yet let no one say he was not a mundane man, for he gives us the Welsh for *port, sherry, whisky, brandy, burgundy, claret,* and even *Rhenish wine.* And do you know that there are ten words in Welsh for *fashion*? But none, apparently, for *tomato, bathroom, cutlet,* etc.

It quickly appeared, on perusing the Welsh-English section, that Dr. Richards's English was somewhat idiosyncratic, for he gives us an English translation of a Welsh word, 'to render prospective.' I have pondered on this phrase, and the only person I can imagine using it is the secretary of the local branch of a political party who, having handed the Committee members a short list of would-be candidates, asks: "Which of these people shall we render prospective?"

Then there is the word *arfogwl,* which apparently means 'a dried skin on a post with pebbles in it,' with no further explanations as to why it should be hanging on a post and why, in

heaven's name, it should contain pebbles. I therefore went out to try to find one in the hope that the object might reveal its raison d'être. I was not successful, and I must warn would-be searchers that I very much doubt whether there is a dried skin with pebbles in it hanging on a post within three miles from Llanrust. They had better look elsewhere.

A closer study of the English-Welsh section soon brought to light the fact that not only did Dr. Richards know a large number of English words which do not appear in recognized dictionaries I consulted but that, clever man that he was, he was able to translate them into Welsh. Words like *dishersion, extillation, restagnate, claricord, contramure,* and, of course, *discubitory.* All these words look as if they meant something. The word *discubitory* took my fancy; neither Chambers nor Webster having been able to enlighten me, I consulted Dr. Richards himself, by the simple process of looking up in the Welsh-English section the Welsh word which Dr. Richards had given as the translation of *discubitory* in the English-Welsh section. I looked up therefore the word *lledorweddle* and was informed that it meant . . . 'discubitory.' However, there was an alternative definition: 'partly lying down.' This I took to mean 'in a semi-recumbent position.' I had it now, of course. *Discubitory* means 'lying down whilst propping oneself on one's elbow.' This word has now taken its place in my vocabulary, and I use it now and then nonchalantly in conversation. To date, no one has asked me what it meant.

To mark the centenary of this remarkable book and help revive interest in its author, I hereby undertake to hand over a prize of one hundred pounds to the first person who challenges me with the words: "You are Michel Vercambre the eminent scholar who discovered the meaning of the word *discubitory* and I claim the prize of one hundred pounds." The challenger must be carrying

at the time a copy of Dr. Richards's Welsh-English pocket dictionary. The 1890 edition.

SIC! SIC! SIC!

"Geranium 'John Elsley'—A lovely prostate ground cover."
From among "Most Recent Offerings," by Wayside
Gardens, spring 1992 catalogue. Submitted by
Florence Madison, Westerly, Rhode Island.

Never Ask a Uruguayan Waitress for a Little Box: She Might Apply Her Foot to Your Eyelet

JOHN R. CASSIDY

The English-speaking nations may believe themselves to be divided by their common language, but their plight doesn't even approach that of the Spanish-speaking peoples. The visiting American who says *bum* inopportunely or the Englishman who urges Americans to *keep their peckers up* may perhaps suffer mild embarrassment, but neither of them will experience the show-stopping thrill induced by a Cuban lady who gratefully acknowledges to the Buenos Aires civic organization, "Yes, your welcoming committee fucked me right in the door of the airplane."

Unless coached beforehand, any visitor from a northern country of Latin America is likely to have at least one experience like that before he learns that in the Rio de la Plata area, the elsewhere perfectly decent verb *coger* 'to pick up, grasp, catch, gather' is

taboo. In those southern lands, *coger,* which is the verb our Cuban lady used, has come to have only one meaning, an obscene one, and the verb has therefore been lost to the *rioplatenses* for civil discourse. A comparable situation might be for English to lose the use of the word *get* because overemphasis on its minor generative meaning has shouldered out all other uses. It is difficult to imagine the ends we would have to go to to avoid the use of the lost word, but it is exactly that kind of a struggle that occurs every time somebody in gaucho country has to express precisely what *coger* would say if he could use it.

The northerners rail at this silliness, but in doing so they forget the beam in their own eye. The people of many of the northern countries have inflicted on the verb *tirar* 'throw, pull, stretch, discard, shoot, publish, etc.' the same fate that *coger* has suffered around the Rio de la Plata. In fact, when you compare the space taken up in dictionaries, you are led to conclude that *tirar* is an even greater loss to the language than *coger.*

How is a traveler to know these things? Having lived in several Latin American countries and Spain and having traveled in every one of them, I have suffered a few linguistic bruises myself, and I conclude that no ordinary mortal can foresee all the possibilities for embarrassment, especially since most of the bothersome differences seem to be in the areas of food and sex, neither of which boons one wishes to forswear. One must eat. But no matter how fluent one's Spanish, one may find eating in restaurants an unexpected struggle during the first few days in a new Hispanic country. It might surprise many Americans to know that, even without much knowledge of Spanish, they would understand a typical Mexican restaurant menu more readily than a Chilean would, because in Chile a *taco* is the 'heel of a shoe' or 'a billiard cue', and the Chilean never heard of *enchiladas, frijoles,* or *tamales.* [The American should not be complacent, however. He

or she may recognize the word *tamales* on the menu, but if only
one is wanted, the customer must ask for a *tamal,* not a *tamale*.]
Our Chilean visitor may see *tomates* on the menu and of course
knows what *they* are, but he or she may be in for a surprise,
because it will be green. If you want a ripe tomato in Mexico,
you must order a *jitomate.* If the Chilean complains, the Mexican
might justifiably claim a sort of proprietorship over the words,
whose structure implies their origin in the ancient world of the
northern part of what is now Hispanic America, along with *agua-*
cate, elote, ayote, pataste, zapote, and *peyote,* to name but a few,
which are, respectively, an 'avocado', an 'ear of corn', a 'squash',
'another variety of squash', a 'fruit', and a 'high'.

It is true that an American in England might stumble over
treacle or *corn* and might not have the faintest idea what a *Cornish*
pastie is, but he or she would at least recognize the ingredients
of the pastie if a Briton named them. In contrast, if a Uruguayan
tried to describe to a Mexican the ingredients of the beloved
boiled dinner, the *puchero,* the Mexican would not understand
the words for *corn on the cob, sweet potato, beans,* and *beef ribs.*

As far as I know, English speakers everywhere generally agree
on the words for *potato, tomato, bacon, sweet potato, butter, lard,*
chops, grapefruit, strawberry, peach, banana, pineapple, avocado,
beans, and *green pepper.* (*Sweet potatoes* are also called *yams,* of
course, but most English speakers are familiar with both names.)
Hispanics are not unanimous about any of the words for those
foods nor about many others too numerous to list here, and as a
general rule you will not be understood if you use the wrong
variant for your current location. As is the case with *tomate* and
jitomate between Chile and Mexico, so it is among the various
nations with regard to 'potato' *patata, papa;* 'bacon' *tocino, pan-*
ceta; 'sweet potato' *batata, boniato, moniato;* 'butter' *manteca,*
mantequilla; 'lard' *manteca, grasa de cerdo;* 'chop' *costilla,*

chuleta; 'grapefruit' *toronja, pomelo*; 'strawberry' *fresa, frutilla*; 'peach' *durazno, melocotón*; 'banana' *plátano, banana, guineo, mínimo*; 'pineapple' *piña, ananá*; 'avocado' *aguacate, palta*; 'green bean' *habichuela verde, judía, chaucha, haba*; 'beans' *habichuelas, frijoles, porotos*; 'sweet pepper' *ají, chili para relleno, pimienta*; 'corn on the cob' *elote, choclo*.

Sometimes the struggle for comprehension involves both food and sex in the same word. In many countries of Latin America, *cajeta*, a creamy caramel spread, made from milk and sugar, is used on pancakes or toast or as an icing or filling for cakes, candies, and cookies; but woe to the sweet-toothed Mexican who asks a waitress in Montevideo if she has *cajeta*. She will not know he means *dulce de leche*: she will understand him to be asking her if she has a cunt. On the other hand, if the Mexican slips and says *chingada*, which might burn the ears of a Mexican waitress, the Uruguayan will not bat an eye, because she will not know the word at all. Many Americans whose Spanish is a rudimentary Tex-Mex assume that *¡chingada!* and its bowdlerized form *¡chihuahua!* are universal expletives among Hispanic peoples, but it is not so. Even where a certain sexual allusion is common throughout the Hispanic world, the words that express it may not be the same for all regions. Spanish speakers everywhere cite testicles both to label a man a hero and to call him an idiot. To say that a man has *pelotas* or *bolas* 'balls' or *huevos* 'eggs' is to qualify him as a brave and most admirable he-man. [I never use the word *macho* anymore because the English-speaking world has adopted it and ruined its noble connotations.] But if a man is *pelotudo* or *boludo* or *huevón*, it means he has outsized testicles, that is, he is stupid or subhuman.

Every region of the Hispanic world has its own collection of words for human genitalia, and sometimes these words are transferable to other regions, but more often they are not. In Buenos

Aires, for example, the penis is known variously as *la pija, la pistola, la poronga, el nabo* 'turnip', or *el mongo*. [Those who assert that language can be sexist may note with perplexity that the most commonly used words for penis, testicles, and beard, attributes which characterize men as men, are of feminine gender in Spanish, whereas the words for a woman's breasts, except for the indelicate *tetas*, are masculine (*senos, pechos*).] One can imagine the impact on the public of Buenos Aires the day a careless or mischievous typesetter set up a headline chronicling the doings of the famous General Slim, known east of Suez as *Monghi Slim*. The headline stood out blatantly on the newsstands, and even those who spoke no English could understand from the words MONGO SLIM VICTORIOUS that he had won and what somebody thought of him.

I have heard fewer names for female genitalia, and that may be because the shape offers fewer opportunities for similes than the male organs. As noted, *cajeta* is used in one region. Although in some other countries it means 'caramel syrup', its original Spanish meaning is a 'small box', and the sexual application is obvious. *Concha* means 'shell' and is also apt. *Vaina*, a descendant of *vagina*, is perfectly acceptable in most Hispanic countries and means exactly what its Latin root meant, 'sheath'. Like *vagina* everywhere in the modern world, *vaina* in Colombia has come to be used for one human organ; but whereas *vagina* is clinical and acceptable in most circumstances, *vaina* is obscene in Colombia. Anyone who has spent time there can testify that Colombian males use the word with the same emphasis, intent, and effect as English-speaking males of all nations use the word *fuck* in locker rooms and barracks.

Some years ago the State Department assigned a friend of mine, who is fluent in Spanish, to a tour of duty in Bogotá, a city he did not know. He was accompanied by his wife, Vina. Now, when one uses the word *señora* as an adjective in Spanish, it can have the meaning 'magnificent, grandiose'—as in *¡Es una señora casa!* 'It is a tremendous house!' For many days, my friend's new Colombian friends were either too embarrassed or too mischievous to tell him that he was introducing his wife ("Señora Vina") to Colombian society as "my magnificent cunt."

Anyone who has tried to enter into a foreign language in another land has experienced or heard about those moments when the innocent use of a word suddenly submerges the speaker in a shocked silence.

It happened to me. A group of close friends took me partridge hunting in Uruguay, and I had an excellent day. My friends argued good-naturedly among themselves and with me about whether this *yanqui* was really that much of a crack shot or whether it was all *puro ojete. Ojete* means 'eyelet', but it was obvious from the context that they were saying I was unbelievably lucky. *Pues bien,* at a cocktail party in Montevideo a few days later, I was holding forth to a mixed group of Uruguayans on the marvels of their country's game birds, and this kind of praise invariably garners a sizeable and attentive audience. After announcing the number of birds I had bagged, I modestly admitted in a clear and ringing voice that it had been nothing but *puro ojete.*

Reflexively, a friend standing nearby said, "What did you say?"

And so, I said it again.

By now, the glassy eyes around me told me something was wrong. Later, I learned that in Uruguay, *ojete* means only one thing—'asshole'. In defense of my hunting companions, they had not tried to play a trick on me. They assumed that I knew what the word meant, just as they assumed that I knew that the most vivid way to call a man phenomenally lucky is to say that he has a huge asshole.

Uruguay was also the scene of a slip that I think must stand as an all-time classic. A young woman from a northern country (Ecuador, I think) was visiting a posh country club near Montevideo. She was of that green-eyed, blonde Spanish type one sees so frequently and with such pleasure on the streets of Madrid, and her face was matched in beauty by a superb body. The bikini had not yet shrunk to the string size of today's models, but she was nonetheless giving the males around the club pool a pleasant afternoon contemplating the contents of a provocative bathing suit. Needless to say, a large number of young males had gathered to enjoy the spectacle.

In the midst of the almost palpable lust, she eased herself gingerly into the water. She wasn't serious about swimming; it was simply a continuation of the show. After paddling about daintily and seductively for two or three minutes, she got out and stood dripping divinely at the edge of the pool. But when she took off her bathing cap and fluffed her golden tresses, she discovered that they were damp. Whereupon she exclaimed, "*¡Ay, mira mi cabello! ¡Y apenas me mojé la concha!*"

In her native region, *concha* means 'skin', and so she was not saying anything extraordinary from her point of view. But to the dumbfounded Uruguayans, she had exclaimed, "Darn it, look at my hair! And I just barely got my cunt wet!"

I wonder if she still blushes when she remembers, as I still feel embarrassed about having proclaimed the size of my asshole at an Uruguayan cocktail party. She and I belong to an exclusive club from which any normal person would, in fact, wish fervently to be excluded. If I had any way to get in touch with her, I'd tell her it helps to write about it. Or, if she prefers not to do that, then my advice, in her own dialect, would be to relax and try to maintain a thick *concha*.

SIC! SIC! SIC!

"... the underground parking garage will probably never see the light of day." From *University of Toronto Magazine,* summer 1990. Submitted by Gordon B. Thompson, Etobicoke, Ontario.

From Za-za to San-san: The Climate of Japanese Onomatopoeia

DAVID GALEF

Bells in Japan ring with a *jan-jan* sound; roosters cry *koke-kokko*. "Even the dogs in Japan," remarked one long-term foreign resident, "speak Japanese." True enough: The sound of barking is written as *wan-wan*, not all that far from canine reality. But what is one to make of *bata-bata*, the sound of beating wings, or *goro-goro*, approximating the rolling of a barrel? This is *giseigo*, the Japanese version of onomatopoeia, where the sound of a word imitates its meaning.

Japanese onomatopoeia is really divided into two groups, *giseigo* and *gitaigo*. The three characters which make up *giseigo* mean 'mimic-voice-language', really a word imitating a sound. The word *bū-bū*, for example, means 'to complain or grunt' because it is the sound a pig makes. *Gitaigo*, on the other hand, is an attempt to represent the sound of an action, subtler and more abstract than *giseigo*. An interesting instance of this second grouping is *sassato,* which means 'quickly' or 'promptly'. While possibly disconcerting to the foreigner trying to learn Japanese, these expressions add a lot of color to an otherwise polite, honorific language. In fact, a Japanese speaker's style has a lot to do with the amount of *giseigo* and *gitaigo* he uses: the more sound-expressions, the more vivid the speech.

Since the world of nature figures so prominently in Japanese life, numerous expressions exist to capture the seasonal phenomena. A light wind makes a *hyū-hyū* sound; as the wind picks up, it becomes *pyū-pyū*; and a gale makes a rhythmic *byū-byū* sound. For those who like to form lexical rules, the *h* to *p* to *b* sequence usually represents stronger and stronger force. While *pata-pata,* for example, may be the flap of little wings, *bata-bata* might represent a helicopter's massive dislocation of air. The *k* to *g* switch follows the same pattern. The familiar syllabic repetition represents a continuing state. For the Japanese, even smoothly flowing actions have this alliterative repetition.

Rain, so quintessentially Japanese, comes in a variety of forms: *za-za* is a downpour, heavy slanted drops soaking one to the skin. *Potsu-potsu* is a medium rain, striking the roof tiles, perhaps with a pinging sound. Finally, as the rain tapers off to a drizzle, the sound modulates to a polite *shito-shito.* The clouds roll away (*goro-goro)* and the sun shines brilliantly, *san-san.* Later, at night, the stars come out, twinkling *kira-kira.* And once in a great while, a shooting star may go flashing *pika-pika* toward the horizon. The Japanese natural world has its own distinct personality.

The Japanese represent their moods in a variety of sounds, as well. In moments of exasperation, they grimace *muka-muka,* or gnash their teeth with a *giri-giri* sound. Nervousness makes them *waku-waku,* and real fright causes them to tremble *buru-buru* all over. The *shiku-shiku* sound of sobbing can be heard right through a Japanese screen. In the neighboring house, someone is smiling *niko-niko* as he listens to a funny story. The punchline is delivered, and he gives out a big *gera-gera* belly laugh. In the next room, however, someone is exhausted *(kuta-kuta)* and trying to sleep. A half hour later comes the *gū-gū* of gentle snoring. Japanese households can be very noisy and complex in a quiet, simple way.

This is not to say that English onomatopoeia is so plain, and in fact there are some interesting cross-cultural equivalents. A *pocha-pocha* Japanese child becomes *roly-poly* in America.

The *kera-kera* laugh, a step down from the rollicking *gera-gera,* approximates 'giggle' in English. *Jara-Jara* in Japan is as good as a jingle in New Jersey. As for the annoyed *humph, fun* (pronounced "foon") is a much-used Japanese equivalent. The Japanese terms, however, extend to a variety of what English-speakers would consider silent actions: *jiro-jiro* is 'to stare in fascination', the way many Japanese still do at foreigners.

The world of abstract actions, *gitaigo,* is more of a puzzle to nonnative speakers. The literal meaning of *gitaigo* is 'mimic-condition-language', or mimesis, though the phonic connections seem less obvious than with the reduplicated words. Why does *pittari* mean 'to fit perfectly' or *sokkuri* 'to be exactly alike'? The word *gisshiri* 'squeezed in' or 'packed full' has resonances of the English *squished,* but why does one resolve a matter *shikkari to* 'firmly or decisively'? For the most part, these are words not representable by Chinese ideograms, so the etymology is unclear. Written in the phonetic *kana* syllabary, they appear to antedate the importation of Chinese characters by several hundred years: sounds before signs. Questioning a number of Japanese on the subject produces the response that words like *hakkiri* ('clearly, obviously') simply sound like their denoted conditions. Such is the essence of any onomatopoeia, and though *gitaigo* tends to be more adverbial in usage than the general *giseigo,* it may simply be that the Japanese have a more refined phonic sense. The onomatopoeic *giseigo* always makes good intuitive sense: *bara-bara*, which is the sound of an object breaking into pieces, has come to mean 'scattered' or 'on all different levels'. "This English class," a Japanese instructor might say of his students, "is *bara-bara*."

Though it would be an exaggeration to say that there is a Japanese sound-word for every occurrence, a full list would be extremely long. This is a country where trains rattle along *goton-goton* and buzzers go *bun-bun*. On the train, a lively *pichi-pichi* young girl is kicking and struggling *jita-bata*, while an old man with his clothes *boro-boro* (in tatters) looks on. It sounds like a scene from Japanese comics, which in fact rely heavily on *giseigo* for their impact. The American *pow* and *zap* seem uninspired by comparison. The Japanese for *pow*, incidentally, is *pachin*, while a ray-gun's *zap* is *bii-bii*, coincidentally the sound of a baby's crying.

The association of onomatopoeia with comics is not accidental. *Giseigo* and *gitaigo* remain informal, sometimes pungent expressions, bespeaking easy usage. That is not to say they are slang. Even the staid *Kenkyūsha Dictionary* admits their lexical validity. Still, the words retain a nonrigorous quality, not entirely fit for serious scholarship. Far better to get a sense of them *bura-bura*: 'wandering around aimlessly, looking at the sights with no fixed destination in mind'.

Hocus Pocus

WILLIAM BRASHEAR

And [then] I stood on the royal stump and
blessed them in the sacred Altrusian tongue,
"Arooaroo halama rama domino,
shadrach meshach abednego."

—Garrison Keillor, *Lake Wobegon Days*

The thought of Uncle Louie speaking in tongues was
fascinating . . . what if he stood up and said, "Feemalator,
jasperator, hoo ha ha, Wamalamagamanama, zis boom bah!"

—Ibid

Exotic, strange-sounding, and unintelligible words, whether authentic and foreign or artificial and spontaneously made up on the spot, are an age-old and pandemic device for creating an aura of mystery, holiness, or magic. The use of genuine foreign languages is called *xenoglossia*. Familiar examples are the ancient languages, Latin, Coptic, Hebrew, and Greek, used in modern liturgies. However, the peculiarity of incantations and prayers is nothing new. It is attested in Babylonian, Egyptian, Greek, and Latin religious and magical texts preserved on clay tablets, papyrus, parchment, gems, and strips of metal thousands of years old. In ancient Hittite religious texts, Accadian words provide the mysterious, exotic sounds; in Latin it is Persian words; in Greek, Hebrew and Aramaic; in Hebrew prayers, Greek was used.

Glossolalia is the technical term for artificial languages, or "speaking in tongues," as it is more commonly known. To cite just a few ancient examples, an Assyrian incantation for retrieving a fugitive slave begins with the following nonsense sequence: *en ki-su-al-lu-ki . . . ki-ku-al-lu . . . ki na . . . gi-na-al-qi* (*Orientalia* 23, 1954, pp. 52–53). An Egyptian spell contains this gibberish: *edera edesana, ederagaha edesana, marmu edesana, emui edesana, degejana edesana, degabana edesana.* Another one: *paparuka paparaka pararura.* (*Ägypten and Ägyptisches Leben*, A. Erman and H. Ranke, pp. 406–407). A spell in Latin for alleviating sore throat prescribes chanting: *crissi crasi concrasi* (*Marcellus*, XIV, 24); another for healing dislocated joints: *motas vaeta daries dardaries astataries dissunapiter . . . huat hauat huat, ista pista sista, dannabo dannaustra . . . huat haut haut, istasis tarsis, ardannabon dannaustra* (*De re rustica*, Cato, p. 160). The Babylonian Talmud recommends reciting *baz bazia, mas masia, kas kasia, scharlai and amarlai . . . bazach bazich bazbazich* to prevent skin rash.

Hundreds of Greek and Coptic magical texts from Egypt (dating from the first century B.C. to the eleventh century A.D.) are replete with concatenations of *voces magicae*, some with up to a hundred letters, such as the more mellifluous: *melibou melibau melibaubau, touchar souchar, nennana sennana, samousoum souma soume soumeia meisouat srouat . . . rouat,* or the cacophonous: *chuchbachuch bauachuch bakaxichuch bazabachuch bachaxichuch bazetophoth bainchoooch.* (Psycholinguists like F. Trojan even trace relationships between word sounds and word meanings, the deep, dark vowels like *o* and *u* having an awesome, threatening, secretive nature on the one hand, and on the other the lighter ones like *e* and *i* often referring to the gentler, pleasanter things—whether in Indo-European or Chinese phonetics.)

Some of these ancient nonsensical magical words enjoyed exceptional longevity. *Meriut, mermeriut* in a Greek magical text of the third century A.D. reappear in medieval French Catholic and Eastern Syriac church liturgies as *mermeut.* Echoes of one Greek curse text written in the third century A.D. can be found in a Greek manuscript written almost fifteen hundred years later. More recently, Goethe in his *Reineke Fuchs* (11. Gesang) wrote: "und sie legt' ihm die Hand auf Haupt and sagte die Worte" ('and she laid her hand on his head and spoke the words'): *nekrast negibaul geid sum manteflih dnudna mein tedachs.* Thus, Garrison Keillor's boy narrator, with his *arooaroo halama rama,* is simply continuing a universal tradition, hallowed by generations of priests, magicians—and children—through the millennia.

There is no law against combining bogus, *ad hoc,* "foreign" words and the real thing in one breath, just as Keillor's narrator does in his "Altrusian" blessing, juxtaposing what is obviously nonsense next to genuine Latin *(domino)* and Hebrew *(shadrach, meshach, abednego).* Likewise, in ancient Greek magical texts snippets of Egyptian, Hebrew, Aramaic, Coptic, and Babylonian words and proper names commingle in happy abandon with endless concatenations of gibberish, producing a veritable Babelian babble to challenge the ingenuity of Indo-European and Semitist scholars alike two thousand years later, as they wrangle with these more-than-sesquipedalian creations of Greco-Egyptian magical fantasy. For example, the Greek palindrome *Aberamenthooulerthexanaxethreluoothnemareba,* according to one philologist, is Egyptian for 'Powerful One of the Waters, Thoth, God of Rain, O Sovereign: Rain of God, Thoth, of the Powerful Waters'.

Keillor, by incorporating the names of the three youths in the fiery furnace into his blessing, is merely following in the footsteps of some of his forebears in esotericism, the Copts of early Christian Egypt, who often invoked Shadrach, Meshach, and

Abednego alongside such fantasy figures as Thoulal, Moulal, and Boulal in their magical charms. (In all probability we owe to the Coptic Christians the invention, and to the Coptic magicians the dispersion, of the names of the three wise men, who make their first appearance, as Melchior, Thattasia, Bathesora, in Coptic magical texts in the sixth through eighth centuries A.D.)

Aside from the linguistic challenges they pose, these ancient artificial noncewords, with their sonorous, cantillating, rhyming, and rhythmical variations on phonetic themes, have intrigued and fascinated scholars who try to divine the rules governing their formation. For example, variations on a theme involving *homoiarcton* and *homoioteleuton* (similar beginnings and endings; see Keillor's "feema*lator*," "jasper*ator*") is a common device. A Greek magical spell for conjuring up a deity (seventh through eighth centuries A.D.) begins with the following nonsense sequence, *armapophar, astramuphar, astramuchur,* and continues with a series of transmutations typical of magical texts. Taking off from *armapophar,* the author transmuted the beginning to *astra-* and the ending to *-muphar.* For the next variation he combined and retained *astra- + mu-* but then altered the ending to *-chur.* Later on one finds: *Chla, Achla, Achlamu, Chlas!,* showing variations on the theme *Chla.* Another jingle in the same text runs: *otra peruth, . . . methor baruthar, eseluth* with the obvious themes *per-, bar-, -uth, -uthar, -ethor,* setting the tone in this ancient version of a magical patter song or jazz scat.

Another theory is that this mumbo jumbo may represent a kind of ancient pig Latin which, if properly decoded, might actually make sense. Hidden anagrams might be lurking there, awaiting the alert scholar to come along and detect them. Taking the example cited above: *otra perouth* might be transmogrified Greek for *o pater, therapeue* 'O Father, heal!'

Going a step further, linguists have noted the similarity between the sonorous sound manipulations of such artificial words in magical incantations and children's game songs. Children—and, in earlier times, illiterates—often took snippets of liturgical texts which they had heard in church on Sunday, adapting sing-song versions of them for their own irreligious and irreverent use on Monday. According to some scholars, the universally known and applied designation for magic, *hocus pocus,* may ultimately derive from the Latin Eucharist formula and represent a muddled version of Christ's words in the Vulgate New Testament (1 Cor. 11.24): *hoc est corpus meum* 'this is my body'. Likewise, *abracadabra*, it has been suggested, might stem from Hebrew *habracah dabrah* 'pronounce the blessing'.

Children around the world hold these alliterative and rhyming nonsensical sequences in great respect and are careful to incant them with meticulous exactitude. Furthermore, they seriously believe their jingles are genuine foreign languages—for example, Chinese—and hallowed by hoary antiquity. While their Chinese etymology may be doubted, "that these rhymes are centuries old is not to be lightly dismissed" (I. and P. Opie [*Children's Games in Street and Playground,* Oxford 1969, p. 44]), the well-known example *ene tene mone mei* (Germany 1847), *eena meena mina mona* (England 1895), *ina mina maina mau* (Norway 1959).

In *Verbatim* (I, 1 and I, 2, respectively) Roger Wescott and Paul Lloyd discussed rhyming, rhythmical, or alliterative "word chains," otherwise known as "coordinates" or "binomials" and "trinomials," which exist not only in English but in other languages as well. For example: *kith and kin, wrack and ruin*; in German: *mit Kind und Kegel, drauf und dran*; in French: *sain et sauf.* Alongside such fixed combinations, which seem to adhere to their own rhythmic and phonetic rules, are the playful, non-sensical, purely rhythmical and melodious formulations, which distinctly recall the ancient incantatory cantillations characteristic of Egyptian, Greek, and Roman and latterday hocus pocus. In English: *hunkydory, namby pamby, nitty gritty, higgledy-piggledy, heebie-jeebies, inky-dinky, itsy-bitsy, teeny-weeny*; in German: *Kuddelmuddel, Techtelmechtel, Krimskrams, Simsalabim, Holterdipolter*—to cite just a few.

These perhaps *quondam ad hoc* expressions, now part and parcel of our respective daily languages, adhere to the same general rhythmical and phonological rules as the nonsense words in the magical texts. Hans Winkler, the German Semitist, noted in 1935 that glossolalia, incantations, and children's chants all display certain common tendencies, namely, (1) the repetition of a given motif *(feemalator, jasperator; touchar souchar; astramuphar, astramuchur)*, and (2) the economical use of the vocal apparatus. Repeating a word or syllable or sound puts the least strain on the voice. Yet human creative ingenuity is not satisfied with repetition; it wants something new. Thus, once a pleasing motif has been discovered, the next least exerting is to reproduce it with a slight variation. Winkler discovered that the first element of binomials, whether nonsense or not, often begins with a laryngeal or velar phoneme which is formed in the back of the mouth (i.e., aspirated and unaspirated vowels). Taking the [preceding] examples, *hunkydory, higgledy-piggledy, hanky-panky, hocus pocus, heebie-jeebies, hodgepodge, hokey-pokey, inky-dinky, itsy-bitsy, Holterdipolter, Hülle und Fülle,* as can be noted, the second element tends to be a repetition of the first, beginning, however, with a labial *(p, b, f, m, v, w)*. Winkler called this the "*aleph-beth* rule" and demonstrated its practically universal validity, citing evidence from both medieval and modern gaming rhymes in European and Semitic languages alike. Going a step further, he found that nonsense trinomials generally continue with a word beginning with a palatal *(ch, g, j, k)*. As early as 1835, Richard Lepsius, the German Egyptologist, had pointed out the curious fact that the Hebrew alphabet contained no fewer than three groups of letters which adhere to this rule: (1) aleph, beth, gimel, daleth, (2) he, waw . . . heth, teth, (3) ayin, pe . . . koph . . . taw.

This evidently primordial phonetic series has continued to persist through the ages and is obviously as eminently appealing to Keillor's youthful narrator today as it was to his forebears several millennia ago and half a world away. By initiating his glossolalic cant with *beth-* element words *(feemalator, wamalama)* and continuing with palatal variations on their respective themes *(jasperator, gamanama)* the boy is apparently responding to the same primal urge that motivated the anonymous creators of our alphabet to begin their artificial series of sounds with *aleph, beth, gimel,* and *daleth*—and not with something like *zis boom bah!*

Epistola

In Mr. William Brashear's "Hocus Pocus," the "nonsensical magical words" from Goethe's *Reineke Fuchs, "nekrast negibaul geid sum manteflih dnudna mein tedachs"* make sense when the words are read backwards (with some anagrammatical liberties):

Schadet niemand und hilfet, Man mus(s) die Gläubigen stärken, which freely translates into 'Harm nobody and help, one must strengthen the believers'.

JACOB DE JAGER
Salt Lake City

Where'd That Come From? Etymologies

The sad thing about etymologies is that the better the story, the less likely the etymology is to have any connection, however remote, with the true and complete history of the word. In *Verbatim*, we try to strike a balance, avoiding both the credulous reporting of folk etymologies (although they are damn good stories!) and the tedious listing of long chains of words that descend from some proto-proto-proto word that means 'dirt'. Here, then, are some tales of etymology and etymologists that are at least mostly true and at least mostly entertaining.

Our Playful Vocabulary

BURT HOCHBERG

In compiling a list of English words that originated in games, but not in sports, I began by trying to separate games from sports to avoid wasting time on irrelevant research. Trying, but not quite succeeding. The more I investigated the matter, the less clearly I understood what it is about a game that makes it not a sport, and vice versa. Even chess, the quintessential game, cannot be definitively categorized. In the Soviet Union, for example, it is considered a sport; can we insist that it is not?

Lacking an unequivocal guideline, I decided that every borderline game/sport that added anything interesting to our vocabulary was, for my limited purpose, a game. Bowling, golf, and croquet are included, though many people consider them sports.

This list does not pretend to be exhaustive—that would have been an unrealistic ambition in view of the large debt that our language owes to games. I have omitted many common expressions because of their obviousness (especially phrases with *play* and *game*), others because of their rarity or obscure origins. Many terms that originated in games were listed by Stephen Hirschberg in *Verbatim* [XII, 3]; they are not repeated here.

The game categories, and the terms within each category, are arranged alphabetically. Terms that apply to no specific game are given in the *Miscellaneous* category at the end of the list.

Board and Table Games

Atari This Japanese word, familiar as the name of a [former] leading American home computer manufacturer, is from the game of go, where it signifies a threat to capture one or more of the opponent's pieces. Like the warning *check* in chess, it is not spoken during serious play.

back to square one Back to the starting place. The phrase was popularized—at least in England—by radio broadcasters of cricket matches who hoped to make the game comprehensible by referring to grids which had been printed in newspapers. The broadcasters borrowed the image from a board game (probably snakes and ladders) in which an unlucky dice roll sends a player's token to the beginning of the track. *Hopscotch* (q.v.) has been suggested as another possible source.

domino theory If communism is allowed to take root in one country it will inevitably spread to neighbouring countries. So goes the *domino theory,* a metaphor based on the parlor trick of standing dominoes on end in such a way that pushing over the first one topples the one behind it, and so on *ad Dominum.*

endgame The characteristic final phase of certain games, particularly chess and backgammon; metaphorically, any final phase, such as old age.

Go to jail, go directly to jail, do not pass go, etc. From Monopoly; sometimes used as a wry enumeration of the consequences of bad luck or of a bad move or decision.

kibitz The flycatcher (also called lapwing, pewit, and other names) is an insectivorous bird with an irritating cry. *Kiebitz,* the German word for this fellow, is the source of the German verb *kiebitzen* 'to look over the shoulder of a card player'. The Yiddish version *kibitz* has several meanings, all of them well established in English: 'comment while watching a game (typically cards or chess); second-guess; banter, wisecrack, or tease'.

Bowling

Bowling Green The name of several towns in the United States, and of a section of lower Manhattan. I do not know about the other towns, but New York's Bowling Green got its name from the fact that it was a level grassy area (a green) where people bowled.

debut, debutante The French word *but* means 'goal, aim, target' and also 'point (in a game)'. *Debuter* 'to make the first play', was originally used in old forms of billiards and bowling, and probably other games.

kingpin The *kingpin* (or one-pin or headpin) is the most important pin in the starting array because its action influences that of all the other pins. The term is used also for a person in the highest position of authority.

Card Games

above-board Wrote Samuel Johnson: "In open sight; without artifice or trick. A figurative expression, borrowed from gamesters, who, when they put their hands under the table, are changing their cards."

deal from the bottom of the deck A form of cheating.

deuce Generally, two of anything construed as a single unit (such as a two-dollar bill). In card games where the ace is high, the deuce is the weakest card. In craps an opening roll of deuce (two ones, or "snake eyes") loses immediately. The unluckiness of deuces may be why *deuce* came to signify misfortune or evil or the devil himself (see the *OED*). The meaning of *deuce* to signify a tied score is found only in tennis and table tennis.

discard Originally (and currently), to play or otherwise divest oneself of a card.

fast shuffle A method of setting up a *stacked deck* (q.v.). Generally, any deceptive, underhanded tactic.

finesse The meaning of *finesse* as an elegantly tricky or evasive stratagem originated in whist (and was later incorporated into bridge, a descendant of whist), where it is a technical maneuver in the play of the hand.

joker (in the deck) Anything, as a clause in an agreement, that changes the purpose, effect, or nature of something, often unexpectedly or surreptitiously.

7-Up One story has it that this brand of soft drink was named for the popular card game seven up (also known as *all fours* and *old sledge*). According to another story, *7-Up* was so named because it was introduced in a novel seven-ounce bottle and because its maker wanted to exploit the popularity of Bubble-Up, a competing soft drink. A spokeswoman for the 7-Up Company, in St. Louis, could not confirm either story; the name's origin, she said, is unknown.

Shoot the moon   In the game of hearts, players lose points for every heart they're stuck with at the end of the hand. But in the most popular version of the game, a player dealt the right cards can *shoot the moon*; that is, try to take all the hearts (plus the queen of spades) to earn a bonus. If the attempt fails, of course, the player will end up with a handful of losers. As a metaphor, the phrase means to risk all for the ultimate prize.

singleton   One of anything, as distinct from other things within its group ("a set of twins and a *singleton*"). The term originated in whist, where it refers to the only card of its suit in a hand, and is in common use in bridge.

stacked deck   A deck the cards of which have been secretly arranged—for example, by a *fast shuffle*—for the purpose of cheating. The victim (by extension, any victim) has the *cards stacked against him,* a situation in which he is powerless.

vie   This word, from the Old French *envier* (whence also *envy*), once meant, among other things, to 'place a wager in a game'; specifically, the card game gleek (see the *OED*).

Carnival Games

close, but no cigar   Cigars were once prizes in many carnival games.

gimmick   A *gimmick,* or *gaff,* is a secret device used to control a dishonest game, such as a wheel of fortune. Its meaning off the lot is 'any trick, device, or stratagem employed to increase something's interest or appeal'.

play fast and loose   The old fairground game fast and loose (sometimes called *the strap game*) wasn't exactly dishonest—it merely played on the gullibility of the suckers, as so many carny games do. A strap would be folded in half and rolled up with the two ends on the outside.

A sucker would be invited to bet that he could place a stick in one of the inside loops so that when the two ends of the strap were pulled apart the stick would be caught ("fast"). A sucker being a sucker, the stick was always in the clear ("loose"). *To play fast and loose* now means to behave in a deceitful or irresponsible manner.

shell game   This old gambling game (earlier known as *thimblerig*), in which the operator openly places a pea under one of three walnut shells, then rapidly shifts the shells around and challenges a sucker to bet on the location of the pea, has given its name to any kind of chicanery or subterfuge.

Children's Games

animal, vegetable, or mineral   A phrase used to express doubt that the basic nature or purpose of something has been definitely established. It comes from the word-guessing game Twenty Questions, where the only hint given the guessers is the word's category—*animal, vegetable, or mineral.*

blind-man's buff   Any activity the practitioners of which seem not to know what they are doing. The *OED* cites figurative uses of the term going back to 1590. In the game, a blindfolded player tries to catch other players who are "buffing" (buffeting; i.e., 'playfully harassing') him.

dibs   *Dibs,* short for *dibstones,* were animal knucklebones (or pebbles) used in the game of dibstones, also called *jackstones* or, more usually nowadays, *jacks.* The meaning of *dibs* to stake a claim to something (as in "I have *dibs* on the crossword puzzle") may or may not be related to that game. The *Random House Dictionary* says it is, but Wentworth and Flexner, in *Dictionary of American Slang,* say it comes from *divvy,* a slang form of *divide.*

getting warm   From the game Hunt the Thimble (known also by many other names), in which one player hides an object and tells the "hunter" whether he is getting closer to it ("warm") or farther from it ("cold").

hide-and-seek (or hide-and-go-seek)   A simple game in which one or more players hide themselves, and others try to find them. Figuratively, *to play hide-and-seek* is to maneuver evasively.

hopscotch   A rapid series of moves from place to place, literally or figuratively by hopping. *Scotch* is from an old French word meaning 'scored line' or 'mark'. In the game hopscotch, a player tosses an object into a numbered grid and then tries to retrieve it while hopping sequentially into every area of the grid on one foot (except the one where the object lies) without stepping on a line or losing his balance.

leapfrog   To advance (ahead of others) by jumping. In the game, players take turns leaping over the bent backs of players in front of them in a continually advancing chain.

musical chairs   In the game of musical chairs (known also as *going to Jerusalem*), music is played while the players circle two rows of chairs, placed back to back and numbering one fewer than the number of players. The object is not to be left without a seat when the music stops.

Croquet

mall; Pall Mall   Pall Mall, a street in an elegant district of London, owes its name to Charles II's favorite game, Pallamaglio (an ancestor of croquet), which used to be played in an alley (now called The Mall) in nearby St. James's Park. (Pall Mall cigarettes were so named to suggest the upper-crustness associated with that district.) The game got its name from the Italian *palla* (whence *ball*) and *maglio* ('mallet'). The current *mall* (a shopping center) is a direct descendant of the alley where Pallamaglio was played.

Dice Games

hazard   This gambling game, a predecessor of craps, gets its name from the Arabic *az zahr* 'the die'.

raffle   An old game using three dice; the winner of the stakes was the player who rolled either three like numbers, or the highest triplet if there were others, or the highest pair if there was no triplet. The word came to be used for various kinds of lotteries.

Golf

stymie   Before the rules were changed in 1951, a player could not lift another player's ball that lay between his own ball and the cup. That situation was called a *stymie,* and the term came to mean any block or obstruction.

tee off; teed off   To *tee off* is to begin the play of a hole by driving the ball off the tee. It has several figurative uses: 'to begin anything; to attack or denounce; to strike hard'. *Teed off,* aside from being the past tense of *tee off* in the above senses, is an adjective meaning 'annoyed' or 'angry'. The *Webster's Third*

New International Dictionary (WID3) relates it to the golf term, but other sources think that it an offspring of *ticked off* (which has been traced to WWI British navy slang) and should be spelled *t'd off*, or that it is a euphemism for *peed off*, itself a euphemism for *pissed off*.

Marbles

knuckle down   Marble games are played by shooting marbles with the thumb while the knuckles of the other fingers rest on the playing surface for stability. In games, *to knuckle down* is 'to prepare to shoot a marble' in that way; figuratively, it means 'to apply oneself seriously'.

Pool and Billiards

carom   An angled rebound. The meaning comes from Billiards, where a *carom* is a shot in which the cue ball is made to rebound so as to hit two other balls. *Carom* is a shortening of *carambole*, an obsolete three-ball game with a similar object. The origin of *carambole* is the East Indian carambola tree and its fruit, but their connection with the game is obscure. Were the fruits used as balls in a primitive version of the game?

Puzzles

jigsaw puzzle; piece of the puzzle   A common metaphor, especially in detective fiction, used to describe the intricate fitting together of facts or other elements to achieve completeness.

Miscellaneous Games

game not worth the candle   A lost cause. Before the invention of the electric light, it was said that to continue a hopelessly lost game would be to waste the candle used to illuminate it.

handicap   The origin of this word was *Hand-in-Cap*, an old lottery game in which two players and an umpire put forfeit money in a cap. The umpire then stated the difference in value between two articles that the players offered to exchange with each other. If neither player then put up more money, the umpire took the forfeit stake and the articles were not exchanged. If both players upped their offers, the umpire took the money and the articles were exchanged. If only one player increased his offer, that player won the stakes and there was no exchange.

high jinks   Originally, various tavern games in which patrons would be challenged to sing or perform a silly task or drink a quantity of ale (or whatever) on penalty of some forfeit. The tasks and who would do them were sometimes decided by dice. *High jinks* (often spelled *hijinks*) now refers generally to any boisterous play.

jeopardy   In Old French, *jeu parti* meant 'evenly divided game'; hence, 'an uncertain outcome'. In English, *jeopardy* took on the meaning of 'danger or risk'.

ludicrous   From the Latin *ludus* 'game, play', *ludicrous* once meant 'frivolous or characteristic of play'. The meaning has shifted somewhat to 'laughable or absurd'.

SIC! SIC! SIC!

"Regardless of anything to the contrary in this booklet, if your medical insurance terminates for any reason including death, you . . . may elect within 30 days . . . to continue such medical insurance. . . . From *Group Insurance for 1–14 Employees,* Consolidated Group Trust, The Hartford, p. 70.

On Again, Off Again, Finnigin

J. WALTER WILSON, M.D.

I have before me a small tan-colored book of poems published by Strickland Gillilan in 1917 entitled *Including Finnegan.* The fly leaf is inscribed "To J. Walter Wilson with the undying regard of a regular feller who knows another regular feller thoroughly but loves him still; also when he isn't still." This was inscribed to my father who was [Gillilan's] companion on several vaudeville circuits.

Gillilan's name is virtually unknown, but he should be forever remembered because the Finnegan poem added to the English language the phrase *off again, on again,* which most of us hear and use frequently in the mistaken belief that it refers to something or someone who changes direction rapidly and often. In fact, it refers to the thousands of persons who fled from Ireland's potato famine in the 1840s, whose men almost always became policemen or railroad workers. Thus it is an old railroad story. It is written in one of the more difficult rhyming styles and contains the longest succession of trisyllabic rhymes I have ever encountered.

Finnigin to Flannigan

Superintindint wuz Flannigan;
Boss av th' siction wuz Finnigin.
Whiniver th' cyars got off th' thrack
An' muddled up things t' th' divvle an' back,
Finnigin writ it t' Flannigan,
Afther th' wrick wuz all on agin;

That is, this Finnigin
Repoorted t' Flannigan.
Whin Finnigin furrst writ t' Flannigan,
He writed tin pa-ages, did Finnigin;
An' he towld just how th' wrick occurred—
Yis, minny a tajus, blundherin' wurrd
Did Finnigin write t' Flannigan
Afther th' cyars had gone on agin—
That's th' way Finnigin
Repoorted t' Flannigan.
Now Flannigan knowed more than Finnigin—
He'd more idjucation, had Flannigan.
An' ut wore 'm clane an' complately out
T' tell what Finnigin writ about
In 's writin' t' Musther Flannigan.
So he writed this back. "Musther Finnigin:—
Don't do sich a sin agin;
Make 'em brief, Finnigin!"
Whin Finnigin got that frum Flannigan
He blushed rosy-rid, did Finnigin.
An' he said: "I'll gamble a whole month's pay
That ut'll be minny an' minny a day
Befure sup'rintindint—that's Flannigan—
Gits a whack at that very same sin agin.
Frum Finnigin to Flannigan
Repoorts won't be long agin."
Wan day on th' siction av Finnigin,
On th' road sup'rintinded be Flannigan,
A ra-ail give way on a bit av a currve
An' some cyars wint off as they made th' shwarrve.
"They's nobody hurrted," says Finnigin,
"But repoorts must be made t' Flannigan."

An' he winked at McGorrigan
As married a Finnigin.
He wuz shantyin' thin, wuz Finnigin,
As minny a railroader's been agin,
An' 'is shmoky ol' lamp wuz burrnin' bright
In Finnigin' shanty all that night—
Bilin' down 's repoort, wuz Finnigin.
An' he writed this here: "Musther Flannigan:—
Off agin, on agin,
Gone agin.—Finnigin."

SIC! SIC! SIC!

"There are no national temperatures today due to transmission difficulties." From the *St. Petersburg Evening Independent.*

"My Name Is Hanes"

GERALD COHEN

One of the tasks of etymologists is to spot etymological treatments that have lain unnoticed in obscure places and to bring them to the attention of other scholars. Presented below is one such item that I noticed [one] summer in the course of my research on slang. It appears in the New York newspaper *The Subterranean*, 15 November 1845, p. 4, col. 1, where it was reprinted from the *Evening Star*. A check of the *Dictionary of American English* and Mathews' *Americanisms* ... shows no mention of *My name is Hanes*, and this expression has therefore apparently been overlooked by scholars of American English.

There are thousands of people in this country who make use of the common expression "My name is Hanes" when they are about leaving a place or party suddenly, yet few know from whence the expression is derived. A more common saying, or one in more general use, has never been got up. We hear it in Maine, in Georgia, in Maryland, and in Arkansas—it is in the mouth of the old and the young, the grave and the gay—in short, "My name is Hanes" enjoys a popularity which no other cant phrase does—be it our next care to give its origin.

Some forty-five years since, a gentleman by the name of Hanes was travelling on horseback in the vicinity of Mr. Jefferson's residence in Virginia. Party spirit was running extremely high in those days. Mr. Jefferson was president, and Mr. Hanes was a rank federalist, and as a matter of course, a bitter opponent to the then existing administration and its head. He was not acquainted with Mr. Jefferson, and accidentally coming up with that gentleman, also travelling on horseback, his party zeal soon led him into a conversation upon the all-absorbing topic. In the course of the conversation, Hanes took particular pains to abuse Mr. Jefferson, calling him all sorts of hard names, run(ning) down every measure of his administration, poked the non-intercourse act at him as most outrageous and ruinous, ridiculing his gunboat system as preposterous and nonsensical, opposed his purchase of Louisiana as a wild scheme—in short, took every leading feature of the day, descanted on them and their originator with the greatest bitterness. Mr. Jefferson all the while said little. There was no such thing as getting away from his very particular friend, and he did not exactly feel at liberty to combat his argument.

They finally arrived in front of Mr. Jefferson's residence, Hanes of course, not acquainted with the fact. Notwithstanding he had been vilified and abused "like a pickpocket," to use the old saying, Mr. Jefferson still, with the true Virginia hospitality and politeness, invited his travelling companion to alight and partake of some refreshments. Hanes was about getting from his horse, when it occurred to him that he should ask his companion's name.

"Jefferson," said the President blandly.

"What! Thomas Jefferson?"

"Yes, Sir: Thomas Jefferson."

"President Thomas Jefferson?" continued the astounded federalist.

"The same," rejoined Mr. Jefferson.

"Well, *my name is Hanes!*" and putting spurs to his horse, he was out of hearing instantly.

This, we are informed, was the origin of the phrase.

SIC! SIC! SIC!

"Proceeds from sales of carved ducks go to handicap children." A sign in a Greek pizzeria in Peabody, Massachusetts. Submitted by Nell Wright, Lynnfield, Massachusetts.

On Blue Moons, and Others

NICK HUMEZ

Nature has favored us with a single large satellite with two felicitous peculiarities: It always turns the same face towards us, and it appears exactly the same size in the sky as our

sun. The latter property makes a total solar eclipse, if we are fortunate enough to see one, one of the most astonishing events of our lives: After an alarming prelude of the sun being seemingly nibbled away to a tiny sliver by a giant but invisible mouth, our world is plunged into a shadowy half-light as the mercury plummets and birds fall silent, a time just long enough for us to have serious doubts about the rightness of things and of our sanity before the flash of "Bailey's Beads"—the glint of sunlight between the peaks of the moon's mountains—as the bright crescent emerges again, gradually waxing into the warm daystar we take for granted most of the time. It is a profoundly unsettling experience, even for those of us who pride ourselves on our rationality and scientific sophistication; its terrifying effect on societies unfamiliar with its cause and unable to predict its recurrence can scarcely be imagined.

And a solar eclipse is just one of the spectacular celestial effects to which our moon kindly treats us. This [article's] title, however, has less to do with any intrinsic lunar property and much more with how we reckon time, and specifically how we reconcile the relation between the natural cycle of the moon (about 29½ days to circle the earth completely, and thus to go through its changes from new to full and back to new again) and the month, which, despite its name, does not necessarily bear a direct one-to-one correspondence to what astronomers now sometimes call a lunation.

A "blue moon" today means the second appearance of a full moon within a (Gregorian)[1] calendar month. This is rare (hence "once in a blue moon") but by no means impossible given months of thirty and thirty-one days. In 1999, in fact, blue moons were not rare at all, there being two of them in twelve months: one in January (the moon was full on January 2 and January 31) and another in March (having had full moons on March 2 and March 31; February having had no full moon at all). On the other hand, having two of them in a year is itself a rare thing: The next year this will happen is 2018, and the next after that in 2037.[2]

It appears, however, that this meaning of "blue moon" is a relatively recent one. In [an] issue of his electronic newsletter World Wide Words[3], Michael Quinion, citing an article by Philip Hiscock in the March 1999 issue of *Sky and Telescope Magazine*, notes that the current definition of the expression has been widespread only in the late '80s and '90s after it appeared on a card in the popular game *Trivial Pursuit,* which cited as its source an item in a children's almanac published in 1985, which itself drew on a radio program of 1979, which referred to a quiz in *Sky and Telescope* in 1943, which in turn referenced an item in the *Maine Farmer's Almanac* of 1934—"and there the trail goes cold," Quinion says, adding that the oldest reference in the chain defines a *blue moon* as the second one not in a calendar month but in a zodiacal house (which, since these change every 365¼ days, or a little over 30, make such an event a little less likely but again far from a once-in-a-lifetime proposition).

Clearly one must delve deeper, and Quinion has obligingly done so, finding a 1528 citation (in a piece charmingly entitled *Rede and Be not Wrothe*), "Yf they say the mone is blewe, we must believe that it is true."[4] This would suggest not just rarity but hens'-teeth impossibility. However, there are occasions when the moon really does appear blue, thanks to smoke or dust in the atmosphere from a very large volcanic event, such as the explosion of the Indonesian island of Krakatau in 1883, or the eruption of Mt. St. Helens in 1980. (Large forest fires or the massive brush conflagrations of Third-World slash-and-burn agriculturists, can also produce this effect.)[5]

Rare does not mean irregular: Clever readers of paragraph three above might guess that the next double-blue-moon year after that will be somewhere around 2056, and they will be right. This is because the common denominator of a 365-day solar year and a 29-day lunar month yields a cycle of 19 solar years (= 235 lunations). If there's a blue moon in March of 2018, there should be one in March of 2037, too.

The lack of a good fit between a solar year and one based on cycles of the moon has led to several work-arounds, depending on the culture. The Jewish calendar has twelve months of 29 or 30 days (Tishri, Marheshvan, Kislev, Tebet, Shebat, Adar, Nisan,

Iyar, Sivan, Tammuz, Av, and Elul); the discrepancy with the solar year is trued up seven times in a nineteen-year cycle by inserting an extra month, called Second Adar, between Adar and Nisan, whose first day in antiquity used to be the official beginning of the year. (It has since been switched to the first of Tishri, celebrated as the feast of Rosh Hashonah.) This allows months to stay lunar but keeps the year more or less in tune with the sun and the fixed stars.

Muslims also observe a lunar month—literally observe it, in fact, since the month starts with the actual observation of the new moon's crescent, and that can vary by as much as two days depending where on earth one is doing the observing—and dates in the Islamic calendar start at sunset, not at midnight. Thus, as astronomical dating expert Khalid Shaukat points out[6], a person whose Gregorian birth date was 31 August 1952 might have any of four Islamic birth dates: Zul-Hijja eight, nine, ten, or even eleven, depending on the time of day, hemisphere, and latitude of his or her birth.

There are twelve months in the Muslim year: Ramadan, Shawwal, Zul-Qada, Zul-Hijja, Muharram, Safar, Rabi I, Rabi II, Jumada I, Jumada II, Rajab, and Sha'ban. Each starts on the evening of the first visibility of the lunar crescent. However, unlike the Jewish calendar, there is no provision for intercalary months; after Sha'ban comes Ramadan and the cycle starts all over again. In consequence, the Islamic year is ten or eleven days shorter than the Gregorian one. Dates being reckoned from the Hegira or Hijjra, the year of the Prophet Mohammed's flight from Mecca to Medina (A.D. 622), the current year is A.H. 1420, though in Gregorian years the Hegira was 1,387 years ago. Both "month" and "year," then, far from being absolutes, assume the status of cultural constructs.

It is in the nature of the moon to appear ever changeable.

Perhaps that is one reason why men in love with binary categories, from ancient Mesopotamia to modern Manhattan, have made the sun male and the moon female, whether Shamash and Ishtar in Babylon or Apollo and Artemis/Diana in Greece and Rome. Another reason may be that courtship is often carried on more conveniently at night, and the moon becomes both the lamp to guide men to the seductive female Other and, by extension, the Other herself, the madwoman in the celestial attic.

Of the 110 lunar citations in *Bartlett's Familiar Quotations*, at least a quarter refer to the moon's pale light, its inaccessibility, its silence, its barrenness, and its association with irrational behavior of dogs and people. Beauty is linked with calamity, or at least peril: A *mooncalf* is a freak or a fool; the insane are *moonstruck* (or *lunatic*). We may get a touch of *moon-blink*, a momentary blindness supposedly caused by sleeping out in the open and exposed to the moon's rays. (To be *moon-blind*, on the other hand, refers not to people but to horses, and probably derives from the cloudy appearance of the lens of the eye.) Sexuality lurks in such expressions as *mooning*, i.e. displaying the bare buttocks, a prank particularly favored by adolescent boys as an act of male bonding; women, on the other hand, may euphemistically refer to their *moon-time*, the average human menstrual cycle and the lunar cycle both being very close to four weeks.[7]

Moonshine is illicitly distilled corn liquor, also called *white lightning*; a *moonlighter* is one who works on the side, often on the swing or graveyard shift, in addition to and contrast with his or her "legitimate" day job. *Moonraking* is woolgathering, but also another word for smuggling, from the tradition that those in England who raked a pond to retrieve smuggled goods concealed in it, if surprised by the authorities and asked what they were doing, would play the simpleton and claim that they were attempting to rake up the moon reflected on the water's surface.

No article on blue moons would be complete without mentioning a song dear to the hearts of American baby boomers reading this article (in whose intracerebral auditory synapses the introductory "BAU-pa-pa-BAU-pa-BAU-pa-BAU-BAU . . ." must surely have been lurking throughout most of the preceding paragraphs). The Marcels' rendition of "Blue Moon" leapt from the charts to our hearts as the 1950s skidded around the corner into the '60s with a squeal of rubber and a roar of Hollywood glasspack mufflers. Other versions of the song were recorded by Elvis Presley and Bob Dylan, but none with the manic drive of the Marcels' up-tempo doo-wop cover.

In the 1980s "Blue Moon" was adopted as a team anthem by English soccer fans loyal to the Manchester Blues, and hence came to be sung ironically and derisively by adherents of opposing teams. New topical lyrics sometimes were substituted for the classics. After a famous win over the Rags in 1989, Blues fans gleefully sang to the fans of the opposition, "Blue Moon, / You started singing our tune, / You won't be singing for long, / Because we beat you 5-1."[8]

Words in Print, Words and Print: The Written Word

Reading is one of the greatest pleasures known in this modern age. Pity the poor Neanderthal: Outside, the howling storm; inside, a nice fire, a chunk of half-cooked meat, a comfy fur rug, but no novel to lose herself in. The pleasure that we get from reading explains why we become so irritated when that pleasure is interfered with—by poor translations, printers' errors, stolen books or, as these essays illustrate, by our own mental interference with the author's words on the page.

The Twenty-third Psalm and Me, or Has the Nightingale Become a Crow?

GRACE HOLLANDER

The Lord is my shepherd; I shall not want.
He maketh me to lie down in green pastures:
He leadeth me beside the still waters.
He restoreth my soul: He leadeth me in the paths of
righteousness for His name's sake.
Yea though I walk through the valley of the shadow
of death, I will fear no evil: for Thou art with me:
Thy rod and Thy staff they comfort me.
Thou preparest a table before me in the presence of
mine enemies: Thou anointest my head with oil;
my cup runneth over.
Surely goodness and mercy shall follow me all the days of
my life: And I will dwell in the house of the Lord forever.

—*King James Version,* 1611

The Lord is my shepherd; I shall want nothing.
He makes me lie down in green pastures, and leads
me beside the waters of peace;
He renews life within me, and for His name's sake
guides me in the right path.
Even though I walk through a valley dark as death,
I fear no evil, for Thou art with me,
Thy staff and Thy crook are my comfort.
Thou spreadest a table for me in the sight of my enemies.

Thou hast richly bathed my head with oil,
and my cup runs over.
Goodness and love unfailing, these will follow me all the
days of my life: and I shall dwell in the house of the Lord
my whole life long.

—*New English Bible*, G. Drover and (Sir) W. D. Hardy,
Oxford University Press, 1970

Stupid me! I always thought that there was only one translation of the twenty-third Psalm until the other day when I
happened on the *New English Bible* (1970) and saw that "my
head was richly bathed in oil." "Bathed in oil"? Odd! I remembered "anointed." Is *anointing* 'bathing'? I couldn't find such a
definition in the thesaurus. I looked up the Hebrew word, *dis-
hanta*. Found no 'bathed'. It bothered me, this image of a man
having his head bathed in oil in a very French barber shop (where
men have their heads massaged in oil to prevent baldness) instead
of the image of the making of a king, like David, who was the
anointed of God. Why did this translator feel he had to change
"anoint his head" to "bathe his head"? Perhaps the translation
comes from some very important commentator but it hardly creates a "sublime" image and surely does not achieve the quiver
mentioned in John Brough's translation of the Sanskrit poem:

> *Of what use is the poet's poem,*
> *Of what use is the bowman's dart,*
> *Unless another's senses reel*
> *When it sticks quivering in the heart?*

Nor does the psalm sing as Henry Ward Beecher put it in "Life
Thoughts," "like a nightingale . . . of small homely feather singing

shyly out of obscurity" filling "the air of the whole world with melodious joy greater than the heart can conceive."

What were the translators of the *New English Bible* thinking? The editors tell us, "The translators have endeavored to avoid anachronisms and expressions reminiscent of foreign idioms. They have tried to keep their language as close to current usage as possible while avoiding words and phrases likely soon to become obsolete"; a most ambitious and delicate program to attempt for the entire Bible. And how does it apply to the twenty-third Psalm? Isn't the metaphoric shepherd an anachronism to a television generation? And what of "anoint his head"? No one does that anymore—not even in England where there are still occasional coronation ceremonies. Are "waters of peace," "valley dark as death," "thy staff and thy crook," current usage? I miss the translator's search for the quiver and the nightingale!

That started my own search. What had other translators done with this "sunny little psalm" that "has dried many tears and supplied the mould into which many hearts have poured their peaceful faith" (Maclaren in A. Cohen, *The Psalms*, 1945)?

In *From One Language to Another* (1986) Jan de Waard and Eugene A. Nida decry the "clinging to old-fashioned language even though the meaning has radically changed" and as a deplorable example points to the retaining of "The Lord is my shepherd, I shall not want" even though *want* no longer means to 'lack' but rather 'desire' and continues with, "Thus many persons understand this traditional rendering to mean, 'The Lord is my shepherd whom I shall not want'." Can you believe it? Can it be that these experts are wanting in judgment?

Perhaps it is because I am just one of the "ordinary readers with no special knowledge of the ancient East" [*New English Bible*, 1970] that I want more than anything else "a quiver in my heart" when I read the twenty-third Psalm and confess to being rather shocked to find that "the Lord" is no longer my shepherd. Writes the translator [*The Psalms*, 1976]: "I abolished 'the Lord' but felt unwilling to call God, Yahweh. I know no one who actually prays in English to that name." I know many who pray to the name "my Lord" and some who are "willing" to pray to their Father, to the Almighty, to the Eternal One. God's ineffable name as told to Moses is unutterable [Exodus 6:3] so why make an issue of it? Why not choose the one that is closest to the nightingale? The *King James Version* chose "The Lord is my shepherd" and it sings! That liquid "L" sounded with that almost awe-full "-ord", "LLL-AWE-RD" followed by the soft "sh" in shepherd and its "rd" alliteration with the "rd" in *lord* entwine this twosome in my soul. Isn't that what "the Lord is my shepherd" is all about—entwining my soul?

Is it a better translation for me because each word is perhaps a trifle closer to the original Hebrew or to the original Ugaritic stem? When I read the psalm what I want is that quiver in my heart. Do I get it when "I shall not want," four simple one-syllable words, swaying in iambic rhythm, with the *shall* sliding irresistibly into the breathy *w* of *want* calling up the memory of God's "breathing the breath of life" [Genesis 2:7] and man becoming a "living soul" is "improved" to "I shall lack nothing" with its jagged *k* sound, its materialistic, vacuous *nothing*, or changed to "I have everything I need" to which "Well, whaddaya know!" can be the only response?

Recognizing that the *King James* translation is "The noblest monument to English prose" [*Oxford Annotated Bible*, 1962], many translators, in prefaces to their "new," "modern" versions have written apologetics explaining why they felt they had to retranslate and how they proposed doing it.

In *The Psalms,* the translator writes in his preface, "I have tried not to substitute without necessity new English phrases for what was old and well-loved, but unity and modernization of language as well as the true meaning of Hebrew have often made changes inevitable." Is "He will bring me into meadows of young grass" really any closer to the Hebrew than "He maketh me to lie down in green pastures"? Is not "He maketh me to lie down in green pastures" old and well-loved? Does the modern reader really lack the great "erudition" necessary to be able to understand a few old English words and forms—What about "My country 'tis of thee"?—and is it indeed true that, in the rather awkward phraseology of the translator, "the language is not altered with doing without thou and thee"? Not altered? For my quiver I prefer doing with *thou* and *thee*! The loving yet formal *thee* and *thou* and the closing *-eth* syllable create a melody, a rhythm, a smooth cadence truly reflecting our beloved shepherd's care, and ignite a feeling of intimacy with him, a mutuality of feeling that the *-s* ending completely wants—Excuse me!—lacks.

Just compare the overtones and associations of the psalm with the *-th* and the *-s* endings:

-s ENDING	OVERTONE	*-th* ENDING	OVERTONE
He makes me	'forces me'	He maketh me	'persuades me'
He leads me	'holds a tight rein'	He leadeth me	'I follow willingly'
My cup runs over	'a coffee cup in a dirty saucer'	My cup runneth over	'a goblet, maybe a grail'

To my ears, *restores my soul* with its -z sound in the middle of the alliteration is irritating and divisive, while the *-th* in *restoreth my soul* smoothly slides along, bringing the alliterative -s's together, etherealizing the restoring and uniting it with my soul. Besides the acoustically melodious vibrations of *restoreth my soul*, its imagery holds that transcendental ingredient, the soul, while *refresh my being* [1966], *revive my drooping spirit* [1969], *gives me new strength* [1970], *renews life within me* [1970], or *renews my life* [1979] are all soulless images arousing only mundane connotations.

"Keeping abreast of the times and translating into the language we use today are two slogans wisely adopted" [*Old Testament of the Jerusalem Bible*, 1966]. What is so "wise" about it? The worshipers of the Golden Calf were keeping abreast of the times, and the language we use today is a Tower of Babel from which elegance and sublimity seem to be deliberately omitted. This translator has replaced "He leadeth me beside the still waters" by "To the waters of repose he leads me." What are "waters of repose"? Are they abreast of the times? or are they the "language of today"? Since the translator may not "substitute his own modern images for the old ones" how can the *shepherd* metaphor retain its old-fashioned pastoral simplicity when its sense and the reader's senses are jarred out of the authentic Bible-time setting and are forced into a frame of the "language we use today"? Seen any shepherds on Broadway lately or even mentioned in the *New York Times*?

Are not visual images-made-modern pedestrian, colorless substitutions? "Though I pass through a gloomy valley, I fear no harm" is like "Though I pass through Wichita on a rainy day on the way to California, I won't have an accident in my automobile"; "Yea, though I walk through the valley of the shadow of death, I will fear no evil" is no casual passing by but step-by-step pacing through life with death constantly threatening and the devil's evil lure contemned, reminding us of Adam and Eve who, tempted by the devil, were enticed and ate from the tree of Good and Evil (not harm!) [Genesis 2:9].

Most of our modern translators seem to be allergic to or very much afraid of death or else have little real faith in the shepherd's taking care of them as they walk through life to ultimate death. In the following outline of thirteen psalms translated since 1937, the preoccupation with darkness and the elimination of any reference to death is conspicuous. The Hebrew word circumvented and about which there is some commentary discussion is *zalmaveth, zal* meaning 'shadow' and *maveth* meaning 'death', the combination translated in the *King James Version* as "the shadow of death," a quivering image.

DATE	REFERENCE TO *dark*	REFERENCE TO *death*
1937	the darkest valley	eliminated
1964	valley of dense darkness	eliminated
1966	a gloomy valley	eliminated
1966	in total darkness	eliminated
1969	a valley of deepest darkness	eliminated
1969	nothing lurking in the dark ravine	eliminated
1969	the valley of darkness	eliminated
1970	a valley dark as	death
1970	dark valley	eliminated
1971	valley of deep darkness	eliminated
1976	valley of the darkness of	death
1976	a valley overshadowed by	death
1977	the valley of	death
1982	the valley of deepest darkness	eliminated

Is it at all possible "to balance the lofty beauty of the heavily nuanced text with an easily understood English" [*Siddur Kol Yaakov*, 1984]? Is "I shall not lack" any easier than "I shall not want," "tranquil waters" easier than "still waters," a "valley over-shadowed by death" simpler than the "valley of the shadow of death," "tormentors" easier than "enemies," and "long days" easier than "forever"? Just what is "easily understood English"?

Some translators have set themselves an almost transcendental goal—to answer the question, "What thought did the person who first recorded these words really intend to express?" [*Jewish Publication Society*, 1979] That is a thought to conjure with. What did David (or was it someone else?) intend when he wrote or sang the Twenty-third Psalm? How can we ever know exactly what he intended? And does it really matter? Whatever the original intention, however literally exact the translation, it misses, unless it sticks quivering in the heart.

The "Wicked" Bibles, or Let Him Who Is without Sin among You Cast the First Line of Type

RAY RUSSELL

Does the Bible condone adultery, or urge us to hate our wives? Did Adam and Eve wear pants? As I discovered while doing research for [a] novel, it depends on which Bible you read.

There was an edition that seemed not only to condone adultery but to *command* it. That Bible, the handiwork of a pair of printers named Barker and Lucas, was published in England in 1631. It was a handsome volume, as well it should have been, for Messrs. B and L were the King's printers.

But it had one little flaw: A three-letter word, *not*, was missing from the Seventh Commandment, making it read "Thou shalt commit adultery." The careless printers of the book that became famous as "The Wicked Bible" were fined three hundred pounds, which effectively put them out of business.

Ten times that amount was the fine imposed on another firm of printers, during the reign of Charles I, for perpetrating what has come to be known as "The Fool Bible." Their slip-of-the-typestick occurred in Psalm 14, which came out reading, "The fool hath said in his heart there is a God"—instead of "there is no God."

At Cambridge in 1653 was printed the justly nicknamed "Unrighteous Bible." It was marred by two bloopers, both concerning righteousness. In 1 Corinthians, it asked the question, "Know ye not that the unrighteous shall inherit the Kingdom of God?" Obviously a *not* is missing from between *shall* and *inherit*— probably dropped on the floor by the same gremlins who lost the Barker and Lucas *not* twenty-two years before. As if that weren't bad enough, in this edition's version of Romans may be seen, "Neither yield ye your members as instruments of *righteousness* unto sin." Of course, *unrighteousness* is the correct word. This proves, perhaps, that the power of positive thinking can be carried too far.

Absent negatives appear to be the single most prevalent kind of error, and they always succeed in completely reversing the Scriptural meaning. "And there was no more sea," we are told in Revelation—except in a certain 1641 edition which has, "And there was more sea."

It wasn't Jesus who, in the garden of Gethsemane, told His disciples to "Sit ye here, while I go and pray yonder." It was Judas—at least according to an edition of 1611.

Eight thousand copies of one Bible were printed and bound in Ireland in 1716 before it was discovered that the command, in John, to "sin no more," had come out as "sin on more," a directive with somewhat more appeal to chronic sinners.

"The Parable of the Vinegar" (instead of "Vineyard") appears in a chapter heading of Luke in a 1717 Oxford printing. Philip, rather than Peter, is singled out as the apostle who will deny Jesus, in Luke of the 1792 "Denial Bible." Poor Luke again gets its lumps in "The Forgotten Sins Bible" of 1638, where "Her sins, which are many, are forgotten" may be seen, rather than the correct "forgiven." "If any man come to me, and hate not his father and mother . . . yea, and his own wife also . . ." So begins another passage in the long-suffering Luke, as given in the so-called "Wife-Hater Bible" of 1810. Here, one letter is the culprit—*w*. It should be *l*, and the phrase should read "and his own life also. . . ."

"The Murderers' Bible" of 1801 slips in *murderers* for *murmurers* in a line from Jude: "These are murmurers, complainers." "Who hath ears to ear, let him hear" is the way a line in Matthew is misrendered in "The Ears to Ear Bible" of 1810. "The Discharge Bible" of 1806 reads, in Timothy, not "I charge thee before God" but (you guessed it) "I discharge thee . . ."

Sexual identity has been in question more than once. *He* is substituted for the correct *she* in what today some might call "The Male Chauvinist Bible," but which is more commonly and more simply known as "The He Bible." This was the first of the two editions of the *Authorized Version*, 1611, and its sin was to say, in Ruth, "And he went into the city" instead of *she*. Another mix-up of gender happened in a much more recent edition of

1923 which contained a table of affinity with the stern admonition, "A man may not marry his grandmother's wife," a feat which the *New Yorker* might call Neatest Trick of the Week.

An edition organized by Anglican Archbishop Matthew Parker, and therefore known affectionately as "The Bishop's Bible," made its first appearance in 1568 and was gratifyingly popular. Its third edition, however, published in 1572, didn't fare so well. Nothing was wrong with the words, but the decorations left a lot to be desired. The printer used highly ornamental initial letters at the beginnings of several books of this Bible, which would have been a splendid idea if the letters hadn't been left over from printings of Ovid's *Metamorphoses* and other classics of pagan literature. The greatest offender was the graphically pictorial letter that met the eye at the beginning of Hebrews—a vivid depiction of the god Zeus, disguised as a swan, offering his amorous attentions to the lady known as Leda.

Depending upon your point of view, these howlers might be considered either the work of the Devil, or Freudian slips—the printer's unconscious advocacy of adultery, wife-hating, Leda-chasing, or what-have-you.

But by no means do all such mistakes result in "wicked" texts. Many are simply amusing. Take "The Camel's Bible," for instance. In Genesis of this 1823 edition, "Rebekah arose, and her camels"—in place of *damsels.* Or "The Standing Fishes Bible" of 1806, which tells us, in Ezekiel, "And it shall come to pass that the fishes shall stand upon it." As much as one hates to dispel that lively image of our finny friends standing upright on their tails, it must be disclosed that the right word is *fishers.*

The second edition of the Geneva Bible, 1562, is known as "The Placemaker's Bible," for good reason. In Matthew, it converts a great utterance into "Blessed are the placemakers, for they shall be called the children of God." Again, one letter is the villain—a mischievous *l* which replaced the first *e* of *peacemakers.*

The largest number of typos crops up in "The Lions Bible" of 1804, so named because, in 1 Kings, it speaks of "thy son that shall come forth out of thy lions," instead of *loins.* But there are other disaster areas, as well: "The murderer shall surely be put together," rather than *put to death* (from Numbers); and "For the flesh lusteth after the Spirit," instead of *against the Spirit* (from Galatians). And there are many more.

Eccentric translations, rather than printing errors, make armfuls of other Bibles worthy of note. There are, for example, two "Bug Bibles." Miles Coverdale's Bible of 1535 has earned that creepy sobriquet; and so has the Bible printed in Antwerp two years later as the translation of a certain Thomas Matthews, which was probably a pen name for one John Rogers. In both editions, a passage in Psalm 91 is presented as "Thou shalt not nede to be afrayed for eny bugges by night." In most other English-language Bibles, it's *terror by night.*

Today, the thought of Adam and Eve wearing breeches may provoke us to laughter, because the word conjures up images of trousers or pants, complete with pockets and zippers, cuffs optional. But in the Geneva Bible, mentioned above, the appropriate passage in Genesis is given as: "And they sowed figge-tree leaves together, and made themselves breeches." The same word is used in other early Bibles; and in all of them, it was almost certainly meant in the sense of 'aprons' or 'loin cloths' (or, possibly, 'lion cloths').

Translations have played havoc with the well-known *balm in Gilead,* too. The phrase, which occurs in Jeremiah, is rendered in the 1609 Douai Bible as "Is there noe rosin in Galaad?" Perhaps you prefer treacle over rosin? Take your pick: both "The Bishop's Bible" and Coverdale's Bible offer treacle in place of the more generally accepted *balm.*

Those Bibles are legion which tell us that a rich man will have more trouble entering Heaven than a camel passing through a needle's eye. Considering, however, that the Greek for *camel (kamēlon)* bears a striking resemblance to the Greek for *rope (kamilon)*, isn't it likely that the latter, earthier, better, more realistic, less outlandish image was lost in translation?

But printers, more often than translators, have been to blame for bloopers in the Bible, so it's only fair that they pointed the accusing finger at themselves in an edition published about 1702. In this version's Psalm 119, David, instead of complaining that "Princes have persecuted me without a cause," says, "Printers have persecuted me. . . ." That edition is now known as (what else?) "The Printer's Bible."

Epistola

In regard to "The 'Wicked' Bibles," the writer struck, perhaps unknowingly, directly upon the cause for all the typographical errors when he wrote, "Depending upon your point of view, these howlers might be considered . . . the work of the Devil. . . ."

All the errors cited were indeed inspired by the Devil, but as in any good corporate structure, the work was delegated to a subordinate. His name was Titivillus, and he has been known to have been at his task since about the middle of the Middle Ages.

He was probably created by the whimsy of the medieval monks who decried the carelessness of their fellows in the monasteries of Europe. Monks lulled by the repetitiousness of life, recitation, and work were prone to mumble the words of the service, jumble the words of the hymns, and make atrocious spelling errors in the works they copied in the scriptoria. Titivillus was a demon who reportedly lurked about monasteries and made

Titivillus

notes on all these errors. Obliged by the Devil to collect a thou-sand sacks of such notations daily, Titivillus carried them to Hell, where each transgression was recorded against the erring monk for consideration when he died and would be considered for re-location in Heaven or Hell.

Titivillus apparently had difficulty locating so many trans-gressions and hit upon the idea of enticing scribes into making recordable errors, whereupon his success surpassed all bounds. In fact, late in the fourteenth century, he became (in a manner of speaking) the Patron Demon of professional scribes in London. Overworked, the guild of scribes claimed that the inordinate number of errors in their work was the result of Titivillus's spell—thus exonerating themselves from any responsibility.

Titivillus was forced to diversify when printing came into full fashion and the number of scribes decreased. He became fascinated with the possibilities available in print shops. If Mr. Russell is collecting Bible bloopers, he may not be aware of his monument to Titivillus's skills:

Sixtus V, pope from 1585 to 1590, apparently unaware of Titivillus, authorized a printing of the Vulgate Bible translated by Jerome. Taking no chances, the pope issued a papal bull automatically excommunicating any printer who might make an alteration in the text. This he ordered printed at the beginning of the Bible. He personally examined every sheet as it came off the press. Yet the published Vulgate Bible contained so many errors that corrected scraps had to be printed and pasted over them in every copy. The result provoked wry comments on the rather patchy papal infallibility, and Pope Sixtus had no recourse but to order the return and destruction of every copy. [from *Medieval Calligraphy—Its History and Technique,* Marc Drogin. Abner Schram Ltd., New Jersey, and George Prior Associates, London.]

Titivillus is, or course, still with us, as any scribe or printer will testify.

Verbatim readers who are interested in a quite serious and detailed study of Titivillus might turn to Margaret Jennings's "Tutivillus—The Literary Career of the Recording Demon," published in *Studies in Philology—Texts and Studies,* 1977, volume 74, number 5, University of North Carolina Press, December 1977. There are other, more obscure references to this delightful demon, which I'd be happy to share with anyone interested.

By the way, the two variant spellings of the demon's name are not the latest examples of his handiwork: His name has traditionally had a multiplicity of spellings (or misspellings?).

MARC DROGIN
Exeter, New Hampshire

[Editor's Note: Readers of Verbatim *who are moved to consternation by the inordinate number of typographical errors in a given issue will be relieved to know the reason for them. In the future, please direct correspondence concerning same to P. D. Titivillus or to his employer, the Archfiend himself.]*

SIC! SIC! SIC!

"VOLUNTEER TUDORS NEEDED." From an ad in the *Sentinel-Standard* (Ionia, Michigan), 19 January 1988. Submitted by Lloyd Walker, Greenville.

Red Pants

ROBERT M. SEBASTIAN

While writers whose business it is to be witty often fail to produce, grave authors occasionally are mirthful when laughter is farthest from their minds. From a lifetime of undisciplined reading with innocent pencil in hand and malice prepense in mind, I have gleaned a harvest of what I am pleased to denominate *Red Pants* items, a sampling of which follows. My designation derives from a splash of vivid writing in Francis

Thompson's *A Corymbus for Autumn,* in which he proclaims how "day's dying dragon" was

Panting red pants into the West.

In this trousers category, Thompson must share the limelight with Coleridge by virtue of the line in *Kubla Khan*:

As if this earth in fast thick pants were breathing.

Even Shelley may stake a claim, if only in the pajama division of this sector, thanks to his description in *Epipsychidion* of how

. . . the slow, silent night Is measured by the pants of their calm sleep.

Since everything is to be found in Shakespeare, it is not surprising that on at least two occasions the Bard has contributed his own *Red Pants* nuggets. In *Antony and Cleopatra* (act 4, scene 8, lines 14 et seq.) Antony commands the wounded Scarus to

. . . leap thou, attire and all,
Through proof of harness to my heart, and there
Ride on the pants triumphing.

And in *Othello* (act 2, scene 1, line 80) Cassio utters the fervent prayer that Othello might

Make love's quick pants in Desdemona's arms.

A variation on this theme occurs in Alba de Céspedes's *The Secret* (translated from the Italian by Isabel Quigly: Simon and

Schuster, New York, 1958, page 114) where she confides that "I still had a whole afternoon before me to spend, and I used it to tidy up my drawers. . . ." One may well wonder what Miss Stowe had in mind when, in *Uncle Tom's Cabin* (chapter 5), she narrates how "Mrs. Shelby stood like one stricken. Finally, turning to her toilet, she rested her face in her hands, and gave a sort of groan." In this same vein, the mirthless Milton adds his bit to the general hilarity of nations when, in describing Mount Etna in book one of *Paradise Lost* (lines 236–7), he penned

> *And leave a singed bottom all involved*
> *With stench and smoke: . . .*

And in chapter 6 of *Vanity Fair,* when Blenkinsop, the housekeeper, sought to console Amelia for Joe Sedley's jilting of her dear Rebecca, Thackeray confides (indelicately?) that Amelia wept confidentially on the housekeeper's shoulder "and relieved herself a good deal."

Chuckles often emanate from the British employment of a term in a sense at variance with American usage. There is that oft-quoted example, near the opening of *Trial by Jury,* where Defendant asks, "Is this the Court of the Exchequer?" and having been assured that it was, Defendant (aside) commands himself to "Be firm, be firm, my pecker." The British, of course, do not giggle at this bit of Gilbertian dialogue, since to them *pecker* means 'courage', as in the phrase "to keep your pecker up." Two of the more common examples of British American divergence of usage are *screw* and *knock up.* In *Vanity Fair* (chapter 39), the niggardly Sir Pitt was not nearly the aerial acrobat your American sophomore might fancy him to be when he "screwed his tenants by letter." He was simply making extortionate exactions upon his wretched lessees. Similarly, when in chapter 34 of the same novel, Mrs. Bute reminds her husband that "You'd have been screwed in gaol, Bute, if I had not kept your money," she was not speaking of pleasures deferred. In *Bleak House* (chapter 27) Grandfather Smallweed, referring to Mr. George, warns Mr. Tulkinghorn that "I have him periodically in a vice. I'll twist him, sir. I'll screw him, sir." In Kipling's *The Light That Failed* (chapter 13), Torpenhow urges Dick to attend a party that night. "We shall be half screwed before the morning," is his dismal sales pitch to Dick.

In chapter 6 of *Vanity Fair,* Thackeray reports on Joe Sedley's drunken avowal to wed Becky Sharp the next morning, even if he had to "knock up the Archbishop of Canterbury at Lambeth," in order to have him in readiness to perform the ceremony. In *Great Expectations* (chapter 6), we learn how "... Mr. Whopsle, being knocked up, was in such a very bad temper." And who could blame him?

Many a raucous snigger has been sniggered from the pure-minded use of a word that suggests unmentionable parts of the human body. It does not take a too-wicked mind to read into such terms meanings of a lewd nature. Who can, for instance, blame a youth with but a mildly evil disposition from guffawing when he reads in Pater's *Marius the Epicurean* (chapter 5) a reference to Apuleius's *The Golden Ass* noting that "all through the book, there is an unmistakably real feeling for asses..."? In Scott's *The Bride of Lammermoor* (chapter 7), one reads about a boy "cudgelling an ass," and one goes back over the passage to reassure himself that it does not contain a typographical error for "cuddling."

One may be indulged a giggle even though he is sure that Isak Dinesen did not intend an impropriety when she recorded in *Out of Africa* (part 5, chapter 4) how "Fathima's big white cock came strutting up before me." And one is certain that Kenneth

Rexroth, in his *American Poetry in the Twentieth Century* (Herder and Herder, New York, 1971) did not intend to hint at closet biographical matter when, in chapter 1, he wrote that "Whitman's poems are full of men doing things together," or, later in the same chapter, when he referred to "Whitman's joyous workmen swinging their tools in the open air." College freshman still read with fiendish glee the first line in canto 1 of Spenser's *The Faerie Queene* (and never mind the title!) that tells how

A Gentle Knight was pricking on the plaine.

In his poem *Mr Nixon* (from *Hugh Selwyn Mauberley*), Ezra Pound's Mr. Nixon advises kindly

Don't kick against the pricks,

although the identities of the latter are not divulged.

One is entitled to speculate on what outrageous proposal the narrator had made in Proust's *Remembrance of Things Past, volume 2—Cities of the Plain* (translated by C. K. Scott Moncrieff—Modern Library, New York, 1934, page 90) to cause the Duchess to say, "Apart from your balls, can't I be of any use to you?" There is a famous letter penned by Rupert Brooke to his friend, Edward Marsh, from somewhere near Fiji (page 463 of *A Treasury of the World's Great Letters*, Simon and Schuster, New York, 1940) in which he relates how he sends his native boy up a palm tree, where he "cuts off a couple of vast nuts . . ." (macho victim not disclosed). In the first chapter of *Uncle Tom's Cabin*, Miss Stowe offers a dialogue between Haley and Mr. Shelby, part of which goes, " 'Well,' said Haley, after they had both silently picked their nuts for a season, 'what do you say?' " In *Bleak House* (chapter 24) Dickens may cause some readers to blush when he wrote of Mr. George's blush that "He reddened a little through his brown."

We must move ineluctably to a consideration of perfectly reputable words which, having acquired sexual connotations, cause adolescent—and often adult—hilarity, even when read by a person of only mildly prurient mind. In Forster's *A Passage to India* (chapter 31) a vivid picture is created by the sentence "Tangles like this still interrupted their intercourse." Pages later (chapter 37), it is acknowledged that "He, too, felt that this was their last free intercourse." Apparently from then on, it was going to have to be cash or credit card only. In *The Bride of Lammermoor* (chapter 5), we are informed that the heroine "placed certain restrictions on their intercourse," a limitation that might have been more usefully set in that same author's *Rob Roy* (chapter 7) where we are told of the chance that the narrator and Miss Vernon might be "thrown into very close and frequent intercourse."

A variation of this theme is found in Robert Browning's *The Flight of the Duchess* (section 5):

> *—Not he! For in Paris they told the elf*
> *Our rough North land was the Land of Lays,*

even though it is generally acknowledged that Paris is numero uno in this area of human activity.

More picturesque are the references to erections. An arresting one occurs in *A Passage to India* (chapter 21) in which Forster describes a small building as "a flimsy and frivolous erection," while in *The Mayor of Casterbridge* (chapter 16) the Mayor himself "beheld the unattractive exterior of Farfrae's erection." A phrase can paint an astonishing picture for the reader.

Consider Dickens's sharp image in *Bleak House* (chapter 54) when he describes how "Sir Leicester leans back in his chair, and breathlessly ejaculates. . . ." Or, in *Nicholas Nickleby* (chapter 47), where that admirable novelist graphically portrays how old Arthur Gride "again raised his hands, again chuckled, and again ejaculated." And in his short tale, *Lionizing,* Edgar Allan Poe is quite candid in describing the reaction of one of his characters: " *'Admirable!'* he ejaculated, thrown quite off his guard by the beauty of the manoeuvre."

Alas for perfectly lovely words that acquire pejorative meanings over the years! Earlier in this century, *pansy* became a derogatory epithet to describe an effete male, thereby cheapening forever lines like Shelley's noble image in *Adonais* (verse 33):

His head was bound with pansies over-blown,

not to mention Poe's odd allusion in *For Annie*:

With rue and the beautiful Puritan pansies.

Or, more slap-stickish, E. F. Benson's action picture in *Lucia in London* (chapter 8): "Georgie stepped on a beautiful pansy."

Of more recent vintage is *gay*. Nobody used to snicker at Chaucer's line (number 5818) in *The Prologe of the Wyf of Bathe*, in which that harried dame asks:

Why is my neghebores wif so gay?

In his poem *The Menagerie*, one of William Vaughan Moody's characters advises:

If nature made you so graceful, don't get gay,

while in *Othello* (ah, the Bard again!) in his dialogue with Desdemona and Emilia on the praise of women, Iago refers to the
kind that

> Never lack'd gold, and yet went never gay.
>   (act 2, Scene 1, line 150)

And what in the world is one to make of William Butler
Yeats's startling revelation in his poem "Lapis Lazuli" (from *Last
Poems*) that

> They know that Hamlet and Lear are gay.

Indeed it is an amusing, albeit utterly wasteful pastime to pur-
sue the quest for *Red Pants* examples. May good cess befall all
such quixotically misguided readers! One caveat: never assume
blithely that an odd word or suspicious phrase is as lubricious as
it sounds. In *The Bride of Lammermoor* (chapter 6) Bucklaw
vows, "I will chop them off with my whinger," and one feels
quite let down when he learns that a whinger is but a whinyard,
which is merely a short sword.

Funny Words

We could fill a whole chapter with funny words—*discombobulate*, *pooky*, and *bushwah* come immediately to mind—but *Verbatim* has been home to some truly funny writing and funny subject matter. Spoonerisms and Irish Bulls have long been particular favorites of *Verbatim* readers; student bloopers are perennial. Needless to say, football chants are a little peripheral to English usage and linguistics, but the wonderful thing about a language magazine is that because almost everything can be described in words, interesting (and hilarious!) topics such as this one can be shoehorned in without too much fuss.

British Football Chants

PETE MAY

Only in Britain would Manchester United's David Beckham have to suffer several thousand football fans chanting "Posh Spice takes it up the arse!" sung to the tune of the Pet Shop

Boys' "Go West." Since he married Spice Girl Victoria Adams, poor Beckham has been the butt of much obscene chanting. It started off when West Ham fans chanted "Posh Spice is a dirty slag [prostitute]!" at Beckham and he responded with aggressive gestures.

This was a mistake. Even if the chants do come from fat blokes with a hang-up about anal sex, most of them can be mollified by a humorous response; the worst thing a footballer can do is show anger, because he will then be baited even more. Beckham has suffered so much from fans envious of his millionaire status, celebrity marriage, and good looks, that the Professional Footballers' Association chairman Gordon Taylor recently called for fans to lay off Beckham. Posh Spice herself has shown more of a sense of humour, and has even said in an interview that "I want to say to them 'actually I don't!' "

The first thing that will strike a newcomer at a British football match (it's called *soccer* in the United States but, although the word is recognised in Britain, it is rarely used) is the number of taboo words used in chants, such as *wanker* (an English term for a masturbator), *arse, shit, fucking* and *cunt*. The record for swearing is probably held by the Arsenal fans' dirty ditty (sung to the tune of the 1960s hit "My Old Man") of "My old man said be a Tottenham fan; I said fuck off, bollocks, you're a cunt!"

Although many clubs had songs from prewar times, chants really developed in the mid 1960s. It was a time when British society was much more restrained by notions of class and "the stiff upper lip," and for many fans, chants were a glorious release from dull jobs and social convention. At first they were just impromptu terrace choirs singing pop songs such as "You'll Never Walk Alone," as at Liverpool. But slowly they developed into adaptations of tunes that quickly spread across the whole country.

Posh Spice

Weekly football matches presented a splendid opportunity for mainly working class males to revel in obscenity, merged with a juvenile delight in using such words in the company of several thousand other fans. They emphasise tribalism, but there is more to chanting than that. For most fans there has always been something pleasingly childish and very funny about thirty thousand fans simultaneously chanting "The referee's a wanker!" particularly when it's picked up on TV recordings.

There's also something of the adult nursery rhyme about footie chants. I first noticed while looking after my one-year-old daughter how much she enjoyed football chants adapted to child-care needs: For example, nappy changing was accompanied by chants of "On with the nappy, we're going on with the nappy," a variation on the "Sing when you're winning, you only sing when you're winning!" chant.

In a similar fashion to how a toddler spots an animal, there was an incident at Liverpool in the 1960s when a cat ran on the pitch. The fans would normally chant "Attack! Attack! Attack! Attack! Attack!" at their team, but when the feline appeared they instantly chanted "A cat! a cat! a cat! a cat! a cat!" Another chant that would be recognisable in a nursery school is that of "Ee-aw! Ee-aw!" directed at any player deemed to be a "donkey"—a clumsy, untalented performer.

And, as in nursery rhymes, there's a strong sense of rhythm, as exemplified by Manchester United's fans' staccato homage to Eric Cantona. "Oooh aah Cantona! I said oooh aah Cantona!" Some of the repetition is also reminiscent of children's songs—a popular chant of the 1980s was sung to the tune of "The Dambusters' March" and directed at the successful but reviled Leeds United. It went: "Leeds, Leeds and Leeds and Leeds and Leeds, Leeds and Leeds and Leeds and Leeds, Leeds and Leeds and Leeds, we all fucking hate Leeds!" (Not too difficult to learn the words to that one.) And the chant of "Big nose, he's got a fucking big nose!" aimed by rival fans at Southampton's Matt Le Tissier is an example of pure playground humour.

The British football chant is also closely aligned to pop culture—although the odd chant is sung to the tune of something more traditional, such as the anti-referee tirade of "Who's the wanker in the black?" which is sung to the tune of the hymn "Bread of Heaven."

In fact, chants are a living memorial to some now-forgotten bands. Who would remember "one-hit wonders" Chicory Tip were it not for the immortalisation of their 1970s hit, "Son of My Father" as a football chant? It started off as a declaration in favour of a particular player, such as Leicester City fans' "Oh Frankie Frankie Frankie, Frankie Frankie Frankie Worthington!" This was immediately modified by opposition fans to "Oh wanky wanky wanky, wanky wanky wanky Worthington!"

Nearly thirty years later the tune is still used. When Teddy Sheringham moved from Tottenham to Manchester United in pursuit of trophies but suffered a barren first season, Arsenal fans taunted him with chants of "Oh Teddy Teddy Teddy, went to Man United and you won fuck all!"

When United won the Treble (English League Championship, FA Cup and European Cup) [one] season this chant no longer applied, but rival fans quickly adapted it to "Oh Teddy Teddy Teddy! Went to Man United and you're still a cunt!"

Another relatively unknown band, Middle of the Road, have also gained footballing longevity through their song "Chirpy Chirpy Cheep Cheep." Its chorus of "Where's your mamma gone?" was often changed to "Where's your fatboy gone?" and directed at the clubs of Paul Gascoigne, a former England midfielder with a well-chronicled weight problem.

While the initial chant can be simply prosaic, insulting or abusive, many develop to become fine examples of a genuinely adaptive wit. For example, players are often greeted by the cry of "One Denis Bergkamp, there's only one Denis Bergkamp! (insert player's name of choice)" sung to the tune of the Spanish song "Guantanamera."

When England played in the 1986 World Cup with two defenders named Gary Stevens in the squad, this was cleverly adapted by England fans to "Two Gary Stevens! There's only two Gary Stevens!" Even better was the version from Kilmarnock fans in Scotland. They sang "Two Andy Gorams, there's only two Andy Gorams!" at the Rangers goalkeeper, who before the match was said to be "mentally unattuned." When a fat player is spotted he is taunted with "One Teletubby, there's only one Teletubby!" a reference to the podgy characters in the preschool children's programme.

In turn, the song became "Sing when you're winning, you only sing when you're winning!" directed at the opposing fans who sing when they take the lead. When sides played Grimsby, a side from a port, their fans chanted "Sing when you're fishing, you only sing when you're fishing!" The Grimsby fans liked this so much that they began themselves to sing "Sing when we're fishing, we only sing when we're fishing!" and a group of supporters even entitled their fanzine *Sing When We're Fishing.* Another version was "Score in a brothel, you couldn't score in a brothel!" used when a player misses with his shot.

A variation on the numbers theme came at the beginning of the current season when West Ham had just signed the Costa Rican striker Paulo Wanchope, pronounced "one-chop." The opposition Spurs fans responded with the chant of "You've only got Wanchope!" this time to the tune of "Blue Moon."

Sometimes a chant is tailored exactly to the play. One of the silliest is "Whoooooah! You're shit! Aaargh!" This occurs when a goalkeeper takes a goal kick. A group of fans will give an extended "Whoooooah" during his extended run-up, followed by a staccato "You're shit! aaaargh!" as he kicks the ball.

Chants reflect the social climate of England. In the 1970s and 1980s, when there was a big problem with football hooliganism, there were aggressive chants such as "You're gonna get your fucking heads kicked in!" In the 1970s, skinhead fans indulged in "aggro," short for *aggravation*. "Aggro" was enshrined in a song sung to the opening section of Gary Glitter's "Hello, Hello, I'm Back Again!" This chant went: "Hello, hello, West Ham aggro, West Ham aggro, hello hello . . ." and would accompany the first sign of trouble in any part of the ground. Another chant from that time is "Come and have a go if you think you're hard enough!" which has gained retro-chic and [became] the title of the letters page in the British lads' mag *Loaded*.

But in the 1990s, all-seater stadia, higher prices, and Sky TV coverage have meant the game has become largely free of trouble, and it is now an increasingly middle-class and trendy sport. In the 1980s only real fans would admit to following football, but today celebrities and intellectuals have all been desperate to declare their love of the game. In this climate chants have centred less on violence and more on humour, encouraging your side and denigrating the opposition.

Where once there was outright hostility there now tends to be irony. These days a bad piece of play from the opposition causes taunts of "You're not very good, you're not very good!" to the tune of the old London song "Knees Up, Mother Brown."

One of the most popular chants of the past decade has been the Arsenal fans' adaptation of the chorus of The Pet Shop Boys' "Go West." This started off as simply "One–nil to the Arsenal!" a song that celebrated Arsenal's frequent victories by this very score. This was rapidly adapted by other fans to "You're shit, and you know you are!" Numerous other versions followed, including "One-nil to the referee!" when a ref was thought to be biased and the already described Beckham/ Posh Spice insults.

When Aston Villa striker Stan Collymore was exposed in the

British tabloids as having beaten up his girlfriend (the TV pre-
senter Ulrika Jonsson) in a Paris bar, fans ridiculed him in their
usual merciless fashion. At first there were chants, again to the
tune of "Go West," of "You're shit and you slap your bird [girl-
friend]!" Even worse, when Collymore checked into a clinic and
stated he was suffering from depression, he was mocked with
chants of "You're mad and you know you are!"

When the comedians Baddiel and Skinner recorded the excellent pro-England song "Three Lions" for the 1996 European
Championships, its chorus of "It's coming home, it's coming
home, it's coming, football's coming home," became another
fans' classic. Although it was soon made cruder and used in
chants such as "You're full of shit, you're full of shit, you're full
of, Tottenham's full of shit!" When star striker Alan Shearer left
Blackburn for his native Newcastle, the club's fans were taunted
with "He's fucked off home, he's fucked off home, he's fucked
off, Shearer's fucked off home!" With similar crudity, Chelsea's
adaptation of "The Red Flag" to "We'll keep the blue flag flying
here" was altered by the club's rivals to "Stick your blue flag up
your arse!"

Black humour is a particular English strong point. After all,
very few clubs actually stand a chance of winning anything, as
there are only three major trophies, so the stoic acceptance of
adversity has long been a source for songs. A goal drought can
cause chants of "Will we ever score again?" (to the tune of "Bread
of Heaven"). Even Vera Lynn's "We'll Meet Again" was adapted
by long-suffering West Ham fans to "We'll score again, don't
know where, don't know when, but I know we'll score again one
sunny day!"

Fans are becoming ever more surreal. When Manchester City
were struggling in division one, the club's fans started singing, to

the tune of "Knees Up, Mother Brown," "We're not really here! We're not really here! We're not really, we're not really, we're not really here!"—surely a classic of its type.

In short, the British football chant is adaptable to just about any event that might happen on or off the pitch. Chants are subject to a kind of natural selection, which is why the best have survived for decades. They are frequently crude, childish and decidedly non-PC—but they're also the reason many of us find live football such an enticing experience. And if you're still mystified by this Brit disease, then there is a football chant that can be utilised. It expresses intellectual scepticism and goes: "You what, you what, you what, you what, you what?"

Learn to Spike Lunars

ROBERT ARCHIBALD FORD

Each time I visit Oxford, I walk past the Bodleian Library, pass under the Bridge of Sighs, and turn down the narrow lane that leads to Oxford University's New College, treading the same path as the late venerable Reverend Doctor William Archibald Spooner. In my head and on my tongue, spoonerisms spring forth. I recall a childhood favourite from my father's sparse joke repertoire: "Church usher to errant worshiper, 'Mardon me padam, but you are occupewing the wrong pie. May I sew you to another sheet?' " Slips allegedly uttered by Spooner himself bring a smile: "Who has not felt in his heart a half-warmed fish to live a nobler life?" Transpositions come to mind that appear daily in the thoughts of every dedicated spoonerist: *darking bogs, a lanely lone, the lissing mink.* Each of these metatheses evokes a chuckle of delight.

The good Dr. Spooner, a kind man with white hair and cherubic face, served New College for a half century as distinguished scholar and able administrator. He denied having made the slips of the tongue that made him famous, and his contemporaries agreed that most legendary spoonerisms were invented by imaginative New College undergraduates. Eyewitnesses claim, however, that the concept began with Spooner's twice-spoken chapel announcement: "The next hymn will be 'Kinkering Kongs Their Titles Take.' " Others claim he once actually said: ". . . in a dark glassly." A colleague recalled a discussion in which Dr. Spooner referred several times to "Dr. Friend's child" when he meant *Dr. Childe's friend.* Equally famous (though as an Irish bull) is his question of a former student shortly after World War I: "Was it you or your brother who was killed in the war?"

Spooner admitted "occasional infelicities in verbal diction" but became openly irritated when his name was associated with oral transpositions. When introduced as the "Dean of Kew Knowledge" at a college social function, he responded with outspoken displeasure.

In the decades since Dr. Spooner's death, the phenomenon of transposed sounds has found a firm place both in spoken and written language. A spoonerism, or more technically, a metathesis, is the transposition of letters, syllables, or sounds in a word or phrase. More often, they take an oral rather than a written form. Writers employ them, however, as a useful comedic device, and accidental faux pas occasionally appear in printed material.

Following exhaustive research and practice, I divide spoonerisms into two general categories based upon their structure and their function. Structural categories depend upon changes in the sound of words or upon their appearance in written form, particularly the effect upon spelling. Functional groupings deal with meaning, either overt or implied, both before and after transposition. Analysis of these groups enables one to determine what might be called "good" as opposed to "bad" spoonerisms. (Many critics maintain *all* are "bad.")

Perfect or true spoonerisms are correct in both sound and spelling when transposed. Laborers are *tons of soil,* in place of *sons of toil,* not only sounds right and spells right, but has meaning in its revised form. The best spoonerisms produce an element of humor or irony, as this one does. Sound, spelling, meaning, and humor all combine to make great spoonerisms.

Partial spoonerisms occur when transposition produces only one meaningful word. A *treckled spout* in the lake for *speckled trout* is interesting, perhaps even amusing, but it lacks the satisfaction and punch of a true spoonerism. As one plays the transposition game, many partial spoonerisms come to mind, but they must be discarded quickly, if you me what I seen.

Auditory spoonerisms preserve the right sound when transposed, but require varied spelling when written. Thus, a spoonerized loose-leaf *note book* becomes *boat nook,* not "bote nook" when written. Dr. Spooner's proverbial *half-warmed fish* for *half-formed wish* has a totally different sound and meaning if written as "half-wormed fish," requiring the spelling to be changed. Since sound and mental image are the keys to good spoonerisms, auditory types are most acceptable.

Visual spoonerisms appear to be correct in written form, but transposition produces the wrong sound. For example, when *warm food* becomes *farm wood,* the result is neither meaningful nor pleasing to the ear. *Farm* does not rhyme with *warm,* and the sound of *wood* differs greatly from *food.* While the term *form wooed* has good sound, it loses its effectiveness, because there is no real meaning in the phrase. Strictly visual spoonerisms must be rejected.

Meaningless spoonerisms may be amusing in sound, but do not create real words. Spooner's original *Kinkering Kongs* for *Conquering Kings* falls into this category along with the comment attributed to him that the story of the flood was "barrowed from Bobylon." His apochryphal statement of compassion for the *duff and demb* brings a smile but creates no new meaning in the transposed words. Because they give great pleasure both to ear and mind, however, meaningless transpositions are acceptable, even relished, by all spoonerists.

Mirror spoonerisms occur when transposition simply reverses word order, usually with little change in meaning. In this phenomenon, the words rhyme. Thus, a *great date* becomes a *date great*. Mirror types are somewhat rare, seldom have new meaning, and usually are uninteresting. I recall a college dean who was addressed as *Dean Greene* to his face. Behind his back, however, irreverent junior faculty referred to him as the *Green Dean*.

Spoonerisms can be classified on a functional basis as either useless or useful. Useless spoonerisms produce correct words which, unfortunately, neither amuse nor have current meaning. If a *stack of plates* is changed to a *plaque of states,* the result is, to say the least, puzzling. *Plaque* is a word, and *states* is a word, but no meaning attaches to the term since there is no mental connection. Useless spoonerisms must be avoided and characterize their creators as rank novices or amateurs.

Useful spoonerisms substitute a common or meaningful phrase for another when transposition occurs, as when "the movement was dealt a *crushing blow*" becomes "the movement was dealt a *blushing crow*." Changing "there's a *cozy nook* in my kitchen" to "there's a *nosey cook* in my kitchen" not only introduces a totally new meaning, but also injects humor. Having achieved these desired results, a sense of satisfaction and well-being settles upon both speaker and listener.

A gratifying subset of the useful category includes the obscene spoonerism, either intentional or accidental. Transposition produces a vulgar term or phrase. Think what the clever spoonerist can do with "the painting is *foul art*," or perhaps even better, *fowl art*. Could one resist tampering if Joyce had written "She was a bit of *awful lass*," or if Shakespeare had penned "Thy chatter is but *showful wit*!" Obscene spoonerisms represent the pinnacle of spooner-type wit (or is that *wooner-type spit*?).

Making up spoonerisms is a pleasant form of addiction. The malady is similar to that of the clever little tune that becomes imbedded in the mind and demands to be hummed: The more one tries to forget, the stronger is the sense of impulsive and involuntary recall. Unlike other lifelong addictions, however, the spoonerist incurs no cost, inflicts little pain upon others, and can engage in his or her passion anywhere at any time, greatly enriching the quality of life. No one ever recovers, but under the circumstances, who wants to? As I often say: "To spooner not to spoon?"

I'll probably try dying!

SIC! SIC! SIC!

"2: The new British Library—sitting comfortably on enlarged piles." Sidebar headline in the *New Scientist*, 27 March 1986:28. Submitted by Cornelius Van S. Roosevelt, Washington, D.C.

The World according to Student Bloopers

RICHARD LEDERER

One of the fringe benefits of being an English or History teacher is receiving the occasional jewel of a student blooper in an essay. I have pasted together the following "history" of the world from certifiably genuine student bloopers collected by teachers throughout the United States, from eighth grade through college level. Read carefully, and you will learn a lot.

The inhabitants of ancient Egypt were called mummies. They lived in the Sarah Dessert and traveled by Camelot. The climate of the Sarah is such that the inhabitants have to live elsewhere, so certain areas of the dessert are cultivated by irritation. The Egyptians built the Pyramids in the shape of a huge triangular cube. The Pramids are a range of mountains between France and Spain.

The Bible is full of interesting caricutures. In the first book of the Bible, Guinesses, Adam and Eve were created from an apple tree. One of their children, Cain, once asked, "Am I my brother's son?" God asked Abraham to sacrifice Isaac on Mount Montezuma. Jacob, son of Isaac, stole his brother's birth mark. Jacob was a patriarch who brought up his twelve sons to be patriarchs, but they did not take to it. One of Jacob's sons, Joseph, gave refuse to the Israelites.

Pharaoh forced the Hebrew slaves to make bread without straw. Moses led them to the Red Sea, where they made unleavened bread, which is bread made without any ingredients. Afterwards, Moses went up on Mount Cyanide to get the ten commandments. David was a Hebrew king skilled at playing the liar. He fought with the Philatelists, a race of people who lived in Biblical times. Solomon, one of David's sons, had five hundred wives and five hundred porcupines.

Without the Greeks we wouldn't have history. The Greeks invented three kinds of columns—Corinthian, Doric, and Ironic. They also had myths. A myth is a female moth. One myth says that the mother of Achilles dipped him in the River Stynx until he became intollerable. Achilles appears in *The Iliad*, by Homer. Homer also wrote *The Oddity*, in which Penelope was the last hardship that Ulysses endured on his journey. Actually, Homer was not written by Homer but by another man of that name.

Socrates was a famous Greek teacher who went around giving people advice. They killed him. Socrates died from an overdose of wedlock.

In the Olympic Games, Greeks ran races, jumped, hurled the biscuits, and threw the java. The reward to the victor was a coral wreath. The government of Athens was democratic because people took the law into their own hands. There were no wars in Greece, as the mountains were so high that they couldn't climb over to see what their neighbors were doing. When they fought with the Persians, the Greeks were outnumbered because the Persians had more men.

Eventually, the Ramons conquered the Greeks. History calls people Romans because they never stayed in one place for very long. At Roman banquets, the guests wore garlics in their hair. Julius Caesar extinguished himself on the battlefields of Gaul. The Ides of March murdered him because they thought he was going to be made king. Nero was a cruel tyranny who would torture his poor subjects by playing the fiddle to them.

Then came the Middle Ages. King Alfred conquered the Dames, King Arthur lived in the Age of Shivery, King Harold mustarded his troops before the Battle of Hastings, Joan of Arc was cannonized by Bernard Shaw, and victims of the Black Death grew boobs on their necks. Finally, Magna Carta provided that no free man should be hanged twice for the same offense.

In midevil times most of the people were alliterate. The greatest writer of the time was Chaucer, who wrote many poems and verses and also wrote literature. Another tale tells of William Tell, who shot an arrow through an apple while standing on his son's head.

The Renaissance was an age in which more individuals felt the value of their human being. Martin Luther was nailed to the church door at Wittenberg for selling papal indulgences. He died a horrible death, being excommunicated by a bull. It was the painter Donatello's interest in the female nude that made him the father of the Renaissance. It was an age of great inventions and discoveries. Gutenberg invented the Bible. Sir Walter Raleigh is a historical figure because he invented cigarettes. Another important invention was the circulation of blood. Sir Francis Drake circumcised the world with a one-hundred-foot clipper.

The government of England was a limited mockery. Henry VIII found walking difficult because he had an abbess on his knee. Queen Elizabeth was the "Virgin Queen." As a queen she was a success. When Elizabeth exposed herself before her troops, they all shouted, "hurrah." Then her navy went out and defeated the Spanish Armadillo.

The greatest writer of the Renaissance was William Shakespear. Shakespear never made much money and is famous only because of his plays. He lived at Windsor with his merry wives, writing tragedies, comedies, and errors. In one of Shakespear's famous plays, Hamlet rations out his situation by relieving himself in a long soliloquy. In another, Lady Macbeth tries to convince

Macbeth to kill the King by attacking his manhood. Romeo and Juliet are an example of a heroic couplet. Writing at the same time as Shakespear was Miguel Cervantes. He wrote *Donkey Hote*. The next great author was John Milton. Milton wrote *Paradise Lost*. Then his wife died and he wrote *Paradise Regained*.

During the Renaissance America began. Christopher Columbus was a great navigator who discovered America while cursing about the Atlantic. His ships were called the Nina, the Pinta, and the Santa Fe. Later, the Pilgrims crossed the Ocean, and this was known as Pilgrims Progress. When they landed at Plymouth Rock, they were greeted by the Indians, who came down the hill rolling their war hoops before them. The Indian squabs carried porpoises on their back. Many of the Indian heroes were killed, along with their cabooses, which proved very fatal to them. The winter of 1620 was a hard one for the settlers. Many people died and many babies were born. Captain John Smith was responsible for all this.

One of the causes of the Revolutionary Wars was the English put tacks in their tea. Also, the colonists would send their parcels through the post without stamps. During the War, the Red Coats and Paul Revere was throwing balls over stone walls. The dogs were barking and the peacocks crowing. Finally, the colonists won the War and no longer had to pay for taxis.

Delegates from the original thirteen states formed the Contented Congress. Thomas Jefferson, a Virgin, and Benjamin Franklin were two singers of the Declaration of Independence. Franklin had gone to Boston carrying all his clothes in his pocket and a loaf of bread under each arm. He invented electricity by rubbing cats backwards and declared, "A horse divided against itself cannot stand." Franklin died in 1790 and is still dead.

George Washington married Martha Curtis and in due time became the Father of Our Country. Then the Constitution of the

United States was adopted to secure domestic hostility. Under the Constitution the people enjoyed the right to keep bare arms.

Abraham Lincoln became America's greatest Precedent. Lincoln's mother died in infancy, and he was born in a log cabin which he built with his own hands. When Lincoln was President, he wore only a tall silk hat. He said, "In onion there is strength." Abraham Lincoln wrote the Gettysburg Address while traveling from Washington to Gettysburg on the back of an envelope. He also freed the slaves by signing the Emasculation Proclamation, and the Fourteenth Amendment gave the ex-Negroes citizenship. But the Clue Clux Clan would torcher and lynch the ex-Negroes and other innocent victims. It claimed it represented law and odor. On the night of April 14, 1865, Lincoln went to the theater and got shot in his seat by one of the actors in a moving picture show. The believed assinator was John Wilkes Booth, a supposingly insane actor. This ruined Booth's career.

Meanwhile in Europe, the enlightenment was a reasonable time. Voltare invented electricity and also wrote a book called *Candy*. Gravity was invented by Isaac Walton. It is chiefly noticeable in the Autumn, when the apples are falling off the trees.

Bach was the most famous composer in the world, and so was Handel. Handel was half German, half Italian, and half English. He was very large. Bach died from 1750 to the present. Beethoven wrote music even though he was deaf. He was so deaf he wrote loud music. He took long walks in the forest even when everyone was calling for him. Beethoven expired in 1827 and later died for this.

France was in a very serious state. The French Revolution was accomplished before it happened. The Marseillaise was the theme song of the French Revolution, and it catapulted into Napoleon. During the Napoleonic Wars, the crowned heads of Europe were trembling in their shoes. Then the Spanish gorillas came down from the hills and nipped at Napoleon's flanks. Napoleon became ill with bladder problems and was very tense and unrestrained. He wanted an heir to inherit his power, but since Josephine was a baroness, she couldn't bear children.

The sun never set on the British Empire because the British Empire is in the East and the sun sets in the West. Queen Victoria was the longest queen. She sat on a thorn for sixty-three years. Her reclining years and finally the end of her life were exemplatory of a great personality. Her death was the final event which ended her reign.

The nineteenth century was a time of many great inventions and thoughts. The invention of the steamboat caused a network of rivers to spring up. Cyrus McCormick invented the McCormick raper, which did the work of a hundred men. Samuel Morse invented a code of telepathy. Louis Pasteur discovered a cure for rabbis. Charles Darwin was a naturalist who wrote the *Organ of the Species.* Madman Curie discovered radium. And Karl Marx became one of the Marx brothers.

The First World War, caused by the assignation of the Arch-Duck by a surf, ushered in a new error in the anals of human history.

SIC! SIC! SIC!

"Moped injuries are clearly one of the top causes of major head injuries in this area ... some major fractures require amputation. The injuries sustained in the accidents may not permit the person to do athletics forever." From the
UCLA Bruin, 23 November 1987. Submitted by
John Paul Arnerich, Los Angeles.

When Everything Was Everything

JOE QUEENAN

On September 27, 1967, *The Consumer's Report on Banality* listed the expression "Everything is everything" as the single most popular cliché in the continental United States, with "If you're not part of the solution you're part of the problem" a close second, and "You can be in my dreams if I can be in yours" a strong third. By the following September, only "You can be in my dreams . . ." continued to appear in the Top Ten (number eight), while "If you're not part of the solution . . ." had dropped to number sixty-seven, right behind "You can't fight City Hall" and "It takes one to know one," (tied for number sixty-five). Incredibly, "Everything is everything" was not even listed in the top three hundred American clichés. By the spring of 1969, all three phrases had vanished from the national idiom, a phenomenon which has recently sparked great interest inside the academic community. How, specialists would like to know, was it possible for three inanities of such a spectacularly fatuous nature simply to drop out of the language like that, as if they had never existed? Was it merely a question of overuse? Or does the answer lie deeper, perhaps rooted in the dark folds of the national psyche?

In his provocative work *Clichés to Live By and the Death of the Sixties*, Anaxamander O'Flaherty, a necro-ethnolinguist at the University of Altamont, suggests that the expression "Everything is everything" succumbed to a natural death brought on by such factors as overutilization, deterioration of relevance, and lack of adaptability to altered states of reality vis-à-vis the American experience. Says he:

It was all right to believe that everything was everything back in 1967 when everything, in a very real sense, was everything. But the escalation of the war, Bobby Kennedy's assassination, and the Chicago riots made it increasingly difficult to go on believing that everything was everything, when it seemed highly unlikely that "everything" was much more than "something." By the time Nixon was elected, it was obvious that "everything" was "nothing."

In *Lowered Expectations and the Politics of Banality*, the follow-up volume to *Clichés*, O'Flaherty suggests that the expression "Everything is everything" could have survived in a modified form (say, as "Everything ain't what it used to be") had habitual users of the remark been willing to "scale down their estimate of the quantitative quality of life in these United States." Their refusal to do so spelt doom for the luckless mouthful of twaddle.

Much more sinister doings are suspected in the demise of the phrase, "You can be in my dreams if I can be in yours." Wotan Schnitzler, in his absorbing *Beyond the Role of the CIA in the Death of My Favorite Cliché*, adamantly maintains that secret federal funding allocated by the Nixon Administration was used to sabotage the youth countercultural movement by utterly discrediting its most revered platitudes. Citing various memos and receipts which [had] come into his possession over the years, Schnitzler contends that thousands of students at major universities were paid thirty to forty dollars a week by the government to say "You can be in my dreams but stay out of my neighborhood," "You can be in my dreams if I can be in your reveries," and "You can be in my dreams if I can be in your 16mm pornflick." Yet though evidence of some government intrigue is irrefutable, Shiloh Sokoloff's thesis, set forth in *What Johnny Can't*

Say, Much Less Read, seems much more plausible; namely, that the sentence "You can be in my dreams if I can be in yours" was simply too hard for most young people to remember. "Chronic drug-abuse ravaged so many collegiate brain cells that only banal expressions without a dependent clause could be summoned forth from the canyons of the mind. *Ergo,* 'What's happening?', 'Hang loose,' and 'Like wow.' "

To this day, no one knows whatever became of the phrase, "If you're not part of the solution, you're part of the problem." As late as March 25, 1969, it was still being heard in strip joints just outside Fresno, California, yet by the following Monday, it had disappeared from the vernacular of the trite, never to be heard again. "Like Henry Hudson, Amelia Earhart, and a couple of other people whose names I forget," says Wendy Bakunin, amateur insipidographer, in her book *Our Vanishing Culture,* "this cliché seems to have literally dropped off the face of the earth. For the love of Mike." Bakunin goes on to say that "If you're not part of the Aleutians, you're part of the problem," an Eskimo separatist rallying cry, may be a derivative form of the expression, but confesses total ignorance as to the current whereabouts of the original catch-phrase, a tight little nugget of piffle so dynamic it was once voted "Hackneyism of the Decade" by the American people. "Everything is everything," on the other hand, has recently surfaced in certain outlying cantons of Switzerland, as the phrase, *"Tout est tout,"* though an application for a license to use the cliché inside France itself has twice been rejected by the Minister of Ephemera, the Government obviously fearing a subsequent decline in the use of *"C'est la vie,"* and *"Plus ça change, plus c'est la même chose."*

As regards "You can be in my dreams ..." The League for the Decriminalization of Overtly Antisocial Behavior last month purchased the legal rights to the triviality, hoping to rent out the phrase "You can beat in my dreams if I can beat in yours" to various sadomasochistic supper clubs. Given this fact, it seems unlikely that the famed remark will ever again be heard in its pure, unadulterated form.

In all this, there is one bright note. Several weeks ago, the National Foundation for the Preservation of Endangered Banality authorized funding to look after shopworn expressions and, where necessary, see that they receive a decent burial, thus sparing them the indignity of outright purging from the American idiom. Furthermore, a Cliché Hall of Fame will soon be erected in Peoria, Illinois, and here will be stored valuable tape recordings of the country's most treasured platitudes being uttered by their inventors (where possible) as well as by those who helped make them famous. Someday soon, if all goes well, the great clichés of the 1960s will be brought home to their final resting place; and then, if only for a short time, everything will once again be everything. Which would, at the very least, be right on.

Irish Bulls in Sundry China Shops

ROBERT A. FOWKES

What is an Irish bull? According to some, it is the product of a kind of unconscious humor, vaguely akin to a malapropism, allegedy endemic to the Emerald Isle. Others have dismissed it as a pure blunder. One definition calls it "the saying that contradicts itself, in a manner palpably absurd to listeners but unperceived by the person who makes it." This is cited by

Sean McCann, *The Wit of the Irish,* London (Leslie Frewin) 1968, page nine, a book that includes half a hundred Irish bulls, mostly very good ones indeed. Perhaps the most sagacious definition is that attributed to Professor Mahaffy, Provost of Dublin University. When asked by a lady seated beside him what the difference was between an Irish bull and another bull, he replied, "An Irish bull is always pregnant" (McCann, 9, also Padraic Colum, *A Treasury of Irish Folklore,* New York [Crown], 1954, p. 35). This definition is reminiscent of certain practices of the Sanskrit grammarians, in that the definition is itself an example of the phenomenon defined.

Sydney Smith said a century ago that a bull was an apparent congruity and a real incongruity of ideas, suddenly discovered— which partly contradicts any notion of unconscious humor, unless the discovery is by somebody else, or is the nature of a "double-take" by the perpetrator. There are doubtless several subvarieties of bulls, some inspired, some contrived; some learned, others illiterate.

The origin of the word *bull* seems unknown. Attempts to connect it with *papal bull* or with Icelandic *bull* 'nonsense', *bulla* 'to talk nonsense' are certainly wide of the mark. Perhaps Irish *buile* 'madness' has something to do with the source—probably not.

The implication of an Irish monopoly of the phenomenon is unwarranted. Nevertheless, many bulls *are* of Irish origin, and of not so naive a character as some proffered definitions might lead us to believe. Parnell once said at a meeting, "Gentlemen, it appears to be unanimous that we cannot agree." And the chap who asserted in a Dublin court, "Your banner, I was sober enough to know I was dhroonk," was perhaps no great fool (McCann 14). A beggar woman who asked for alms with the plea, "Help me, kind sir! I'm the mother of five children and a sick husband" (McCann 15), blessed a charitable donor with the bullish wish,

"May you never live to see your wife a widow!" (In Friedrich Hebbel's play *Agnes Bernauer*, the murdered Agnes is called "widow" by her father-in-law; one hardly dares to call that a *Hebbull*.)

Three bulls in McCann's book have been known to me since long before the appearance of that work. They betoken a far lesser degree of innocence than those given above: "He lay at death's door, and the doctor pulled him through"; "We find the man who stole the horse not guilty"; and "Half the lies people tell about me aren't true!"

Sometimes the bull gives utterance to deep despair at the wretched state of the world: "Such is the corruption of the age that little children, too young to walk or talk, are rushing through the streets cursing their Maker." A similar complaint of more subjective application is, "The trouble with you, my son, is you've no respect for the father that gave you birth!" Or a bull may express with taurine eloquence the feeling of apprehension at impending disaster or the recollection of a menacing fate: "There I stood, thinking every moment would be the next!"

Sometimes doctrinal wrangles are mildly reflected in bulls. A perplexed Dublin woman, on hearing an Anglican priest referred to as "father," exclaimed in nonprotestant protest, "Imagine calling the loikes of him father—a married man with foive children!" Perhaps that could be called a papist bull, though hardly with impunity.

The bull can also be employed in making extravagant comparisons or concocting confused similes: "Talk about thin! Well, you're thin, and I'm thin, but he's as thin as the pair of us put together!" A bull that is heard in several versions has to do with an Irish wake. A prominent figure—political or theatrical or ecclesiastical—has died, and, for some reason, very few people appear at his wake. This prompts one bitterly disillusioned adherent to remark, "Ah, if this had happened during his lifetime, the place would be packed."

The above are of Irish origin, or are said to be. But I have heard bulls from the lips of fellow-Celts across the Irish Sea. It was a Welshman who said, "Why, man, you'll die before I do, if you live long enough!" And a relative of mine from Glamorganshire, South Wales, replied to an American who asked him whether it was true that Welsh houses are cold, and, if so, why, "Well, I suppose they are; they build them out of doors over here, you see." It was also in Wales that I heard this one about a man charged or credited with the traits of a Don Juan, "Why, he's a happily married man, and his wife is too!"

Even England is the source of an occasional bull; for example, "The late Mr. Chambers went to an early grave," which might possibly be termed a John Bull. The Latin class in British public schools was once a source of bulls in the guise of translations, some spurious, some perhaps spontaneous. It is hard to decide how to classify this schoolboy effort, "They fought so hard they lost their arms, and then they used their hands." In a German class in my own college this side of the herring pond a student rendition, "the sweet, timid, yellow-haired face of the maiden," may lack some of the prerequisites for bullishness and may belong rather in the category of classroom boners, but it has some resemblance to genuine bulls too; perhaps it qualifies as a tauroidal.

For bulls are not lacking in this country either. An American bull of venerable vintage is "One of these days you're gonna wake up and find yourself dead!" And another candidate for bulldom is "You'll be a man before your mother," which, if not a bull, is at least a calf. Still another American one is the dire threat "I'll cut off your head and throw it in your face!" Which reminds me of another one in the form of a complaint, "He kicked me in the belly when my back was turned." There's a modicum of violence in our bulls.

Not long ago the radio brought a report of a police department in a New Jersey town that had decided to embrace the tenets of affirmative action with the announcement, "From now on we shall offer police jobs to qualified women regardless of sex." And a law was supposedly once on the books of that state which required that "if two cars approach at right angles at an intersection where there is no traffic light, each shall make a full stop and wait until the other has passed by."

Deans I have known have been capable of exhorting faculty the way an apocryphal dean did at a reception for new members: "I want all of you old-timers to go around and shake hands with every unfamiliar face," which belongs to the type of the Irish podiatrist's bull: "I've extracted corns from most of the crowned heads of Europe." Another feeble faculty bull was the professor's remark to a colleague: "Your book is undoubtedly one of the best I've never read."

A schoolteacher of mine in Pittsburgh remarked, "Some of you children have been absent five times in three days." And the American vaudeville team of Mack and Moran, whose records sold better than hot cakes in the twenties, utilized bulls of a sort in their patter: "Yeah. I'll be there. But how'll I know whether you've been there?" "Well, if I get there first, I'll make a blue chalk mark, and if you get there first, you rub it out."

I once thought I'd detected a bull at a children's concert, when I heard the MC introduce a singing trio thus: "Perhaps I should tell you that these three are twins." Then I found out they were. For the third was from a second set of twins in a prolific family. The bull concerning the wealthy but stingy uncle writing to his nephew away at college has, to my knowledge, appeared in print in three countries, none of them Ireland: "P.S. I had intended, my dear nephew, to enclose a check for ten dollars [or a cheque for five pounds], but as I had already sealed the envelope before doing so, it will have to wait until next time." That is surely as spurious a bull as the old chestnut of the note written to explain the absence of little Joe: "Dear Teacher: Please excuse my son Joseph's absence on Friday, as it was Ash Wednesday. Signed, My Mother."

Humor of the little-man-who-wasn't-there type probably belongs in the same pasture as exhausted bulls, as do riddles like: "What's the difference between a duck?" and its bovine answer. Our gag writers and comedians do not seem to resort to the device of the bull very often. Perhaps it is difficult to make bulls to order. The Marx brothers may have used a bull or two, but I try in vain to recall one, unless Groucho was the author of the following pessimistically timely pronouncement: "Even the future ain't what it was in the past!" That's no bull.

SIC! SIC! SIC!
"I'm sorry I never got to meet him while he was alive."
Leonard Maltin on Andy Devine, from *Entertainment Tonight,* TV program, 20 February 1989. Submitted by Emilio Bernal Labrada, Falls Church, Virginia.

Needless to Say

PETER SYPNOWICH

It goes without saying that the duty of the writer is to explain. In the modern world, there's no denying that everything can in fact be explained. The best prose, therefore, is prose that imposes order. Thus are readers made secure, and, more important, thus is life made simple. Nothing, it is clear, could be more self-evident.

Yet some writers strive instead for eloquence. That is, they try to produce memorable work. But they do so, unfortunately, at the risk of confusing their readers. To start with, their writing is often rhetorical or even evocative. It contains statements, consequently, that allow varying interpretations; inevitably, anything that affects a reader's feelings is bound to produce an unpredictable response. Furthermore, such writers at times resort to humour. Accordingly, they display cynicism, or alas, lead the reader into ambiguity and paradox. Worst of all, these writers sometimes will communicate surprise or wonder. The result is to arouse a sense of mystery. In sum, the effect of such writing is to portray human existence as something vague and complex. More than that, it can actually complicate matters further. On top of all this, we have the unhappy fact that eloquent writing is indeed sometimes memorable, compounding the problem.

In contrast, the effective communicator creates certainty. He or she does this, it is evident, in two ways. First, he rules out irrelevant or erroneous thoughts in the reader. Second, he continually supplies answers. In short, he maintains command, investing his exposition with all the authority that he can muster.

The goal, then, is omniscience. Admittedly, most writers are in reality not omniscient. Not yet, at any rate. But nevertheless, it is within the province of any writer to make a definitive statement on a specific point. This, surely, is sufficient. After all, omniscience can be cumulative. Over time, manifestly, a multiplicity of small omnisciences will add up to total omniscience. It is as if in recognition of this, perforce, that increasing numbers of writers are looking for a way to produce airtight, irrefutable prose. And it is no accident that the English language provides just such a method. I refer, of course, to syllothetics.

The syllothetic system had its origins, no doubt, in the rule followed by the authors of university monographs and government position papers. To wit: first tell them what you are going to say, then tell them what you are saying, and finally tell them what you have said. A sound practice, unquestionably. But it was observed that readers could be effectively directed sentence by sentence. That is to say, the meaning of a sentence could be signaled—and thereby validated—by the use of a sentence adverb such as *moreover, indeed,* or *however.* Essentially, the thrust of the sentence was communicated in advance. In this way readers knew what a writer was going to say before he said it. In a sense, the readers said it themselves.

To be sure, the technique of qualifying sentences with modifiers is nothing new. For instance, many writers had sorted out their expository works with such expressions as *incidentally, on one hand,* and *for example.* In addition, others had followed the practice of enumerating their sentences with *first, second,* and *third,* or *next, then,* and *finally,* or all of these. More noteworthy, some had reinforced their statements with, on the one hand, such key words as *significantly, symbolically,* and *thankfully,* or, on the other hand, such indispensables as *unfortunately, unhappily,* and *alas.* Most significantly, it should be noted, many had gone so far as to advance statements in the form of a premise or a given, e.g., *it need hardly be stated, obviously,* and of course *of course.*

Be that as it may, the foundations of modern syllothetics were cemented, as we now know, with the systematic use of *but* at the beginnings of sentences. There can be no doubt whatever that with this development logical exposition could thereby become relentless. It was discovered—and this should no longer be any cause for wonder—that a sentence containing *however* could also begin with *but*. Moreover, *but* could appear directly in front of *nevertheless*. But this development reached its zenith with the use of *but* as a topper conjunction (see the beginning of this sentence); the topper *but* does not in reality indicate a contradiction, for it always appears at the start of a sentence which is, truth be, in harmony with preceding sentences, but rather it tops the previous statements by pointing unerringly to that which is promised by contradiction, namely illumination. Let's be frank. It was the logical force of *but*, in the end, that began to supply the dynamism of syllothetics, enabling it to combine, as it does, the undeniable energy of the syllogism with the indisputable power of the theorem.

In consequence we have, in syllothetics, a veritable arsenal of instruments that serve to produce coherence and logic in modern prose. For example, there is not only affirmation by demonstration *(ergo, hence, therefore, accordingly)*, but there is also documentation by postulation *(it can be assumed, we can suppose)* and also validation by synthesization *(basically, in truth, in a very real sense)* as well as verification by substitution *(that is to say, in other words, in short)*. Similarly, there is not only confutation by disputation *(on the contrary, notwithstanding, however, nevertheless)*, but there is also negation by concession *(despite, although, allowing that)* and also, not least, refutation by capitulation *(it might be argued, it would be easy to conclude)*.

Syllothetics, it can be seen, is inexorable. Either we have corroboration by escalation *(moreover, on top of that, above all)*, or we have devaluation by declination *(worse, worse still, worst of all)*. On one hand we have substantiation by association *(similarly, in the same way)*; on the other hand we have invalidation by differentiation *(quite a different matter, we cannot compare, something else again)*.

It is hardly necessary to add that syllothetics possesses the capacity to transcend logic. Who can deny it? We have, happily, induction by intuition, the inference that goes beyond mere fact (*one cannot avoid the suspicion, it is difficult to shake off the conviction*), and also, thanks be, attestation by clarification, the proof that is superior to mere evidence (*even so, still, in any event*). Plainly, we are in the presence here of higher truths: Look at ratification by approximation (*for the most part, as it were, broadly speaking*); witness the revelation of amplification (*conceivably, it may even be, it would not be too much to say*).

This brings us, willy-nilly, to the infinite utility of syllothetics. It is a system, broadly speaking, that is impervious to criticism. Certainly it is no passing fad, dependent on vogue words, for despite its infancy it employs such age-old terms as *alas, albeit, perforce,* and *withal.* Nor it can be taxed with pedantry, demonstrably, for on occasion it makes use of colloquial expressions like *for starters, likewise, for sure,* and *no doubt about it.* Above all, though some people might think otherwise, it definitely does not involve clichés. On the contrary. For one thing, a cliché can be defined as an imaginative expression which through repetition has lost its imaginativeness. But syllothetics, in contradistinction, shuns the imagination altogether. More to the point, syllothetics deploys a vocabulary of unparalleled variety. In fact there are well over one hundred syllothetic modifiers. And what is more, additional ones are coming into use every day. Hence the recent discovery, by some writers, that it is possible to syllothesize every sentence.

It is true that there are rational writers, seemingly logical, who make little or no use of syllothetics. They feel, it would seem, that coherence can be obtained without it. They would say, undoubtedly, that one sentence follows another. But the question is, how closely? In syllothetics, it must be pointed out, an expression such as *naturally* or *in other words* not only introduces a sentence but also refers to the previous one. The effect is that at every step syllotheticians have their feet in two sentences, as it were. And by looking backward at all times, it need hardly be added, they appear to be going nowhere of interest. Naturally, nothing is more reassuring to a reader. Nothing, in other words, is more conducive to acquiesence.

It can be argued, you will object, that such a progression is slow, and that, concommitantly, very little is being said. But this objection, however, misses the point. True, syllotheticians aim high; in a word, they seek not merely to persuade but to convince. Still, the fact is that their goals are essentially modest. Let it be remembered that they make no declarations. They restrict themselves to deductions, basing them on references, citations, or precedents, which is a different matter altogether. They may, perhaps, list variables, or, on occasion, identify options; at most, they will establish parameters. But, it must be emphasized, they do not express anything. They articulate, which is something else again. Nor, what is more, do they ever describe. They delineate, which is something entirely different. So it should come as no surprise to be told that, basically, syllotheticians are at bottom unconcerned about how little they might have to say.

It would not be too much to say that it does not at all matter what may or may not be contained in syllothetic sentences. The content lies, rather, in the articulation of the logical relationships between them. But make no mistake about it, that is enough. For, clearly, although it is the writer's duty to explain, the very fact that everything must be explained means, indisputably, that in due course everything will in fact be explained. Ergo, the less said the better.

Already, it is becoming very difficult to deny—all available evidence points to it—that the day is surely coming, withal, when there will remain, truly, no mere coincidences about which one cannot avoid a suspicion or shake off a conviction, when clearly everything will incontrovertibly support a thesis or conversely stand in direct contrast to it, and, overriding all this, there will as a result be not the slightest doubt in our minds about one inescapable conclusion, namely the dawning realization that, there being nothing more to say on the subject, as it were, we therefore will no longer hesitate but rather will necessarily feel compelled to state the obvious. Indeed, we would be remiss in our duty if we failed to mention it. Needless to say.

Wordplay and Word Games

I'm no good at Scrabble. I don't do the cryptic crossword in record time. I rarely fill in the Jumble, try the make-89-words-from-the-letters-in-*refrigerator* puzzle, or play *Botticelli*. I refrain from making puns, for my own safety and the safety and comfort of those around me. But I love to read about these games, and the people that develop and play them. (Just don't ask me for a six-letter word that means "head-scratcher.")

Wordplay

GARY EGAN

Scan any newspaper at random and a predilection for punning headlines is immediately discernible. Take today's *Star* ("Britain's Brightest Daily"), for example: *Fireman's Burning Ambition; Ivana Comes Up Trumps; How to Save Yourself a Packet with Seeds* . . . Go upmarket and read the same story, but with a better class of pun, i.e., *Survey Claims Legalization of Cannabis Has Resonant Grass Roots Support.* Or, in a *Guardian* supplement, perhaps, a pro-feminist piece entitled *Must the Chauvinism Go On?* In similar fashion, a title like *Opera Buffoonery* assumes a greater degree of sophistication in its readers than, say, *Ossie Determined to Earn His Spurs.* (Many English readers will be familiar with Tottenham Hotspur, even if they have never visited White Hart Lane, but fewer will have come across the term *opera buffa*, let alone whistled Mozart's *Abduction from the Seraglio* from the terraces.)

Staying with the quality rags, in addition to the headlines, the articles themselves frequently feature puns. It is not unusual to encounter an art review which opens like this: "Given its penchant for all things scatalogical—of which Duchamp's urinal might be said to form the centrepiece—maybe the Museum of Modern Art should be renamed 'The Cistern Chapel' . . ." Or to see Coppola's *Dracula* castigated thus:

> For once the lupine ferocity of critics who went for the jugular and left teeth-marks all over their reviews may be excused. The box-office takings are a (vam) pyrrhic victory, a triumph of hype over discernment.[*1-2-1 Review*]

For the writer of the sportive essay, wordplay is so common as to seem almost a basic requirement. Take this excerpt from an essay on dogs, for instance:

> When it comes to sucking up to humans, dogs take the biscuit. One of their least fetching characteristics is their willingness to retrieve sticks. ["Have Dogs Backed the Wrong Horse," *1-2-1 Review*]

Or a piece deploring the steamy sex-scenes perpetrated by modern novelists:

They have no truck with plot (unlike the movie moguls of Hollywood's Golden Age who selected plots with the trucker in mind), but they dutifully trot out the same knackered old descriptions of copulation. The reader is treated to a blow-job-by-blow-job account of the hero's sexual conquests but, despite the plethora of climaxes, there's a certain lack of suspense: The reader just knows knickers will be shed in the twist of the tale. ["Writers and Sex," *1-2-1 Review*]

Despite, or perhaps because of its domination of newspaper and magazine headlines, the pun has tended to receive a bad press in more exclusive literary circles. Charles Lamb, for one, dismissed it as "a pistol let off at the ear, not a feather to tickle the intellect." The standard dictionary definition of the pun is something of a put-down: "the use of words to exploit ambiguities and innuendos for humorous effect," as in the comic verse below:

Instead of flushing whenever it's mentioned, we should salute its cisterns' unsung melodies for—no matter how execrable a state it's in—a W. C. puts bums on seats. If only as much could be said for alternative comedians' lavatory humour. ["A Paean to the W. C.," *1-2-1 Review*]

"I'm sorry," she replied, "I know your pride is colossal. And I confess: a multiple orgasm in Basle'd be capital—But how can I be sure the ecstacy-waves will be tidal?" ["Erections Are Universal," *1-2-1 Review*]

Or comic fiction:

Eustace Hewitt emitted the sort of sound a theatre critic makes when tearing a bit-player's performance to pieces. ["People Behave Differently in the Dark," *'U' Magazine*]

English Literature has acknowledged its great satires and comic masterpieces, to be sure, but rarely without a certain reluctance; rarely without giving the impression that comedy, however clever, is in dubious taste. Comedy, acutely aware of this, often appears to be on the defensive where its art is concerned, hence the old adage about every comedian hankering to play Hamlet (another compulsive punster). It is as if some literary elite has decreed that Literature shall be elevating, edifying and, above all, serious. Comedy's gut instinct, by contrast, is that nothing is sacred.

But when a writer puns, it is not always purely for humorous effect. It is necessary to examine the context in which the wordplay occurs. What happens, for instance, when a domestic tragedy is depicted in this way:

Branded by ex-hubby (ex-All-Black & Oxford Blue)
With a hot iron as a lasting token of his esteem,
Leaving Muggins to raise a crop of Enid Blighters—
Crew-cutted & permanently gutted—on a pittance.
[*"Personal Column," Outposts Poetry Quarterly*]

In this case the wordplay is unsettling. A "straight" description of domestic violence (minus the wordplay) might have been less effective. As it is, the reader's sympathies are engaged unexpectedly; taken by surprise, he feels compelled to reappraise the subject matter in question.

It has been noted that comedy's gut instinct insists that nothing is sacred. Literature can cope with this, to a point—but even the politest suggestion that language itself is not sacred causes it enormous anxiety. Wordplay has the temerity to draw attention to language's vulnerability. Puns are essentially disruptive; gremlins loose in linguistic infrastructures, they goose a hitherto sphinx-like text and wink back at the reader. Antipuritan in spirit, wordplay is less interested in making sense of the world than finding pleasure in it, wary of words when they fall afoul of play. However, the dangers ensuing when writers take sanctuary in game playing are undeniable:

> An unco-ordinated woman in her early forties cantered down the porch steps to greet her. A flighty satin evening dress and long thoroughbred nose snubbed the chilly December dusk. ["Baby," *Passages*]

Was that thoroughbred nose always there, or did it only turn up when the writer hit on the verb *canter*? Is the writer straining at the bit to say something about life—or to do something with words? But for those who demand Emotion Before Trickery, it might be pointed out that emotions are often tricky and human nature is usually game.

Puns may be a symptom of language in collision, but who can say that collision is not in collusion with a chaotic cosmos? Being practically untranslatable (watch a Marx Brothers' film with French subtitles sometime), puns effectively scotch the myth of universality. Yet it could be argued that wordplay complements a tragic perspective by its tacit recognition of the fragmented, ambiguous nature of reality. It may be less threatening to linguistic prejudices to believe that every word has a reliable signification, to deny it the right to attach itself to other suppressed meanings, but it should be borne in mind that words are inherently protean and only autocrats resent ambiguity. If it is disconcerting, this may be for the same reason that nudity is found to be disconcerting: It alerts readers to the parts convention attempts to conceal (perhaps that is what is meant by detractors who dismiss wordplay as primitive). The pun's strip-tease shows tantalizing glimpses of language in the buff. That people are irritated or offended does not mean wordplay is trivial or objectionable, only that the dignity of some readers is easily overthrown.

News headlines have brought wordplay into disrepute by their crass application of it: Too often the distorted one-dimensional summary of events, political or otherwise, contradicts the ambiguity signified by the punning title. Far from being vulgar or frivolous or both, wordplay is a complex literary device permitting a richer response to language. Skillfully deployed, the pun does not bandy words, but bandages together (it arises, after all, from a linguistic accident) disparate meanings. Its vivacious, sometimes pugnacious presence warns the reader against taking the text at face value. In short, it is anathema to those who would "skip" because it causes them to pause and reflect.

But there is a difference between a writer pushing words around and a writer being pushed around by words: a difference between the writer who makes language jump through hoops and the writer who jumps through hoops for language: a difference between a pirouette by Pavlova and Pavlov's conditioned reflex. In other words, the pun makes compulsive reading—but it needs watching.

A Quick Fox Jumps over the Cwm Fjord-Bank Glyph Biz

RUSSELL SLOCUM

A *quick brown fox jumps over the lazy dog* is a popular grammar school writing exercise incorporating all twenty-six letters of the alphabet in a thirty-three–letter sentence. For those wishing to shorten the lesson, it may also be the seed of an obsession.

Holo-alphabetic sentences can be addicting. Unpraised holo-alphabaddicts have spent a good deal of time determining that Ezra 7:21 is the only Biblical verse containing all the letters, although it takes 170 letters to do it and excludes *j*, which wasn't around for the translation. But creating a twenty-six–letter holo-alphabetic sentence is the goal of most. Perhaps driven to desperation, Augustus DeMorgan, a nineteenth-century mathematician, used the pre-fifteenth-century alphabet (no *j* and an ambiguous *v*) to reach twenty-six with *I, quartz pyx, who fling mud beds.*

Using the modern alphabet, it has been comparatively easy to create holo-alphabetic sentences of between twenty-nine and thirty-three letters. There's the story of the World War I cryptoanalyst who wrote home requesting, *"Pack my bag with five dozen liquor jugs,"* and the likes of *Quick wafting zephyrs vex bold Jim.* In 1964 a magazine contest for the shortest ended in a tie at twenty-eight letters: *Waltz, nymph, for quick jigs vex Bud*; and slightly more obscure, *Blowzy frights vex, and jump quick.*

Complicated modifiers and implied articles raise the question of what constitutes a valid sentence. But in the heat of condensation, interest in content usually becomes secondary to over-coming the greatest obstacle, the ratio of six vowels to twenty consonants. Bringing the vowelless *nth* into the game better balances the groups, but as the sentences shrink, their meanings often become less lucid. For example: "Endless zigging and zagging through legal loopholes prevented the diminutive employees of an Iranian pyx manufacturer from turning their products into music boxes," or, in other words and twenty-seven letters, *Nth zigs block Qum dwarf jive pyx.* In twenty-six letters: "An esteemed Iranian shyster was provoked when he himself was cheated. An alleged seaside ski resort he purchased proved instead to be a glacier of countless oil-abundant fjords," or *Nth black fjords vex Qum gyp wiz.*

In addition to *nth* there is *cwm* a noun meaning 'a rounded valley or natural amphitheater.' "An eccentric's annoyance upon finding ancient inscriptions on the side of a fjord in a rounded valley" can be phrased as *Cwm fjord-bank glyphs vext quiz.* Telling of his "irritation at being cheated by a promoter's endless balking," a brief chapter 2 in the eccentric's life might read, *Nth balks gyp, vex cwm fjord quiz.*

Although the use of *nth* and *cwm* in a sentence leaves only fourteen consonants to mesh with the six vowels, seemingly incompatible groupings in the former category often appear. In fact, it seems necessary to include *fjord* or *fjeld* in the sentence to keep it at twenty-six letters. An example using the latter word: "A famous singer from a plateau valley (an unnatural wonder) was cheated in a wager concerning the infinite nature of quarks, a business he did not wholly understand"—*Nth quark biz gyps cwm fjeld vox.*

With the ultimate concision attained, it remains only to devise the most comprehensible holo-alphabetic sentence. While some of the preceding may seem contrived, word collections like *Nth cwm fjeld barks gyp quiz vox* make them seem relatively clear. Yet the number of possible combinations of the twenty-six letters is twenty-seven digits long. There must be a few more that make sense.

SIC! SIC! SIC!

"There is no residency requirement for US Senate other than that the candidate be a resident of the state he is running from at the time of his election." From the *Boston Globe*, 1 March 1990:23. Submitted by Robert Loud, Lincoln, Massachusetts.

The Cryptic Toolbox

HARRY COHEN

Seventy-five years ago, the daily *New York World* presented its readers with a new kind of puzzle that consisted of a grid and a list of clues. The Word-Cross, as it was called, started its existence as just another little Sunday supplement feature, with no pretensions to permanence. Yet it was to become the progenitor of the now ubiquitous crossword puzzle. The makeup of the grid has undergone various modifications in the course of time but the rules of the game have remained unchanged. As for the clues, they were called "definitions," and that indeed is what they were. —Or were they? On closer inspection, classic clues appear to be divisible into three groups. First, there are synonyms, like *rooster* for *cock*. Admittedly, there is no such thing as perfect synonymy, but the meanings of many pairs of words are close enough for this term to be used in the context of a pastime like crosswords. Second, a clue may name a class of objects which includes the answer, like *bird* for *cock.* A more specific class, e.g., *male bird,* makes solution easier, whereas a more general class, e.g., *animal,* would complicate the puzzler's task. The third group comprises definitions proper. Such a clue for *cock* might read: *adult male of the domestic fowl.*

Crossword puzzles soon became very popular in America, and perhaps even more so in Britain. But someone must have felt that all this was too simple for our overtrained brains. Straightforward definitions (of all three varieties) were gradually replaced by play on words, ambiguous phrasings, jumble games, and other verbal pranks. A clue for *cock* might thus come to read: *number one in the pecking order dominates hens and crows* (a quizzical statement, unless the word *crows* is read as a verb) or even: *creature with a cow's head and a bullock's rump found in a coop* (first letter of *cow* plus last three letters of *bullock*).

The uninitiated may find these examples too bizarre for words. Still, the idea has caught on so well that most British newspapers now offer two crossword puzzles each day. One is in the classic style, commonly labeled "concise" or "quick." The other is of the newer, playful genre, often referred to as "cryptic"; but this designation is by no means universal. (A well-known American language journal prefers the term "Anglo-American.") In some countries, puzzles of this type are called "cryptograms," a name we shall use from here on. This article is an attempt to catalogue the main tools currently applied by cryptic puzzle-makers and solvers.

A cryptogram clue can be a simple pun, like

A. *A message that goes from pole to pole* (8 letters) = TELE-GRAM

In most cases, however, it consists, as the previous examples suggest, of two elements, each hinting at the answer in its own way. This construction makes sense since each hint by itself is generally so vague or open-ended that it evokes more potential answers than a puzzler's brain can handle. Two such hints, however, have only a few possible answers in common, so that the solver can concentrate on them and pick the most probable one. This quest for the correct answer rests on intricate mental processes which require no elaboration. Our purpose here is rather to devise a classification of the various types of clue elements (CEs) currently in use.

Let us start with the three groups of clues encountered in the classical crossword puzzle: synonyms, superordinates, and definitions. Here are some examples of their cryptic counterparts:

B. *A writer or two* (5) = TWAIN

The first CE (*A writer*) indicates a class to which TWAIN belongs; the second (*two*) offers a synonym of another possible meaning of the answer.

C. *One who counts and recounts* (6) = TELLER

The two CEs are telescoped. Each of them defines a separate meaning of the answer.

These are really old-time clues in new apparel; once wise to the system and having enough vocabulary entries in one's head (or a thesaurus handy on the shelf), it is not too difficult to decode them and arrive at the answer. The going gets tougher, however, as the two meanings of the answer move further apart:

D. *This landlord is quite a character* (6) = LETTER

The mechanism is clear: *landlord* = LETTER, ('one who lets'), and *character* = LETTER, but the two LETTERs differ in both meaning and origin. (Note that some double-dealing has also gone on with the word *character*!) A third layer of camouflage is added in:

E. *Straight commotion* (3) = ROW

The two ROWs differ in pronunciation as well as in meaning and origin.

Just as disorienting are clues where the two meanings of the answer belong to different word classes:

F. *A more successful gambler* (6) = BETTER

To mystify solvers even more, puzzlers may use words in an uncommon but perfectly legitimate sense, especially by attributing to certain words ending in *-er* the quality of agent noun. *Bloomer* (for 'flower'), *butter* (for 'ram'), or even *flower* (for 'river') are recurrent examples, but solvers must always be on the alert for new traps of this type:

G. *More than one anesthetic* (6) = NUMBER

All of the above techniques rest, in one way or another, on the meanings of words. They make up the class of Semantic Clue Elements. Another class, equally important in cryptoland, is that of Graphic Clue Elements. Here, the object of play is the written form of the answer, or, more precisely, the letters of which that form consists. The best known member of this class is undoubtedly the anagram:

H. *Victim of injustice could be grounded* (8) = UNDERDOG

The words *could be* which precede the anagram *grounded* have a special function. They inform solvers (if they get the message!) that an anagram is lurking nearby. Indeed, convention requires that anagrams (and all other Graphic CEs) be accompanied by such flags. On the other hand, the cryptogram composer is free to conceal these signals in all sorts of phrasal hocus-pocus:

I. *Overturned vote overturns all votes* (4) = VETO

Some other anagram flags are *broken, strange, unorthodox, maybe, kind of,* and *a source of.* There are dozens of them, and new ones are being concocted every day.

Many anagrams spread over two or more words:

J. *Brave Tim changed quarterly* (8) = VERBATIM

These are particularly tricky when short words, like articles or pronouns, are involved:

K. *An event is organized for Italians* (9) = VENETIANS

L. *You can't take it with you—neither can I, unfortunately* (11) = INHERITANCE

A subvariant of the anagram is the inversion:

M. *On reflection, the parts will hold together* (5) = STRAP

On reflection is a flag to indicate that *parts* is to be read backwards. Other inversion flags are *coming back, returning,* and *going West.* Purists admit these only for answers that run horizontally in the grid. For the "down" words, they prefer *turning up, traveling North,* etc.

It is worth noting that the first element of clue M. consists of the four words *On reflection the parts.* The comma, correctly inserted between *reflection* and *the,* may mislead, but such punctuational conflicts are considered perfectly legitimate, or even a piquant little feature. We shall return to this point later.

Another type of Graphic CE is the acronym:

N. *The leaders of the unassuming Royal Knights Society can be a source of delight* (5) = TURKS

The leaders of is a flag intended to draw the solvers' attention to the initial letters of the words following it, where the answer lies for the taking. The most common flag for acronyms is, as one would expect, *initially.*

The acronym does not stand by itself in the crypto repertoire. In fact, it is the key member of a whole family of Graphic CEs, all with their own specific flags to indicate whether the answer is to be composed from last letters, middle letters, or other word fragments. An idea of the way they work has been given in one of the introductory examples (the cow-bullock creature).

A relatively new graphic technique is the sandwich. The letters of the answer are left in their original order but spread over two or more words:

O. *Lakeside city located inside the embankment or on top of it* (7) = TORONTO or contained in a single word:

P. *A small capital in Czechoslovakia* (4) = OSLO

Besides *inside* and *in,* common sandwich flags are *part of* and *some of.*

As the above clues demonstrate, a Graphic CE should be accompanied not only by a flag but also by a Semantic CE. This conventional rule also holds for the members of a third class, the Phonic Clue Elements. These are based, just like the traditional pun, on homophony:

Q. *Critique, one hears, of a theatrical entertainment* (5) = REVUE

Somewhat more involved is:

R. *It sounds in one sense (or in none) like simplicity* (9) = IN-NOCENCE

Phonic CEs are not very often used, probably because all suitable flags (*I hear, it sounds, say,* etc.) are so obvious that they threaten to give the game away. In the above tour d'horizon, not all aspects of clue setting have passed in review. Nothing has been said about the artful ways in which abbreviations, chemical symbols, Arabic and Roman numerals, musical notes, etc., may be used in clues. Hardly any attention has been paid to one-element clues. (There are even one-word clues, some of them particularly witty.) No examples have been given of answers that consist of more than one word. More important, no mention has been made of the possibility of chopping the answer into convenient pieces which are separately represented in the clue by anagrams, synonyms, etc.

Just one real-life example:

S. *European city, home of the first person without perverse words* (9) = ?

Solution:

    words = terms (synonym)

    perverse = flag for anagram

  anagram of 'terms' = MSTER

    the first person = ADAM

    without = outside (!)

  ADAM outside MSTER = AMSTERDAM

Clue syntax deserves a more thorough examination than space permits; but perhaps it would be best to comment on some aspects of the ethics of compiling clues.

The first commandment in the puzzlers' bible reads: Thou shalt not waste words. A well-constructed clue comprises only words necessary for conveying, in a deceptive way, the information solvers require to find the answer. Adding fillers to distract them is considered unfair. As for the answer, it is better to avoid very learned or rare words unknown to all but a few lexicographers. The idea is to test the solvers' skill in deciphering clues rather than their familiarity with the recondite recesses of the lexicon. (This being said, one British publication does offer a special obscure-words puzzle, probably for the benefit of glossarial masochists. Little wonder it appears under the name of Mephisto.)

On the other hand, it is admissible, as we have already seen, to throw solvers off the scent with an occasional comma in the "wrong" place. The same holds for other dividers, such as colons, dashes, hyphens, and blanks. Likewise, a bit of juggling with apostrophes, quotation marks, and capitals is permitted, always on the understanding that no punctuation or spelling rules are infringed. And it goes without saying that clue texts may be arranged in such a way that, at first sight, certain words appear to belong to a different inflectional form or word class than is actually the case when the clue is unlocked. In fact, this is an essential part of the fun. This feature has already been demonstrated in the very first example (the cock that crows) and also in clue F. Clue J offers two further instances: At first reading, *changed* is suggestive of being a past tense but after analysis it is identified as a past participle (serving as an anagram flag); likewise, *quarterly* shifts from adverb to noun.

Let us end with a specimen in which several of the above techniques are represented:

T. *Part of his imprint appears in absurd Anglo-Saxon rules, word for word* (6) = ?

Solution: Replace in the second element (*rules word for word*) the last three words by their synonym "verbatim." Well, who rules *Verbatim*? His name (= part of his imprint) appears in *absurd Anglo-Saxon*.

SIC! SIC! SIC!

"Your thumb or fingerprint will be taken." From the
California Driver Handbook, spring 1988. Submitted by
D. Wayne Doolen, Sherman Oaks.

Defile Your Records!

LAURENCE URDANG

When one has been editing dictionaries for as long as I have, a condition of paranomastic fatigue sets in, and, as far as I know, there is no cure for it. It happens in many editorial offices:

Someone comes up with a weird sort of joke that has occurred to him while his mind was wandering through the organization of the materials he was working with. The next thing you know, the joke has become systematized into a game, and the entire staff—all language-oriented—is playing it. One such game was played at *Newsweek* in the mid 1940s, when I was employed there for a while in a capacity that I have tried to forget and that *Newsweek* has probably consigned to the dustbin. It consisted of translating popular English songs (literally) into French and German. *"Ich werde dich warden in einem Taxi, Honig,"* was originally "I'll be down to get you in a taxi, Honey," and *"Y avait un gars. Un gars qui était tout bizarre"* had been "There was a boy. A very strange, enchanted boy." Since some of those songs had actually been translated for consumption abroad, I cannot any longer be certain which were our translations and which the "official" ones. But they were a lot of fun. The best collection I know of that treats a wide range of such translations is *The Astonishment of Words*, by Victor Proetz, which [was] one of the first and most popular books offered through the *Verbatim* Book Club.

Other games—if they can be elevated to that status—abound: In *Verbatim* [III, 4] we featured a solitaire version described by Walter Kidney in "The Seating of Zotz." One game focused on collecting bloopers made by fellow editors. The *American College Dictionary*, for example, defines *yoheave-ho* as, a cry that sailors give when heaving together. One editor on the *Random House Dictionary* (Unabridged) assigned to writing definitions of idioms and to the contrivance of example contexts had great difficulty in keeping the literal separated from the metaphoric. For "get in on the ground floor," she gave the example, *He heard they were building a new factory in the area and wanted to get in on the ground floor*; for "last straw," the example was *The service in this restaurant has been bad before, but this is the last straw*; and for "give someone his head" she wrote, *She wanted to go to college out of town, so her parents gave her her head.* If you were writing that stuff all day long, week in, week out, for months on end you might do worse. I imagine that Tom Swifties were invented in just such an atmosphere.

One of my favorites, though, was one of my own invention, and everyone is invited to play. It's absurdly simple: If clergymen are *unfrocked* and lawyers are *disbarred,* how are members of these trades and professions to be got rid of? A few examples are given, with answers, below.

1. *electricians*
2. *carpenters*
3. *exhibitionists*
4. *vintners*
5. *mathematicians*
6. *wall flowers*
7. *mourners*
8. *Italian fascists*
9. *manicurists*
10. *florists*
11. *casting directors*
12. *prostitutes*
13. *alcoholics*
14. *pornographers*
15. *segregationists*
16. *swearers*
17. *reweavers*
18. *models*
19. *denominationalists*
20. *puzzle-makers*
21. *farmers*
22. *hairdressers*
23. *bankers*
24. *dry-cleaners*
25. *examiners*
26. *ninth-century Scots*

1. delighted
2. devised
3. debriefed
4. decanted
5. deciphered
6. decoyed
7. decried
14. deluded
15. discolored
16. discussed
17. dispatched
18. disposed
19. dissected
20. dissolved

8. deduced
9. defiled
10. deflowered
11. deformed
12. delayed
13. delivered

21. distilled
22. distressed
23. distrusted
24. depressed
25. detested
26. depicted

Epistolae

In reference to "Defile Your Records": An electrician may be discharged, as well as delighted. And I discounted your mathematician at first glance. Some more are obvious: The horseman who is derided, the tree surgeon who debarked, the foundation digger who is debased, the podiatrist who is defeated. A poster painter can be designed, a sports star displayed, an orchestra conductor disconcerted, an archer deranged, and an air-conditioning repairman deducted.

A girl in pigtails can easily be depleted, a single woman dismissed. But how unfortunate when Rover is detailed, or the breeder's top stud desired. A late sleeper should be debunked, that incompetent waiter deserved, and weathermen predicting heavy winds disgusted. Also joining the unemployment ranks are the dissuaded leatherworker, the devoted politician, and many despised CIA employees.

The local judge caused quite a stir when he defined a traffic violator, distorted a lawyer, described the court clerk, and deliberated a free man. A halted battle leaves soldiers defrayed. Ladies in mink can be deferred. An orphan left on his own, then adopted, has been defended; a certain Ontario Indian tribe, losing its identity, is decreed.

The optometrist called on to remove a beam from a patient's eye was demoted when he failed. The Olympic diver upon whom

we depended jumped into the shallow end instead; when he jus-
tified the jump later, he was deified ("if I'd"). A rescued item at
a garage sale is disjunct.

Anyone now in a bad mood from overexposure to puns needs
to be defunct.

SUE HYDE
Jacksonville, Florida

Review of The Mammoth Book of Word Games

WILLARD ESPY

The *Mammoth Book of Word Games*, by Richad B. Manchester, Hart Publishing Company, New York, 1976, paper.
Reviewed by Willard Espy.

Walter Raleigh, not the one who spread his cloak in the mud
for Queen Elizabeth to step on, but the one who didn't, once
remarked:

> *I wish I loved the Human Race;*
> *I wish I loved its silly face;*
> *I wish I liked the way it walks;*
> *I wish I liked the way it talks;*
> *And when I'm introduced to one*
> *I wish I thought What Jolly Fun.*

I feel the same way about most word games. The real reason,
of course, is that I am no good at them; I can't show off by doing

a London *Times* crossword puzzle in four minutes flat. But just in case you are one who *does* like word games, you should have Richard B. Manchester's *The Mammoth Book of Word Games* in your library, or at least in that of your children. The whole family will find it Jolly Fun (there are answers in back, too). Mr. Manchester has accumulated enough challenges to keep you sharpening your pencil for hours; the front cover does not exaggerate when it notifies you that the 510 lubberly pages (8½" × 11") provide *"over a full year's entertainment."*

The first entry is perhaps a bit simpler than most, but it gives you the idea. You are asked to find equivalents containing the word *light* for a list of twenty-five expressions. *"A tower having warning beacon for ships at sea,"* for instance, is a . . . Ah! You are already catching on. At another point, you are asked to reduce big words to little maxims: "Aberration is the hallmark of *homo sapiens* while longanimous placability and condonation are the indicia of a supramundane omniscience" turns into . . . But there! I won't give Mr. Manchester away. There are Word Mazes, consisting of vocabulary puzzles that I am reluctant to penetrate for fear of running into a Minotaur somewhere inside. There are Threezies, where you list all the words you can think of containing certain three-letter sequences. (Mr. Manchester says that at least nine words contain the sequence *Oto.* I could not get beyond *motor.*) There are enough cryptograms to fill a crypt. (I plan to create an insoluble cryptogram some day by substituting two other letters for what I contend to be the shortest verse in English—well, half in English. The wife of the British Ambassador is hostess to the wife of the Spanish Ambassador, and their conversation runs as follows:

"T?"

"C."

It should make a great cryptogram, but I haven't got around to it yet, and neither, I gather, has Mr. Manchester.)

Cryptograms lead on to Jumbles—emigrants, one assumes, from the lands where the Jumblies live; these are anagrams on various themes. There follow Quizzes, which test background knowledge (I didn't dare try them); Picture Quizzes, where you are wrong if you put *porcupine* under the picture of an anteater; Crossword Puzzles, clearly not edited by Will Weng; Across-tics (the pun is self-explanatory); Blankies, which seem to be Jumbles sitting around the fire telling stories; and Initialettes, which in an earlier day were called Categories or Guggenheims. There is more besides.

Word games are an excellent introduction to the delights of English. If you have offspring still on the morning side of pubescence, I hope they will have an opportunity to savor this book before intenser drives supervene. Indeed, whatever your own level of verbal sophistication, you cannot lose by thumbing through these word games; for,

> *You may be introduced to one*
> *That makes you think What Jolly Fun.*

Pairing Pairs

LAURENCE URDANG

The clues are given in items lettered *a–z*; the answers are given in numbered items which must be matched with each other to solve the clues. In some cases, a numbered word may be used more than once, but after all matchings have been completed, one numbered word will remain, and that is the correct answer. Our answer is the only correct one.

a. Deficit may result in early winter	1. Ape
b. Let the shilling remain as auxiliary support	2. Auto
c. Dresser has pullout feature	3. Egg
d. Bloody offspring is no plum!	4. Dog's
e. Potential energy from down east water	5. Body
f. Source of smelly col' cream	6. Mitre
g. Where bishops buy their hats	7. Spring
h. Lay on one of these and you still have nothing	8. Short
i. Descend into the warehouse	9. Tacks
j. Bury soprano up to her waist	10. Dam
k. Able to mimic an hors d'oeuvre	11. Joint
l. Australian stinger	12. Cast
m. Used-car salesman's hint	13. Cutter
n. Dos Passos quartet?	14. Agua
o. Nana, the flunky	15. Suggestion
p. Fleet Street Coiffure?	16. Goose
q. Trouble in Mexico	17. Son
r. P.M. or notorious TV star?	18. Lunatic
s. Hitchhikers pay this	19. Mezzo
t. Pussy's moan for a jewel	20. Bob
u. Insane purpose will get you there	21. Fall

v. Regatta on the Isis or fourth down
w. Such a vessel would surely sink
x. Viceregent subsiding
y. Heavily pressing need
z. Dramatis personae absent. Marooned?

22. Loco
23. Caliente
24. Sad
25. Motive
26. Can
27. Factory
28. Manhattan
29. Stay
30. Sin
31. Transfer
32. Thumb
33. Down
34. That
35. Drawer
36. Inter
37. Wasp
38. With
39. King
40. Punt
41. Cher
42. Stone
43. Fringe
44. Digger
45. Sigh
46. Ol'
47. Away
48. Go
49. Formation
50. Main
51. Iron
52. Cat
53. Proud

Pairing Pairs—Answers

a. Deficit may result in early winter. (8, 21) Short Fall.

b. Let the shilling remain as auxiliary support. (20, 29)
   Bob Stay.

c. Dresser has pullout feature. (38, 35) With Drawer.

d. Bloody offspring is no plum! (10, 17) Dam Son.

e. Potential energy from down east water. (50, 7) Main Spring.

f. Source of smelly col' cream? (46, 27) Ol' Factory.

g. Where bishops buy their hats. (6, 11) Mitre Joint.

h. Lay on one of these and you still have nothing. (16, 3)
   Goose Egg.

i. Descend into the warehouse. (48, 33) Go Down.

j. Bury soprano up to her waist. (36, 19) Inter Mezzo.

k. Able to mimic an hors d'oeuvre. (26, 1) Can Ape.

l. Australian stinger. (44, 37) Digger Wasp.

m. Used-car salesman's hint. (2, 15) Auto Suggestion.

n. DOS Passos quartet? (28, 31) Manhattan Transfer.

o. Nana, the flunky. (4, 5) Dog's Body.

p. Fleet Street Coiffure? (18, 43) Lunatic Fringe.

q. Trouble in Mexico. (14, 23) Agua Caliente.

r. P.M. or notorious TV star? (34, 41) That Cher.

s. Hitchhikers pay this. (32, 9) Thumb Tacks.

t. Pussy's moan for a jewel. (52, 45) Cat Sigh.

u. Insane purpose will get you there. (22, 25) Loco Motive.

v. Regatta on the Isis of fourth down. (40, 49)
   Punt Formation.

w. Such a vessel would surely sink. (42, 13) Stone Cutter.

x. Viceregent subsiding. (30, 39) Sin King.

y. Heavily pressing need. (24, 51) Sad Iron.

z. Dramatis personae absent. Marooned? (12, 47) Cast Away.

Not in Polite Company

H eard any good obscenities lately?" is not a question often
posed. People swear, curse, blaspheme, and run blue at the
mouth, often dozens of times in a day. Some are provoked by
wayward hammers, others by a fallen soufflé. And quite a few,
if you believe the Hollywood gangster movies, have incorporated
(what Benedict Kimmelman calls in his essay) "the ineffable
F——r-letter word" into their everyday speech with no provo-
cation at all. Just one (compound) word like *motherfucker* can
have countless connotations, depending on the emphasis in pronunciation.

Though these emotive words cloud the air, we rarely discuss
them, unless it's to say "Watch your mouth!" The only discussion is a prohibition of discussion, which is unfortunate, since
these powerful expressions are a fascinating part of our language.
Over the years, *Verbatim* has published some attention-grabbing
articles on these attention-grabbing words—articles that have re-
sulted in cancelled subscriptions and letters of commendation in
about equal measure. If you tend to be easily offended, skip this
chapter entirely. It's not for the faint of heart and delicate of
nature. You adventurous types read on!

Meretricious Words,
or the Quean's English

BRYAN GARNER

Meretrix, specioso nomine rem odiosam denotante.

—Plato *(Plut. et Athen.)*

In the English Renaissance, Fortune was commonly personified as a fickle strumpet, as in the scene from *Hamlet* where the protagonist banters bawdily with Rosencrantz and Guildenstern: *The Riverside Shakespeare,* ed. G. Blakemore Evans (Boston: Houghton Mifflin Company, 1974), hereinafter cited in text.

> HAM: Good lads, how do you both?
> ROS: As the indifferent children of the earth.
> GUIL: Happy, in that we are not over-happy, on Fortune's cap we are not the very button.
> HAM: Nor the soles of her shoe?
> ROS: Neither, my lord.
> HAM: Then you live about her waist, or in the middle of her favors?
> GUIL: Faith, her privates we.
> HAM: In the secret parts of Fortune? O, most true; she is a strumpet. (2.2.225–36)

The metaphor suggested itself because Fortune, with her unsteady Wheel, is fickle and inconstant, as strumpets were commonly thought to be. But if strumpets themselves have been inconstant in the popular mind, then it is certainly apt that the fortunes of their distinctive epithets have been equally inconstant, for, historically, speakers of English have licentiously jumped from term to whorish term to describe practitioners of the oldest, most venerable of human occupations.

We have therefore inherited scores of synonyms for *prostitute* that seemingly cover—or, rather, uncover—every possible nuance of the scortatory hierarchy, from the tinselly, grand *courtesan* to the abject, base *slut*. In fact, the synonyms for *prostitute* probably outnumber those of any other comparably specific meaning. Why is this? Perhaps it is because those in the underworld, who are most deeply involved with prostitution, have the raciest argot (almost invariably ephemeral) and wield words more boldly, loosely, and inventively than other speakers. Or perhaps it results from a popular fixation with the less pleasant, seedier aspects of human existence. Then again, it may demonstrate that we are perennially witness to more vice than virtue.

However that may be, and whether we find prostitution a barbarous, abhorrent practice or a desirable societal peccadillo, it is of interest to word lovers to see how the copious English appellations for prostitutes have developed and changed through the centuries. Many of these terms exemplify the witty and ironic creativeness of English speakers; my own favorite in this regard is *laced mutton*, a British slang phrase current in the sixteenth through eighteenth centuries, in which the ambiguity of *laced* is quite effective. It might mean 'bedizened with lace', 'corseted', 'tenderized', 'slightly squiffed' (i.e., 'flavored with alcohol'), or 'savory and zestful'—perhaps all of these. Forthwith the rest of the list, with some cursory notes and explanations made in consultation with the *OED*; with Partridge's *Dictionary of Slang and Unconventional English*, *Dictionary of the Underworld*, *Slang Today and Yesterday*, and *Name Into Word*; with Wentworth and Flexner's *Dictionary of American Slang*; with *Webster's Third New International Dictionary (W3)*; and with Brewer's *Dictionary of Phrase and Fable*.

abbess ironic slang for 'brothel-keeper', ca. seventeenth through nineteenth centuries; *obs.*

abandoned woman *abandoned* in the sense of 'self-abandoned', 'given over to vice'; *euphemism.*

adventuress also has a slightly broader meaning, 'a woman who lives by questionable means'.

bar-girl see *B-girl.*

bawd [Middle English *bawde*, perh. fr. Middle French *baude* 'bold, merry'] 'a procuress'; formerly used of either sex.

bawd-strot [fr. Old French *baudetrot? OED* remarks that *strot* suggests Teutonic *strutt*, and *bawd* Middle French *baud* 'bold'] variant of *bawd; obs.*

B-girl [fr. *bar-girl*] 'a prostitute who meets her prospective clients in bars'; often a B-girl may be employed by a bar to entertain men and induce them to buy a lot of drinks.

bit cf. *piece.*

broad U.S. slang fr. ca. 1910; also means 'woman'; *obsolescent.*

bunter [origin unknown] 'a low harlot and thief'; British, eighteenth through nineteenth centuries, *obs.*

burick [origin unknown] 'prostitute' ante 1851; during the nineteenth century, it was increasingly used to mean 'wife' among Cockneys; *obs.*

cab-moll 'a harlot professionally partial to cabs or trains', ca. 1840–1900.

callet [perhaps, as *W3* suggests, fr. Middle French *caillette* 'frivolous person', after *Caillette*, a French court fool of ca. 1500] *obs.* exc. as Scottish and dialectal English.

call-girl 'a prostitute who arranges her rendezvous over the telephone'; originally, however, 'a prostitute who works in a call-house' (i.e., a brothel).

camp follower 'a harlot who follows a military unit'; cf. **V-girl**.

cocodette [alteration of French *cocodète,* fem. of *cocodès* 'fop, dandy'] 'a high-society French prostitute'.

cocotte [according to *W3,* fr. French (baby-talk) *cocotte* 'hen'] a "forbidden word," wrote Mencken in *The American Language.*

conciliatrix 'a bawd or procuress'; *obs.*

concubine [Latin, literally 'one who lies with (another)'] 'a kept woman'; 'a mistress'; sometimes misapplied for *courtesan.*

corinthian [fr. *Corinth,* a region of ancient Greece] 'a profligate addicted to salacity and dissipation'—used of both sexes in English (but cf. *korinthiazesthai* 'to be a prostitute').

courtesan, courtezan [French 'woman courtier'] 'a prostitute with an aristocratic or upper-class clientele'.

cruiser 'a peripatetic whore'; 'any person who cruises'; *slang.*

Cyprian [fr. Latin *Cyprius* 'native of Cyprus' (reputed birthplace of Aphrodite)] *archaic.*

daughter of joy translation of French **fille de joie.**

debauchee 'one given to sensual excess'; used of either sex in English; a euphemism when used for 'whore'.

demimondaine [French 'inhabitant of the half-world'] 'a courtesan who serves the upper class and strives to maintain the appearance of respectability'; *OED* says that this meaning is improper and recommends 'a prostitute on the outskirts of society'.

demirep 'a woman with only half a reputation'; *slang* fr. eighteenth century.

doll [= *Doll* = *Dorothy*] traditional name for a wanton; 'twentieth-century slang for paramour'.

doxy, doxie [origin unknown] fr. sixteenth century; dialectal as 'girl friend, sweetheart'.

drab [akin to Irish *drabog* and Gaelic *drabag* 'dirty female'] 'a filthy slut'.

erring sister a typical Victorian euphemism.

fallen woman a typical Victorian euphemism.

fancy girl self-evident.

fancy lady self-evident.

fancy woman self-evident.

floozy, floosy, floosey , etc. [Partridge suggests rel. to *flusey* 'female pudend'; he also conjectures (in *Origins*) that *floozy* = *Flossie* = *Flora,* the goddess] legitimately, 'a becoming loose woman', but also, slang, 'a slovenly harlot'.

fornicatress a euphemism when applied to prostitutes; *fornication* 'coitus other than between a man and his wife or his concubine'.

fornicatrix same as preceding entry.

frail sister euphemism.

garrison-hack 'a soldiers' harlot'; nineteenth-century British *slang.*

gin [fr. *gin* 'female Australian aborigine'] 'a black prostitute', U.S. slang, ca. 1920; *obs.*

gold-digger 'an avaricious woman who exploits her femininity to extract gifts and money from men'; U.S. slang, ca. 1915.

gun moll 'the mistress of a gangster or crook', U.S. *underworld slang,* ca. 1931; *moll* here primarily in the sense of 'thief'; *obs.*

harlot [fr. Old French *herlot* 'rogue'] as suggested by the etymon, this word formerly referred more commonly to knavish men (fr. thirteenth century) than to whorish women (fr. fifteenth century); Mencken labels it a "forbidden word."

harridan [perh. fr. French *haridelle* 'old jade horse'] 'a worn-out old harlot'; Dr. Johnson: "a decayed strumpet"; ca. 1700–1864; now refers vituperatively to termagants and shrews.

hetaera, hetaira [Greek for 'companion'] 'one of the highly cultivated courtesans of ancient Greece'.

hooker 'one who hooks or entraps, often in a happy manner'; twentieth century.

hostess see **madam.**

house girl 'a prostitute who works in a bagnio'—as contrasted to a *call-girl* (in the modern sense) or *streetwalker.*

hussy, huzzy [fr. Middle English *huswif*, whence also *house-wife*] a pejorative term since the eighteenth century; denotes a 'loose, brazen woman or a prostitute'.

hustler United States slang fr. ca. 1900.

joy girl perh. a translation of French *fille de joie*; slang (cf. *joy house* 'brothel'.)

kept mistress a common term that may be redundant, since *mistress* usu. means 'kept woman'.

kept woman see preceding and following entries.

keptie like the preceding two entries, 'a woman nicely supported by a man in return for sexual favors'.

lady of assignation in this entry and in the following five, *lady* is employed ironically; cf. **fancy lady.**

lady of leisure see preceding entry.

lady of pleasure see **lady of assignation.**

lady of the evening see **lady of assignation.**

lady of the lake 'mistress'; see **lady of assignation.**

lady of the night see **lady of assignation.**

lewd woman a term of contempt in polite society, hence a pejorative euphemism.

limmer [origin unknown] generally Scottish and dialectal English; *The Scottish National Dictionary* traces the meaning 'prostitute' from ca. 1728, but the *OED* dates this meaning fr. the early sixteenth century; refers also to scoundrelly men.

loose woman a genteelism.

lost woman a genteelism.

mab [fr. seventeenth-century form of *mop*; perh. also a short form of Mabel] slang fr. seventeenth century, now Standard (British) English.

madam, madame *obs.* as 'prostitute'; now 'the head of a brothel'; according to Mencken, the word is "forbidden" in this sense.

malkin [= *Mall* = *Mary* (Partridge); according to the *OED*, a diminutive of Matilda, Maud] 'slattern'; Scottish fr. ca. 1540, obs. in British English exc. as dialectal; also denoted the female pudend (perh. fr. its association with *cat,* hence *pussy*).

market-dame 'a harlot of the marketplace'; colloquial fr. eighteenth century; increasingly Standard English.

meretrix [fr. Latin *merere* 'to earn, gain'] the suffix humorously suggests the service paid for, and the entire word [suggests] *Mary Tricks.*

minion [fr. French *mignon, mignonne* 'favorite or darling'] 'paramour, mistress'; now *literary.*

miss [short for *mistress*] 'prostitute' was one of this word's earliest meanings, though it is now archaic.

moll [= *Moll* = *Mary*] 'a common whore', fr. ca. 1600; in U.S. twentieth-century slang, "any woman regardless of condition," according to Partridge.

mopsy [origin unknown] 'a disreputable and slovenly woman', though earlier a term of endearment; *obs.* exc. as dialectal British English.

mort [origin unknown; euphemistic Latinism for the Elizabethan *die* 'to have orgasm'?] also denote merely 'girl' or 'woman'; fr. sixteenth century, now *archaic.*

naughty pack 'a lubricious woman of questionable reputation', though it can refer to either sex; *obs.*

nightwalker 'any person who roves about at night'.

nun ironic for 'harlot' fr. ca. 1770, though *nunnery* 'brothel' fr. late sixteenth century—hence the ambiguity of Hamlet's cry to Ophelia, "Get thee to a nunn'ry!" (3.1.120); *obs.*

nymph aside fr. mythological association, 'a woman of loose morals'; euphemistic in reference to whores.

nymph of the darkness elegant variation of **lady of the night**.

nymph of the pavement translation of French **nymphe du pavé.**

odalisque [fr. French *odalique*, fr. Turkish *ōdahliq.* 'chamber-maid'] 'a female slave in the harem of a Turkish sultan'.

one of the frail sisterhood a Victorian euphemism.

pack 'a man or woman of low character', hence often applied to whores as well as to others regarded as dregs; *archaic.*

painted woman self-evident.

Paphian 'a devotee of the Paphian Venus; a prostitute' *(OED).* Paphos was a Cyprian city sacred to Aphrodite or Venus and hence became associated with sexual indulgence.

paramour [fr. Old French *par amour* 'through or by way of love'] 'one who loves illicitly'—usu. used of women, and sometimes euphemistically of prostitutes; the word is virtually synonymous with **mistress.**

party doll same as following entry.

party girl 'a young woman employed to entertain men at parties'.

perfect lady British slang for 'anything but a perfect lady' (Partridge); derives either from the claims of prostitutes or from the irony of whoremongers and other men.

pickup humorously suggestive of 'pick-me-up'.

pom-pom girl during World War II, U.S. servicemen used *pom-pom* to mean 'sexual intercourse'.

pro [short for *professional,* not *prostitute* (Wentworth and Flexner)].

pross [short for *prostitute*] low British slang fr. ca. 1880.

prossy [same as preceding] twentieth-century U.S. slang.

punch [akin to the vb. *punch* 'deflower'] late seventeenth to mid-nineteenth century; cf. *punch-house* 'bagnio'.

pure 'a kept woman, wanton', British, seventeenth through nineteenth centuries; *obs.*

purest pure 'a courtesan of high fashion', fr. ca. 1690 to ca. 1830; *obs.*

quean [fr. Old English *cwene,* akin to the etymon of *queen*].

rig [Middle English *riggen,* of uncertain derivation] dialectal English; cf. *riggish* 'sluttish', as in Shakespeare's *Antony and Cleopatra,* where Enobarbus speaks thus of Cleopatra:

> *Other women cloy*
> *The appetites they feed, but she makes hungry*
> *Where most she satisfies; for vilest things*
> *Become themselves in her, that the holy priests*
> *Bless her when she is riggish. (2.2.235–39)*

saleslady U.S. slang fr. ca. 1920.

Saturday-to-Monday 'a weekend mistress'; British *slang* fr. ca. 1900, perh. having arisen as a variation of the earlier week-ender, q.v.; *obs.*

scarlet woman also—ironically—when capitalized, 'The Roman Catholic Church.'

shady lady self-evident.

skit [of obscure origin] 'a wanton', now *obs.* in this dialectal sense; cf. skittish 'capricious, fickle' (and formerly suggestive of 'whorish', as in Shakespeare's phrase "skittish Fortune's hall," *Troilus and Cressida* 3.3.134).

slattern [akin to **slut**] 'a slovenly prostitute'.

slut [Middle English *slutte*] a word with strong connotations of opprobrium—suggests uncleanness.

sporting girl cf. *sporting house* 'brothel'.

street girl self-evident.

streetwalker self-evident.

strumpet [Middle English *strompet,* of obscure origin].

sultana [fr. fem. form of Italian *sultano,* fr. Arabic *sultān*] 'a mistress or paramour of a royal personage, esp. of a sultan'.

tart [Middle English *tarte,* fr. Middle French] originally a term of endearment, this "forbidden word" (Mencken) for comparatively young prostitutes pejorated ca. 1900.

tom 'an old prostitute' or 'a mannish prostitute'; current fr. mid-nineteenth to early twentieth century.

tommy low slang of the twentieth century.

tottie, totty [prob. fr. *Dot = Dorothy*] British for 'a high-class, well-dressed harlot', fr. ca. 1880.

tramp contemporary; also used of men in the sense of 'a begging or thieving vagrant'.

trapes (usu. British), traipse (usu. U.S.) 'slattern,' seventeenth through eighteenth centuries, now *archaic*.

trollop [akin to *trull*] a "forbidden word" (Mencken).

trull [fr. *obs.* German *Trulle* 'prostitute'] *contemptuous.*

unfortunate used of outcasts generally, whether prostitutes, prisoners, or other pariahs.

unfortunate female like the preceding entry, a genteelism.

unfortunate woman like the preceding entry, a genteelism.

V-girl [for 'victory girl'] 'a wartime amateur camp follower or pickup'.

vice girl self-evident.

wanton [fr. Middle English *wantowen* '(one) deficient in discipline'] used of the dissipated of either sex, and commonly of whores.

weekender same as **Saturday-to-Monday;** British, ca. 1885; *obs.*

wench [shortened and pejorated fr. Old English and Middle English *wenchel* 'a child or common woman'] formerly 'a young girl', the word pejorated during the fourteenth century; by the late nineteenth and early twentieth centuries it had become a "forbidden word" and is now used only disparagingly or jocosely to suggest looseness or whorishness.

white slave 'a white woman or girl held under duress for the purposes of commercial prostitution,' as in Bartley Campbell's play *The White Slave* (1857).

whore [fr. Old English *hōre*] even more taboo than other "forbidden words," this term and *slut* are probably the most universal denigrating terms for 'prostitute.'

woman of easy morals like the following seven entries, a euphemism.

woman of easy virtue an ironic phrase, for "easy virtue" is patently a vice.

woman of ill fame self-evident.

woman of ill repute self-evident.

woman of loose character self-evident.

woman of the street(s) self-evident; cf. *nymphe du pavé, trottoise.*

woman of the town euphemism.

working girl euphemism.

young woman of pleasure a loan-translation of French **fille de joie.**

Synecdochic and metonymic terms:

bag a metaphor for the female pudend or womb?

baggage fr. sixteenth century, *obs.* by 1800; Shakespeare used this word several times in this sense, e.g.:

BAWD. The stuff [i.e., whores] we have, a strong wind will blow it to pieces [a pun?], they are so pitifully sodden [i.e., they have been oversoaked in sweat-tubs as treatment for the pox].

PANDAR. Thou sayest true; they're too unwholesome, o' conscience. The poor Transylvanian is dead, that lay with the little baggage. (*Pericles* 4.2.18–23)

barber's chair an allusion to the phrase, "as common as a barber's chair" 'fit for common use' (Partridge); British, seventeenth through nineteenth centuries; *obs.*

bat 'a prostitute who works at night'; British, seventeenth through nineteenth centuries; U.S. *slang,* ca. 1920; *obs.*

bit of fluff twentieth-century slang.

bit of muslin slang of ca. 1873; *obs.*

bit of mutton nineteenth through twentieth-century slang.

bitch 'a lewd or immoral woman; slut,' fr. ante 1400.

blue gown British, ca. 1913; *obs.*

canary 'mistress,' eighteenth through nineteenth centuries; as cant, "harlot"; *obs.*

cat seventeenth through nineteenth centuries; *obs.*

chippy, chippie 'a bold, sexually promiscuous woman,' fr. the primary meaning, "the chipping sparrow"; U.S. slang fr. ca. 1890, and a "forbidden word" according to Mencken.

fox *obs.* in the sense of 'prostitute'; now refers to any eyesome female.

fruit 'readily picked' (like so much fruit), hence 'an easily obliging girl or woman,' since ca. 1910.

glue neck 'a filthy harlot', U.S. slang fr. ca. 1920; cf. *glued* 'affected with venereal disease'.

goods 'a white slave'.

hay-bag 'something to lie upon,' but perhaps also suggestive of an old whore's appearance; fr. 1850, now mainly U.S. slang.

heifer U.S. slang fr. ca. 1920 (cf. *heifer den* 'brothel').

hot beef nineteenth-century slang.

hot meat nineteenth-century slang.

hot mutton nineteenth-century slang.

jade fr. the primary meaning, 'a worn-out horse'.

light skirt 'a loose woman,' late nineteenth through early twentieth century.

loose fish current in nineteenth century; *obs.*

nag same as **jade**.

piece 'girl' fr. fourteenth century; 'harlot' fr. ca. 1580 to ca. 1830.

piece of goods same as preceding.

piece of muslin British, ca. 1875–1910.

piece of mutton seventeenth century to early nineteenth century.

piece of trade self-evident.

pig 'a slovenly whore'; twentieth-century U.S. slang.

rainbow perhaps fr. the colorful dress of prostitutes; British *slang* fr. ca. 1820 to ca. 1870.

rip 'a worn-out worthless horse'; cf. **jade** and **nag**.

skirt 'woman,' but also 'harlot', since to skirt means 'to be a harlot', as does to *flutter a skirt* (Partridge); nineteenth through twentieth centuries.

sloop of war nineteenth-century British slang; obs.

soiled dove twentieth-century southern U.S. slang.

stew 'a whore', but more commonly 'a bordello'.

twist 'a light woman', U.S. slang fr. ca. 1890; *obs.*

wagtail fr. the species of bird—the term is suited to prostitutes in describing a come-hither walk; British slang of seventeenth through eighteenth centuries.

Eponyms:

Aspasia consort of Pericles; though she was not actually a hetaera, "dour biographers call her an adventuress" (Partridge); hence the common conception.

Delilah perfidious and treacherous mistress of Samson.

Doll Tearsheet an apparently luetic harlot in Shakespeare's *2 Henry IV*; Falstaff says to her: "If the cook help to make the gluttony, you help to make the diseases, Doll. We catch of you, Doll, we catch of you." (2.4.44–46).

Jane Shore ca. 1445–1527; mistress of King Edward IV, of William, Baron Hastings (beheaded by Richard III), and of Thomas Grey, first Marquis of Dorset.

Jezebel fr. Queen Jezebel, wife of Ahab—"used figuratively for a bold-faced, evil prostitute or bedizened woman of not invincible virtue" (Partridge).

Kate proverbial name for prostitutes; current ca. 1860, and later used especially for popular harlots.

Kate Keepdown a pregnant prostitute referred to by Mistress Overdone in Shakespeare's *Measure for Measure* (3.2.199–201).

Laïs several famous hetaerae of ancient Greece had this name— one was regarded as the most beautiful woman of her age; "Laïs" was used proverbially as a name for a woman of great pulchritude.

Messalina the dissolute wife of the Emperor Claudius of Rome; "her name has become a byword for lasciviousness" (Brewer).

Mistress Dorothy Pistol's alternative name for Doll Tearsheet in *2 Henry IV*:

PISTOL. Then to you, Mistress Dorothy, I will charge you.
DOLL. Charge me? I scorn you, scurvy companion. What,

you poor, base, rascally, cheating, lack-linen mate! Away, you
mouldy rogue, away! I am meat for your master. (2.4.121–26)

Mistress Overdone another of Shakespeare's suggestively
named bawds; this procuress is introduced in act 1, scene 2 of
Measure for Measure.

Mistress Quickly fr. Shakespeare's *1 Henry IV, 2 Henry IV,*
and *The Merry Wives of Windsor* (she is Hostess Quickly in the
last-mentioned play); the name is perhaps a pun on "quick lay";
her malapropisms in *The Merry Wives* include *fartuous* for *vir-
tuous* (2.2.94), *infection* for *affection* (2.2.111), *erection* for *direction* (3.5.39), and *speciously* for *especially* (4.5.108).

Moll Flanders known primarily as a pickpocket, she is also a
character of loose sexuality who is sometimes misconceived as a
harlot, though she never solicits; fr. Defoe's novel of that name
(1722).

Mrs. Warren in Shaw's *Mrs. Warren's Profession* (1898), the
eponymous prostitute plies her trade to support her unwitting
daughter.

Phryne a Greek hetaera who "acquired so much wealth that
she offered to rebuild the walls of Thebes if she might put on
them this inscription: 'Alexander destroyed them, but Phryne the
hetaera rebuilt them' " (Brewer).

Sadie Thompson fr. the character in *Rain,* Somerset
Maugham's play (itself based on his short story "Miss Thompson") in which a South Seas missionary first proselytizes the harlot Sadie Thompson, and then prostitutes her; he kills himself in
anguish and remorse.

Thaïs an Athenian hetaera of the fourth century B.C. who accompanied Alexander the Great to Persia, later becoming the concubine of Ptolemy I, King of Egypt; another courtesan of this
name lived in Alexandria in the first century B.C. and became a

nun—she resisted being seduced by her converter (perhaps thereby averting for this man the fate of Sadie Thompson's pious lover).

Theodora a Byzantine empress who, according to the *Secret History of Procopius,* which some historians consider a dubious source, was an actress and prostitute before her marriage to Justinian I; originally a Cyprian, she represents the reformed harlot who becomes eminently successful.

Foreignisms not fully naturalized:

bona-roba [Italian] 'good stuff.'

chère amie [French] a euphemism.

dame de compagnie [French] 'a lady of companionship', i.e., one who is paid for it.

fille de joie [French] cf. daughter of joy, pleasure girl, etc.

grisette [fr. French *grisette* 'cheap gray woolen cloth often used in dresses'] 'a working-class girl who combines prostitution with another job'.

lorette [fr. *Notre Dame de Lorette,* a section of Paris] 'one of the select class of Parisian courtesans during the Second Empire'; because of this term and the ironic ambiguity of *nun,* the respectable *Loretto Nun* may invite literary double entendres.

mui-tsai [fr. Chinese for 'younger sister'] analogous to **white slave.**

nymphe du pavé [French] 'a streetwalker'; cf. nymph of the pavement, its calque.

petite dame [French] literally, 'small woman'; akin to *mignonne.*

poule [French] literally, 'a chicken, hen'.

trottoise [French] same as **nymphe du pavé.**

Thunderboxes and Chuggies

DANIEL BALADO-LOPEZ

In semantic terms, the words in the above title belong to a specific domain in the English vocabulary with which every member of the human race achieves intimate familiarity. The naked terms for such a traditionally taboo subject as "the toilet" have always proved too much to bear for polite society, which hastily covered the bare-cheeked shame of them with a blanket of euphemism. The domain is a prolific nursery of such linguistic fig-leaves, and as a result (contrary thing that human nature is) has also fostered many ribald versions. It is not surprising, therefore, that there is an almost inexhaustible supply of paraphrases and synonymous terms in this field, ranging from the most tasteful euphemism to the most flagrant vulgarity. While most of these bear testament to the wonderful versatility of the English language and the rich vein of humor that runs through our culture, some necessitate etymological investigation in order to uncover their roots and, in some cases, to explore changes in meaning. Most, indeed, defy precision in the attempt altogether.

Six hundred years ago, toilet designs, though crude, were what we might term today *latrines* (the Middle English word was *laterin* from Latin *latrina*): planks of wood with circles cut into them, placed over a ditch. Conveniences for the wealthier sections of the community (i.e., those who could afford high-rise property) consisted of straight-drop or long-drop privies. The word *privy* is one of the earliest euphemisms used in England; an anonymous writer at the turn of the fifteenth century advised "whanne he sitteth at privy he schal not streyne him-silf to harde." It is derived from the French word *privé* and the Latin *privatus,* both meaning 'private', and this is the specific sense in which the word entered the English language. The earliest euphemisms documented use of the word in this original sense of intimacy or familiarity between people dates from 1225, and *privy council* (a small group of advisers to the monarch) from 1300, when Edward I established it. It is not surprising, semantically speaking, that the word widened its meaning so quickly since it naturally lent itself (as did *closet*) to the description of a solitary place, one where people performed lavatorial functions.

Privy and *closet* are examples of euphemism by metonymy, which is the substitution of the name of an attribute of a thing for the thing itself: A toilet is a private place, therefore a privy. Similarly, Bombay furniture (a style combining European forms with Indian ornamentation) provided the metonymic euphemism *The Bombay*; the *Oxford English Dictionary* tells us that the name is possibly attributable to the *Bombay chair,* wherein chamberpots were placed, as it was common in the past to have one's chamberpot concealed in a piece of furniture, which could then be proudly displayed. The name *close-stool,* which makes an appearance in Shakespeare's *All's Well That Ends Well* of 1606 and John Florio's *Montaigne* of 1603, was also inspired by the furniture in which it was cased, as was *commode.*

If one is to go by Florio's use of *close-stool,* it seems interchangeable with another, less notorious, term for a privy, the *ajax.* In the sixteenth century, an Elizabethan courtier, Sir John Harrington, invented a water-closet with a flushing system and wrote a book on the subject entitled *A Metamorphosis of Ajax,* published in 1596. The word, however, seems to have existed before that, as Shakespeare uses it, also in close conjunction with *close-stool*, in *Love's Labour's Lost*, c. 1593, and it achieved an entry in Cotgrave's *Dictionarie of the French and English Tongues* of 1611. Its exact origin is unascertained, but it is likely to have been a variant of *jakes* (with the indefinite article preceding it). *Jakes* is also of unknown origin; the most common suggestion for its roots is in the proper name *Jacques* or *Jack*, which is not unbelievable when we consider other examples such as *jerry* and *john*. Shakespeare uses *jakes* confidently in *King Lear* (c. 1605):

My lord, if you will give me leave, I will tread this unbolted villain into mortar, and daub the wall of a jakes with him.

Eric Partridge, in *A Dictionary of Slang and Unconventional English*, suggested that the word dates from 1530 and was standard English until about 1750, when it became a colloquial term. The word was also very much alive in the late nineteenth and early twentieth centuries in the dialect of southwestern England, where it had come to mean any type of filth or litter, according to Elworthy's *A West Somerset Word-Book*. Patridge also says that the term is now obsolete, but to this day the blocks of toilets at my old school, St. Edmund's College in Hertfordshire, are affectionately known as "Jakes Tower."

The origin of *jerry*, like so many of these terms, can only be guessed at. It is slang for *chamberpot* and, like *jakes*, could be the familiar variant of a proper name (*Jeremiah* or *Jeremy*). It is supposed, however, that it is an abbreviation for *jeroboam*, which started off life as a large bowl for holding wine [I Kings 11.28/ 14.16]; the addition of the suffixes *-y*, *-ie*, and *-ey* to the main stem of a word have always been popular ways of forming diminutives. *Jerry* first appeared in Hotten's *Dictionary of Slang* in 1859, defined as "a chamber utensil." In *An Etymological Dictionary of Modern English*, Ernest Weekly suggested an even earlier association with the word *jordan*, a medieval alchemist's vessel and, later, a chamberpot. All these are feasible surmises by the process of metonymy. Perhaps it hails from a shortening of *jerry-shop* (c. 1851), a term used to describe a low beer-house. As the chamberpot is a great friend to those with bibulous tendencies, *jerry* might have become a pet-name for it.

The etymology of the word *loo* is perhaps the greatest mystery of all in this field of vocabulary. The word first gained general usage in Britain during World War II, and possibly came about as a result of fraternizing with French troops, perhaps as a corruption of *l'eau* (water) or *lieux d'aisance* (water-closet), or even as a derivation of the cry (*Garde á l'eau!*, given to warn passersby that someone above was about to slop out (the anglicised form, *gardyloo!*, occurs in this context in a novel by Tobias Smollett as early as 1771). Also at that time, rustic laborers in Italy used to have the number 100 painted on their privy-doors; to go *al numero cento* was an accepted idiom of the day: indeed, children used to have fun replacing the last zero with a one after the privy had been used. The number 100 is not dissimilar in appearance to the word *loo*, and there were plenty of servicemen from the U.S.A. and England in Italy from 1943 onwards.

Among the more incredible explanations (as recorded by Adrian Room, *A Dictionary of True Etymologies*) are a derivation from *ablution* or *luliana* [*Daily Telegraph*, 13 September 1968] and even from *hallelujah*, as prompted by a caption to a cartoon by Du Maurier in *Punch* [22 June 1895], which read "Now we'll begin again at the Hallelujah, and please linger longer on the 'lu'!" A more promising story to note is that of a corruption of the word *lee*: for those working in the country, a place for relieving oneself was always chosen out of the bite of the wind, that is, in the lee.

Terms such as *toilet* and *lavatory* have, like *privy*, undergone pejoration over the years (that is, their meanings have acquired depreciatory connotations). The original meaning of *lavatory* was simply a vessel for washing: In his 1382 translation of the Bible, John Wycliffe talks of washing feet in "a brasun lavatorie" [Exodus 30.18]. Similarly, to perform one's "toilet" in 1681 was "the action or process of dressing or of washing and grooming" *[OED]*. An unclear sense-development of this word is mapped out in the *OED*, but it seems to concede that the modern sense of *lavatory* originated at the start of this century: The (British) Army and Navy Stores catalogue of 1926 lists a *lavatory paper-holder* as one of its items, but it was probably earlier; *The Illustrated London News* reported in 1860 that each ward of the new Florence Nightingale School of Nursing had "its own bathroom, lavatories and closet." While *toilet* and *lavatory* have discarded their original meanings, terms such as *bog* retained their original meanings ('a marshy place') as well as being understood in Britain as a slang synonym for a toilet; it achieved an entry in Hotten's dictionary as early as 1864 as "a privy as distinguished from a water-closet."

Terms which border on the vulgar tend to be onomatopoeic: examples include *chuggie, duffs, dubs, biffy, honk,* and *thunder-box.* The last example (Eric Partridge tells us) is a nickname for a chamberpot originating in India c. 1870, and is "derived from the noise therein caused." By far the most numerous group of terms is that which contains words only with a localized meaning. It would be impossible to compile a definitive glossary for this group, but a few examples follow: *the heads* (naval colloquialism, dating from the late nineteenth century, said to be from the location of the latrines on a ship); *the longs* (pet-name for latrines at Brasenose College, Oxford, from c. 1870, so-called because they were built from funds donated by a certain Lady Long); and *greenhouses* (*Ulysses,* book 8), James Joyce's personal slang for the public toilets after the color of their paint. It is this group that ensures steady growth in this most malleable domain of the English vocabulary, for the resources of the human imagination are limitless.

SIC! SIC! SIC!

"Child grows into sweater." From a headline in the *New York Daily News,* 30 November 1982. Submitted by Bernard Witlieb, White Plains, New York, who comments, *"Perhaps his bones began to knit."*

Assing Around

JESSY RANDALL AND WENDY WOLOSON

The word *ass* appears in American slang in multiple ways with multiple meanings. It has a rich and varied history and can signify anything from *good* to *bad* to *more.* A mildly transgressive word, *ass* is not quite as serious as *shit* or *fuck*—it is more of a humorously vulgar word, but certainly "dirty," especially when paired with the anatomical specificity of -*hole.* And because *ass* is so short it is easily combinable with other words, making it quite versatile. What also lends to *ass*'s character, especially as a curse word, is its sound. The almost hiss of the *ss* allows for particularly colorful emphasis in many expressions.

Historically, the word *ass* referred to the donkey, an animal representing "clumsiness, ignorance, and stupidity"[1] in many early folktales; the word *arse* referred to the buttocks. In England, *arse* is still used more than *ass* to identify that body part. Over time, *ass* gained a third meaning in addition to the donkey and the buttocks: synecdoche for the entire body. The first two meanings are usually employed as insults, and the second has a more general usage.

Ass referring to a four-legged equine has been around since at least the year 1000; as a stupid, clumsy beast since about 1200. Shakespeare wrote in *A Midsummer Night's Dream* (late sixteenth century), "This is to make an asse of me, to fright me, if they could."[2] Sir George Etheridge, in his seventeenth century poem "Song (If She Be Not as Kind as Fair)," wrote "I would not have thee such an ass, / Hadst thou ne'er so much leisure, / To sigh and whine for such a lass / Whose pride's above her pleasure."[3] And as recently as 1998, the word *ass* used even in this relatively innocuous way caused Anne Frank's *Diary of a Young Girl* (written in the 1940s) to be challenged at a Texas middle school: Parents objected to the sentence "what a silly ass I am!"[4] This kind of usage is probably the most common and, the Anne Frank case above notwithstanding, the mildest. It continues to be found today in the mainstream business cliché "When you *assume* you make an *ass* out of *u* and *me.*"

Of course, *ass* is often used to refer to the ass: that is, the buttocks, the gluteus maximus, the hindquarters, the butt, the bottom, the tushy, the rear-end. (We could go on all day with other terms for this part of the body—but such a digression would last for paragraphs.) "He's got a nice ass" is fairly straightforward, as is "he pinched my ass." But then there's being a *tightass,* which suggests literally that the person in question is constipated and figuratively that the person is a prig or a tightwad—refusing to let go of even worthless things such as waste. To "keep a tight asshole," in military terminology, means to stay cool and to avoid panic and the diarrhea associated with it.[5] Having "a stick up his/her ass" has a related but more pejorative connotation—in this case, the person is rigid and anchored, can't relax or have fun.[6]

Strangely, a reference to the ass part of the body can be a statement of skepticism. The response *my ass* expresses the thought "I don't believe you," also known as "you're pulling my leg." (The G-rated version of *my ass* is *my foot*.)[7]

Ass is also used as synecdoche for the entire human body, so that the ass stands for the person to whom the ass belongs: *Get your ass in here, Quit dragging your ass, Watch your ass,* and *Cover your ass* (often abbreviated in professional dialogue as *CYA*). And if you are a *candy-ass,* you are a person who is wimpy, perhaps even feminine, whose ass—and entire body—is easily taken by bullies.

The word can also be used as an adjective-intensifier, as in *cool-ass, lame-ass, dumb-ass,* and the title of the television program *Bob Goldthwait's Big-Ass Show. Ass* here has no positive or negative meaning; it functions like the modifier *very. Ass-out,* in hip-hop culture, has the same meaning.[8] One can also go about things *ass-backwards* (which becomes *back-asswards* or *bass-ackwards*), which is a more extreme form of just backwards.

Similarly, *ass* can be used to intensify verbs: *Freezing your ass off* is worse than just freezing; *falling on your ass* is an exaggerated form of falling, with a certain amount of humor and humiliation attached. *Working your ass off* is the most difficult form of working; there is no further amount you can work. (Conversely, of course, if you do a *half-assed* job—as opposed to whole-assed?— you have taken a cavalier attitude and not done all you should.) The phrase *sitting on your ass* implies more than just sitting— since, after all, on our asses is where we all do that—but adds the sense of laziness: hyper-sitting. Being *on* or *up* someone's *ass* is not just to follow her, but to be literally on her tail—to follow her too closely.

This brings us to the idea of the ass being an unprotected part of the body, a part that gets *kicked* in a fight or *chapped* in annoyance. (This last is primarily a westernism, where people's asses probably could get chapped from riding horses all day.) Having a *case of the ass,* like having a *chapped ass,* is to experience a state of irritation. *Tearing someone a new asshole* means to light into someone, to severely criticize or hurt him, and comes from military references to bullet wounds; but this phrase should not be confused with *to tear ass,* which means to hurry. If one gets a crazy idea and follows through with it, he is said to have a *wild hair up his ass,* which may lead him to fall *ass-over-teakettle,* or *-tit,* in confusion. John Steinbeck wrote in his 1938 *Grapes of Wrath,* "You jus' scrabblin' ass over tit, fear somebody gonna pin some blame on you."

If someone wants to fight you, she might say she's going to *kick your ass*; a boxer in a match can be said to have had his *ass kicked* even though the ass is below the belt and therefore off limits in a fair fight. What the phrase contributes in colorfulness it lacks in intensity—after all, the ass is probably the least painful area to be kicked. The phrase *I'm going to kick his ass* means something different and less severe than the more specific *I'm going to kick him in the teeth* or *kick him in the stomach.* Kicking someone's ass-perhaps shouting *Your ass is grass!*—carries with it an element of playfulness and fun. It is more of a schoolyard boast (as frightening as those may be) than a truly worrisome threat.

Indirectly, *ass* also means the sex organs, especially of women, and becomes synonymous with sex: Men in particular will speak of *getting a piece of ass,* alternately expressed as *a piece of tail.* While the earliest recorded usage of this expression appeared around 1684, more recent occurrences of this phrase are no more genteel: An *ass peddler* was a prostitute or a pimp in the 1940s.[9] This usage has worked its way into literature: John Updike wrote in 1960s *Rabbit, Run,* "Then he comes back from the Army and all he cares about is chasing ass," and Donald Stahl riffed on this usage in *Hokey* in 1968 with, "I've always felt that the quickest way to a woman's heart is up her ass."[10] Interestingly, British English uses *fanny* in a similar way—to mean a woman's vagina. Lawrence Levine, in *Black Culture,* has identified this usage in Black vernacular language as early as the 1910s: "White folks on the sofa, / Niggers on the grass, / White man is talking low / Nigger is getting ass."[11]

These terms are not to be confused with *ass man,* which merely means a man who appreciates and is most attracted to a woman's behind. There is also the more familiar *tits and ass,* shortened to *T and A,* a phrase used to describe something really terrific or cool, as in *That was really tits and ass, buddy*; it can also more directly refer to the pleasure of looking at the actual body parts in question—*Baywatch* is the quintessential T and A television show.[12]

When associated with other parts of the body, *ass* can be particularly demeaning. *Ass-for-face* is a derogatory noun denoting ugliness. But there are other familiar and colorful insults in which *ass* figures prominently. From the refrain *Kiss my ass* to the crude *You asshole,* or, shortened but no less offensive, *a-hole,* (which seems to be applied more to males than to females, despite the equality of ass-ownership by both sexes), there are many unkind things we can say about each other that involve the word *ass.*

These can be related to stupidity or ignorance: When *ass* is connected to speech or thought, it is clearly an insult. *You horse's ass* plays on the sense of donkeylike clumsiness. *Talking out your ass* is talking as if you know what you are talking about when you don't, also known more succinctly as *talking shit.* Similarly, if you're being a *smart-ass,* you're being a wise guy, acting as if you know more than you do. (This expression has a couple of G-rated variations: *smart-aleck, smarty-pants*.) *He's got his head up his ass* and *She doesn't know her ass from her elbow* are other forms of the *ass*-as-stupidity insult. To try to *blow smoke up someone's ass* is to try to fool someone through obfuscation—bullshitting someone, to mix metaphors. While to *pull something out of one's ass* is to create it from out of nowhere.

The list of insults goes on. A person who is annoying is a *pain in the ass* (mildly, *pain in the neck*). Some *ass* insults are scatological—*ass-wipe,* for example. Others are related to sycophantic "brown-nosing": *ass-kisser* (and its reverse, *kiss-ass*), *ass-licker*. A recent e-mail chain-letter of "office vocabulary" included *ass-mosis,* defined as "the process by which some people seem to absorb success and advancement by kissing up to the boss rather than working hard." Most inscrutably, Jimbo calls Nelson *ass-butt* in an episode of the Simpsons, suggesting that the word *ass* is simply a modifier meaning *bad*. But according to contemporary college slang, *butt-ass* means 'very', as in *it's butt-ass cold*.[13]

Even culture brokers themselves have a hard time pinning down the meaning of ass. A recent article in a Philadelphia newspaper[14] claims that *ass* is the new "edgy term to replace *sucky,*" as in "WMMR [a local rock station] is so ass." None of the Philadelphians we have interviewed, however, admits to using this term or even hearing it used, although we all agree that an edgy term to replace *sucky* is highly desirable. We did find evidence to suggest the opposite—that *ass* means *good*, as in the advertisement for a brand of sneakers with a circled *S* logo: "Sketchers—it's the *S*," where the pronunciation *ess* is supposed to sound like *ass*.

Curiously, *ass* can also connote the positive: a *kick-ass* party is the best kind of party. A *badass* is credibly both an adjective and a noun: a person who is tough but cool is a *badass,* and something that is really awesome can also be *badass*. And speaking of fun, *assing about* or *assing around* is an old-ish phrase for having fun or goofing off: Eric Partridge notes that *to ass* (or *arse*) *about* was a common schoolboys' expression by 1910 in Britain, and James Joyce wrote of "arsing around from one pub to another" in 1922s *Ulysses*.[15] (We wonder if this usage relates to "horsing around" or horseplay.) Another Britishism used by schoolboys is the expression *can't be assed* (or *arsed*) to do a particular task, meaning "can't be bothered."

So what, then, can we make of *ass* as used in its myriad contexts of insult, praise, and objectification? For such a small word it gets around, being exchanged in our vernacular language like common currency. It will be interesting to see its twenty-first-century incarnations, although it is probable that they will have precedents dating back hundreds of years. And we're not just talking out our asses when we say that.

Deciphering the Four-Letter Word in a Medieval Manuscript's Satire on Friars

CARTER REVARD

The English may now reclaim from the Scots the honor, if such it be, of being the first to put the popular quadriliteral into writing. As one might expect, however, they used a bastard form of the word, and they wrote it only in cipher: Thus, even though the poem containing this coded occurrence has been in print for a hundred and forty years, the Victorian scholar who printed it with full knowledge of what he was printing, but who left it to his readers to decipher the medieval scribe's code, could certainly have felt that the public would not be corrupted by the word, and it was left to D. H. Lawrence and others to curl the aspidistra permanently.

As for the Scots' claim to primacy in this matter, it rests on the shoulders of William Dunbar, whose poem of ca. 1502 was the first instance which the editors of the *OED's Revised Supplement,* volume 1 (1972), could find of a written use of the word. However, a British Museum manuscript, Harley 3362, contains among its many jokes, proverbs, riddles, and pious poems a group, on folio 24r (old numbering p. 47), which vigorously vituperate friars. Certain lines of this invective are written in a cipher or code, and when deciphered one word among these is *fuccant,* which in context is indubitably our word, though it has been given a mock-Latin form (with participial-*ant*) in keeping with the macaronic language of the lines in which it occurs.[1]

These lines were first printed in 1845 by Thomas Wright, in his *Reliquiae Antiquae* (Vol. 1, pp. 91–92). Since they have not been reprinted, I shall present them here, before discussing their contents, date, and some problems concerning them.

    1 fflen flyys and freris / populum domini male caedunt,
      þustlis and breris/crescentia gramina ledunt.
      Xriste, nolens guerras, / sed cuncta pace tueris,
      Destrue per terras / breris flen flyȝes & freris.
    5 fflen flyȝes and freris / Foul falle hem þys fyften ȝeris,
      ffor'non þat her ys / louit flen flyȝes ne freris.
      Fratres carmeli / nauigant in a both apud Eli;
      Non sunt in celi / quia gxddbov xxkxxȝt pg ifmk—
      Omnes drencherunt / quia sterisman non habuerunt.

10 ffratres cum knyuys / goþ about and txxkxʒv
        nfookt xxʒxkt.

    Ex Eli veniens presenti / sede locatur,

    Nec rex nec sapiens, / Salomon tamen vocatur.

    Pediculus cum sex / pedibus me mordet vbique;

14 Si possum capere / tokl tobl debet ipsem habere.

Lines 1 through 6 here attack friars generally, while lines 7 through 10 verberate the Carmelite Friars of Ely particularly. Wright made the interesting point that in his day, "two lines ... are still popular among schoolboys in the following modified form: *Tres fratres coeli navigabant roundabout Ely; Omnes drownderunt qui swimaway non potuerunt,*" and he further remarked that "the expressions concealed by the cypher ... are rather gross, and do not speak much for the morals of the Carmelites of Ely."[2] This remark set me to examining the cipher, of course, and I succeeded in decoding it. It merely involves substitution of the next letter in the alphabet, so that if the encipherer began with an *a,* he would write *b,* if with a *b,* he wrote *c,* and so on.[3] Thus, in line 8, *gxddbov xxkxx\ʒ\t pg ifmk* is written for *fuccant uuiuis of Heli,* with *fuccant* formed on the same lines as *drencherunt* in the next line (9). The friars of Ely, according to the poem, will never get to heaven, because they are *fuccant* the wives of Ely. To this elegant criticism the rhymer ads that they will all drown because they have no *steersman*—no doubt a double entendre—and further, that friars with knives are going around and swiving men's wives, this being of course the same assertion made by most critics of the ubiquitous medieval friars, as for instance in Chaucer's General Prologue to the *Canterbury Tales,* where he describes the Friar as having his hood *ay farsed ful of knyves / And pynnes, for to yeven faire wyves.*

We observe that our medieval scribe has enciphered not only

fuccant, but also *suuiuit*. Obviously these words were synonymous at this time, and the modern version had not yet pushed
out the older *swive* as yet.[4] But this brings us to the important
question: Just when was the poem written, or at least when was
it written into the manuscript?

Inspection of the script and hand shows that it could have been
almost any time in the middle or later fifteenth century. Use of
þ (thorn) and \ʒ\ (yogh) would seem to rule out a dating in later
sixteenth century, but it is not possible to assign a precise date
on palaeographic grounds alone, and I have not had time to look
for historical references or other evidence that might pin down
the date of transcription. Wright said the date was "of the fifteenth century," and this is Max Förster's opinion also (*Anglia*
vol. 42, 1918, pp. 198, 207), though *Förster* specifies that the MS
is of the latter part of the century, i.e., ca. 1450–1500. And editors
of the *Middle English Dictionary* have also assigned a date of ca.
1500 to the MS.; in my opinion, the date is palaeographically
more likely to have been ca. 1450–75 than 1500. In any event, it
is almost certainly as early as Dunbar's poem, and very probably
earlier by some years.

But a final problem must be spoken to: Why did the scribe
encipher those passages? One might simply think he was keeping
these naughty words away from uninitiated eyes, and perhaps
that is the case. But if so, then why did he also use the cipher in
line 14 (the last one given above) for the words describing what
he will do to the lice biting him if he can catch them? Those
words, as we see by deciphering *tokl tobl*, are just *snik snak*, and
it is hard to see why the poet or scribe should have thought them
obscene enough to put the fig leaf of his cipher over them. Perhaps, of course, *snik-snak* was accompanied by an obscene gesture, of a sort not hard to imagine, and the audience would have
rolled in the aisles at the thought of doing that to a body-louse.

Which brings us, surely, to the realization that the cipher is meant not to conceal as much as to reveal. Like a bikini, it is meant to draw attention rather than baffle it. *Snik-snak* put straightforwardly onto the page is not half so funny as *tokl-tobl* becomes, when one has the *Aha!* pleasure added to the *Yeah!* one: It is the slight stammer of the humorist before he gets the right word out, making the joke funnier. Now, I might be wrong; but the cipher is so *very* simple, and the whole point of a riddle is to have an answer, after all. So it is my opinion that the medieval scribe here was not really showing how shameful the words seemed to him but adding a little extra spice to the joke of using the words about friars. Instead of *obeying* a taboo, that is, the scribe was *exploiting* it: This is a case of what Allen Walker Read (in *Language,* vol. 40, no. 2, April–June 1964, pp. 162–66) has called "a type of ostentatious taboo." In fact, what the scribe was doing is very like what we do when we print "f——k" while expecting that every reader will know that the word meant is— well, you-know-what! We have lately enriched our vocabularies in this area, too, with the word *bleep (bleeping),* which has replaced earlier *blank, blankety-blank,* not to mention *s.o.b.* and the like. Who knows? We may soon see, with returning censorship, ciphers replacing these acronyms and replacements.

SIC! SIC! SIC!

"A person shall not be treated as suffering from physical disablement such that he is either unable to walk or virtually unable to do so if he is not unable or virtually unable to walk with a prosthesis or an artificial aid which he habitually wears or uses or if he would not be unable or virtually unable to walk if he habitually wore or used a prosthesis or an artificial aid which is suitable in his case." From a (U.K.) Department of Health and Social Services explanation regarding mobility allowances for the disabled, as reported in a letter in *The Daily Telegraph*, 30 October 1983. Submitted by Edward G. Taylor, Tangier, Morocco.

The Ineffable F—r-Letter Word

BENEDICT B. KIMMELMAN

In an essay published recently in a history journal, the editor substituted "foul ups" for the correct term I had used in referring to certain incidents witnessed during army days. For quoting a Vietnam-era line of graffiti, "Fighting for peace is like fxxxing (my cryptic spelling throughout) for chastity," the witty columnist Molly Ivins was blasted in a long letter to the editor of *The Progressive*. In contrast, we have the story about the ten-year-old who, caving in to the nagging of his ever-suspicious grandmother, admits that his grandfather did indeed let slip a "dirty" word (*shmuck*) on their fishing trip, but won't quote it: "What I can tell you is that it rhymes with fxxx." And there is the story of the touching letter in a shaky script from a ninety-year-old in the nursing home, thanking the community service people for the gift of the transistor radio with earpiece that freed her from having to share the radio of her roommate, Mrs. Hamady, and now she can tell Mrs. Hamady "to go fxxx herself."

My interest in the life and times of the word stems directly from a recollected bit of army business during World War II. In early 1942, a bizarre directive came down from on high, one of a kind in the memory of army "lifers," or regulars. Issued by Lt. General MacNair, commander of all U.S. ground troops, it stated that less authoritarianism and greater courtesy must thenceforth characterize all orders to enlisted men, and it closed with "the day of the shouting sergeant is over." It was to be read to all formations. Our regimental commander used the opportunity to append an order of his own to all company-grade officers to make special efforts "forthwith" to eliminate the use of obscene language in their commands.

As a junior officer in charge of an infantry medical detachment, this assignment was mine. On a muggy morning in Camp Livingston, Louisiana, the regular business of reveille completed by 6:30, I read out General MacNair's directive.

"Any questions?"

"Question, sir!"

"Yes, Sergeant Willard." This was an "old" national guardsman of thirty, a barker, heart and soul of the outfit.

"May I say, sir," shouting, "that when the day of the shouting sergeant is over, on that day the army will have died, sir!" preceded and followed by the snappiest salute in that man's army.

"Thank you, Sergeant Willard. Now—any questions?"

Nothing but grinning faces. "I will now read the order of the regimental commanding officer. Subject: obscene language. To: All regimental personnel." There followed a paragraph linking decent language and decent conduct. I wound up with, "You know what that means. From now on, the *fxxx* word is taboo! Dismissed!" No questions solicited.

Perhaps three seconds of perfect silence. Then the dam burst.
"Taboo you, Thorp!"
"Where's Taboo-up Metcalf?"
"You're asking for it, Taboo-face!"
"Delgado, get this tabooing morning report to regimental!"
It became a party.

Nearly three years later, in January 1945, I arrived as a POW
at Stalag IV B, in Muhleberg, East Germany, part of a battered
lot of several hundred American soldiers trapped and finally
taken prisoner in the Battle of the Bulge. Stalag IV B housed
mostly British enlisted men, about seven thousand at the time,
and though the camp never attained the notoriety of some other
grim stalags, it entered the literature unnamed in *Slaughterhouse-
Five*, the novel by Kurt Vonnegut. The portrayal of the camp and
the reception by the British POWs, camouflaged though it is, is
so vivid that on reading it when it appeared in 1969—and since—
I have found myself transported back there, frozen feet and all.

. . . out marched 50 middle-aged Englishmen.

They were singing, "Hail, Hail the Gang's all Here" . . .
These lusty ruddy vocalists were among the first English-
speaking prisoners to be taken in the Second World War. Now
they were singing to nearly the last . . . The Englishmen were
clean and enthusiastic and decent and strong . . . They were
adored by the Germans, who thought they were exactly what
Englishmen ought to be.

The Englishmen had never had guests before and they went
to work like darling elves, sweeping, mopping, cooking, bak-
ing . . .

There was silence now, as the Englishmen looked in astonishment at the frowzy creatures they had so lustily waltzed

inside . . . "My God, what have they done to you, lad? This isn't a man. It's a broken kite!"

—*Slaughterhouse-Five or The Children's Crusade*, Delta Book, Dell Publishing Co., 1969, pp. 80–84.

The take-charge British prisoners dazzled us, as they had Vonnegut's Billy Pilgrim. Bedraggled, starving, and exhausted after a final four days crushed in box cars, we were, I learned later, the most disheartening lot of ragmen they had seen in their more than three years of imprisonment. Responding in the tradition of trained British "ranks," they radiated full responsibility, herding us to plank tables, scurrying about like a choreographed swarm of caterers. Their boots were polished and their worn tunics had all their buttons. These were the remnants of the defenders of Tobruk—Tobruk in the North African desert—in the year 1941, when the Allies were losing the war! To me, they were creatures from a lost planet, another world. They served us tea in "Klim" tins, and a cracker each. They indulged our incoherent questions and smiled reassurances. They returned us to life.

An impeccable, mustachioed Sergeant Major MacMahan, gaunt like all the others, wearing the beret and polished insignia of a Scots regiment, stood erect as a flagpole at one end of the barrack hut surveying it all, the angel in charge. To his deputy, carefully doling hot water from a canteen cup into a row of small tins, he snapped, "Mind the measuring now, there's twenty-fxxxing-four to serve 'ere!"

I heard it. Whatever my state till then, I knew I was not now hallucinating. That was the first I had ever heard the word used as a "bridge." It was snapped out loud and clear, after the fashion of the proper British soldier, with none of the slurring so characteristic of the American using it as an adjective. (Compare "y'r *fxn* well told" with "you're *fxxxing* well told, ole boy!") I was in no condition to be charmed. But impressed—I was forever impressed.

After a few days, befriended and coached by these veterans of a different time and a different kind of war, most of us revived enough to make do behind the barbed wire in the blighted landscape. Assigned after some weeks to a few hours per week in the makeshift dental clinic in the prison revier, or hospital, I took to busying myself during the great gaps of empty time by searching out and putting on paper British army-language specials, like *mucker* 'partner', *scoff* 'overeat', *fluff* 'girl', *skilly* 'meal', *griff* 'rumor', *duff* 'dessert'. Most numerous and engaging by far were the novel (to me) uses of the ubiquitous, all purpose Anglo-American word *fxxx.*

Hearing of my hobby, the prison "editor" paid a visit. With a willing little group of helpers he periodically put out the prison "newspaper." This was a wall poster containing innocuous camp news items, all painstakingly penned by hand. A new issue was unveiled to a hungry readership about once every six months. The suggestion by the editor, Eric Hurst, that I work up my lexicon on *fxxx* for the forthcoming issue was a great boost. I felt a sense of real purpose in mining for new specimens in conversations with these old "kriegies" (POWs) from almost everywhere in the world where the King's and everyone else's English and American were spoken. I was also the beneficiary of special contributions from numbers of users and listeners who had never previously felt the pull of scholarship.

Reviewing our completed lexicon, Hurst and his colleagues pronounced it a respectable body of work, acceptable for publication in the newspaper. It never made it, however. Just one week later, elements of Marshal Konev's First Ukrainian Army liberated the camp and to our great joy, the world of the prison newspaper ceased to exist for us.

Though the manuscript remained out of sight yellowing in a footlocker for forty-three years, the work was never completely out of mind, recalled on occasions when some special item caught ear or eye. For example, there was the title of the popular British film of the 1970s, with Dirk Bogarde, *I'm Allright, Jack* (see *Fujiyama*, Lexicon), and the name borne by a boutique in downtown Philadelphia, "Sweet Fanny Adams" (see *Sweet Fxxx-all*, Lexicon). Special mention should be made of the fact that there are some items in this lexicon similar to those in the classic *Dictionary of Slang and Unconventional English*, by Eric Partridge (eighth edition, 1984), which first appeared in 1937. Luckily for the lofty sense of purpose which infused and inspired us, none of us knew of its existence then. Except for the elimination of several redundant items, this is the lexicon produced in 1945.

Lexicon

Fxxx [*Anglo-American*]
Noun. 1. A lesser individual, usually male, undistinguished. Patronizing or pejorative: *He's just a simple (dumb) fxxx. Hello, little fxxx!* (in response to *"What do you say to a little fxxx?"*, anecdotal.)

2. The sex act.

3. An item or transaction of little worth: *a poor fxxx of an alibi.*

Verb. 1. To betray, cheat, destroy, reject, ruin, sabotage, stymie, swindle, terminate, wreck: *Churchill tried to fxxx the deal on the second front.*

2. To engage in the sex act.

Derivatives:

Fxxx her, — him, — it, — them. [*Anglo-American*] Declaration. Command or suggestion to defy, disobey, disregard, reject the claims of—. Dismissive, rather than condemnatory of—: *Fxxx'm! What can a foul ball like that do to you? "Fxxx 'em all, fxxx 'em all, / The long and the short and the tall"* [Opening lines of a familiar song].

See also final example cited under **Fxxxin'**, 1.

Fxxx! [*Anglo-American*] Expletive, oath, or exclamation expressing anger, disappointment, disgust, dismay, rage, as "damn!", with emphasis: *Fxxx! I forgot the password!*

Fxxxin', Fxxx'n [*American*], **Fxxxing** [*British*]. Pres. participle of **fxxx.**

Adjective, adverb. 1. Contemptible, downright, great, notable/notably, outrageous/outrageously, treasured, vexatious: *A fxxx'n terrible* [American], *fxxxing dreadful* [British], *crime! You're fxxx'n well told, Jackson! The sun came out in all its fxxxing glory. Went no place without his fxxx'n walkin' stick. "Fxxx the fxxxing torpedoes, full fxxxing speed ahead,"* as your bloody commodore once said.

2. Used as bridge or connector; new part of speech, to add power or point, enhance tonal quality. Also, **damned, bloody:** *Twenty-fxxxing-four faces to feed. Blame it on your anti-fxxx'n-air craft units, mate.*

3. Participating in the sex act: *If the Lord invented anything better than fxxx'n, He kept it for His-self.* [Army aphorism. American.]

Noun. A crushing (humiliating) defeat, a drubbing, a fleecing, a loss, usually viewed from the receiving end: *We took a right regular fxxxing at Tobruk.*

Derivatives:

F'n, F'ing. Pronounced "effin," "effing." Affected or effete form of **fxxxin',** etc.

N.F.G. [*American*] Abbrev. for *no fxxx'n good.*

Phrase. Noun. An individual, situation or state without any redeeming features; hopeless, incompetent, utterly worthless: *I'm NFG before my coffee in the morning.*

Royal—[*Anglo-American*] Also, **Double—**, **Double—in spades.** [*American*]. *Nouns.* Embellished or emphatic forms of **fxxxing.**

Fxxx-all [*British*]

Compound noun. Nought, empty, state of utter bankruptcy, total disappointment, zero: *The desert is nothing but miles and miles of fxxx-all.*

Derivatives: [*British*]

Fanny Adams, Sweet Fanny Adams. *Noun.* Euphemisms for **fxxx-all.**

F.A., Sweet F.A. *Abbrevs. for* **fxxx-all:** *We had Sweet F.A. for air cover at Dunkirk.*

Go for fxxx-all. *Phrase.* To be done for, finished, obliterated: *Berlin will go for fxxx-all.*

Fxxxer [*Anglo-American*]

Noun. 1. A male individual; one with some minimal identity; a bloke; a joe; faintly noticeable: *The savvy little fxxxer managed to con the medics into a Section 8* ['unfitness disharge'].

2. A frustrating object; a sticky or vexatious problem: *The fxxxer in most PW escape plans is the calories.*

Fxxxface [*American*]

Compound word.

Noun. 1. A fool, a joker, one not held in high regard or likeable: *You can bet ole fxxxface won't be on time* ['won't accomplish—'; 'will fail'].

2. Greeting; form of address, semi-humorously or strongly contemptuous: *What alibi now, Fxxxface?*

Fxxxhead [*American*]

Compound noun.

A cheese head; an easily confused or misled individual; one

"short on the dollar"; scatterbrained; [pejorative, not hostile, implication]: *He'd be just fxxxhead enough to buy that line of who-shot john.*

Fxxx me! [*British*]

Phrase.

Expletive. Announcement of confusion, perplexity, ignorance, as "Damme!" [*British*], "Search me!" [*American*]: *Fxxx me if I know where we're at!*

Fxxx-off! [*Anglo-American*]

Noun (rare). A dodger, evader, shirker, one who is undependable: *That full-time fxxx-off is geared to fly backward.*

Verb. To escape, evade, fade, run, slink away, vanish, when needed: *First incoming shell burst, that clown will fxxx off!*

Fxxxup. [*American.*]

Compound noun. A botcher; bungler; disrupter; failure; one who is ill-coordinated; incapable, or ineffectual; an inept individual; a loser; a spoiler: *That fxxx-up is the boil on this outfit's ass. Section 8 discharge is ordered for this incorrigible company fxxx-up* [From a division surgeon's formal report].

Verb. To confuse; deface; disfigure; disorganize; entangle; make a mess of; snarl; tie up; ruin: *To fxxx up the detail* [classic, American army].

Derivatives:

General fxxx up [*American*] *Noun.* **GFU** (Abbrev.) An individual with a consistent or outstanding record as a *fxxx-up.*

Janfu [*American*] *Noun.* Abbrev. for 'joint army-navy fxxx up'. A failed amphibious military operation considered badly planned and/or executed.

Snafu [*American*]

Noun. Abbrev. for 'situation normal, all fxxxed up'. An obviously ineffectual operation or dire predicament, cynically anticipated because typical; perfect opposite of OK.

Fxxx you! [*Anglo-American*] *Interjection.*

Emphatic negative retort expressing condemnation, defiance, hostility, opposition, refusal, rejection: *As civilians we'll have to get used to using "No thanks!" in place of "Fxxx you!"*
Derivatives:
40! Affected or effete form of **fxxx you.**
402! Anticipated response to **40.**
Fujiyama [*British*] *Phrase.*

Acronym for 'Fxxx you, Jack, I'm all right'. Expression of sole concern for self at expense of partner or ally; abandonment, betrayal.

I'm all right Jack. Alternate form of **Fujiyama.**

Epistolae

In reference to Benedict Kimmelman's article, I should like to submit a polite euphemism in frequent use.

When people try to push ahead of a queue at a bus stop or in a shop, one would politely say to the person, "Get in the far queue."

There is also the famous story of the Fukawi Pygmy tribe who frequently got lost in the jungles of Africa; in order to ascertain their whereabouts, they would stand on another's shoulders to peer over the long grass, crying, "Where the Fukawi?"

RAYMOND HARRIS
London

I am writing primarily to correct and update Benedict Kimmelman's article on the eff-word.

The "popular British film of the 1970s, with Dirk Bogarde, *I'm Allright Jack,*" was, in fact, a popular British film of the late

1950s, *I'm All Right, Jack,* and Dirk Bogarde, who was off in Hollywood being Liszt in the abysmal *Song without End,* wasn't within three thousand miles of it when it was being made.

Further to Mr. Kimmelman's lexicon, I offer a few Australian examples:

fxxxable [*Anglo-Australian*] *Adjective.* Sexually desirable.

fxxxwit [*Australian*] *Noun.* Incompetent person; nincompoop. *You'd have to be a right fxxxwit to print almost every column filler more than once in a small circulation magazine.*

fxxxwitted [*Australian*] *Adjective.* Foolish; stupid. *A fxxxwitted attempt at scholarship without doing thorough research.*

clusterfxxx [*Australo-American*] *Noun.* Collective incompetence, usually by those in authority, bureaucrats, officers; esp. of edicts and recommendations the practicality of which is doubtful, decisions made by committees, etc. *Only a clusterfxxx like the Joint Chiefs would approve an invasion plan that didn't take out the television and radio stations as priority targets.* (To which a British sympathizer might reply, *Absofxxxinglutely!*

Get fxxxed! [*Anglo-Australian*] *Interjection, verb.* Negative reply to an unwelcome suggestion. *If he thinks I going to print his fxxxwitted letter, he can get fxxxed!*

MIKE HARRIS
Palm Beach, New South Wales

Revising the F-Word

JESSE SHEIDLOWER

Writing a book entirely about the word *fuck*, aside from being a good way to guarantee cocktail-party chatter, exposes one to numerous criticisms. Apart from the tiresome "degradation of society" arguments from the puritanical, everyone is familiar with this word in its many forms. Newspapers coyly refer to it with euphemisms and circumlocutions; T-shirt vendors stock shirts emblazoned with its many parts of speech; and everyone has a favorite passage, unusual compound, or offbeat etymological theory to promote.

The original edition of *The F-Word* was a successful project. It included almost all of the important uses of the word, and the introduction gave a good picture of the word's history, both etymological and social. But there is always room for improvement, and so when Random House determined it was time to reprint, we decided that a major revision could be supported. The revision is in progress at the time of this writing, and this is a preliminary report on where things stand.

Historical

Interest in the historical aspect of the word *fuck* has always been high; most reviewers cited various anecdotes from the Introduction. We have accordingly been trying to research and add any relevant or interesting story. The earliest example of *fuck*, appearing in a ciphered version in the fifteenth-century poem "Flen Flyys," has always been a crowd-pleaser, since it is not only in code—suggesting that the word was taboo even at that time—

but describes monks fucking. (Seemingly a popular subject for that era—an early sixteenth-century apostil refers to the poor scribe's "fucking abbot.") The original edition gave sparse details on the background of this poem and translated the cipher without explaining it; even the mainstream *American Heritage Dictionary, Third Edition,* gave more complete treatment. In the new edition, we will give a thorough version of this attestation.

The date of 1926 for the first openly printed use of *fuck* in America—still the earliest we have discovered—provoked the question of the first use of *fuck* in the movies. We are still researching this, but it seems that *fuck* first appeared in mainstream movies around 1970 (*MASH* and *Myra Breckenridge*); it had been used earlier in several avant-garde films. Unlike the literary world, where provocative books such as *Ulysses* or *Lady Chatterley's Lover* led to legal battles over obscenity issues, in the movies, no one tried to place *fuck* onto film until the country was ready for it.

While *fuck* appeared in popular periodicals such as *The Atlantic Monthly, Harper's Magazine, Playboy,* and others by the 1960s, it took a bit more time for the word to, um, penetrate the august pages of *The New Yorker.* The editorship of Tina Brown is usually credited—more usually, faulted—with that journal's frequent use of the word, and though writers did use it frequently under Ms. Brown, in fact *fuck* appeared there, spelled in full, in 1985, during the editorship of the puritan William Shawn, in a short story by Bobbie Ann Mason: "Maybe you have to find out for yourself. Fuck. You can't learn from the past." (3 June, 1985, p. 81).

The etymology of *fuck* has never ceased inspiring comment. The various purported acronymic origins are still the first thing most people think of; we will be expanding our treatment of this, and including the first known appearance of an acronymic etymology (in New York's underground paper *The East Village Other*), in 1967. The most striking recent development has been the popularity of the "pluck yew" story, which conflates the origin of *fuck* with an earlier piece of folklore about the origin of the offensive backhand two-finger gesture. According to the original form of the tale, before the battle of Agincourt, immortalized in Shakespeare's *Henry V,* the French taunted the English longbowmen by waving two fingers at them, saying that those fingers (used to pull back the bowstring) could never defeat the mighty French. After the English annihilated the hapless French (ten thousand dead French to a mere twenty-nine Brits, by Bill S.'s count), the English responded by waving their two fingers back at the French in the now-familiar gesture (the American version limits it to the single middle finger). The recent twist has been to note the fact that longbows are traditionally made of yew wood, and claim that the act of drawing the bowstring was called "plucking yew"; the victorious English not only waved their fingers at the French, but shouted "We can still pluck yew! Pluck yew!" at them. A few convenient sound-changes brought us to our familiar phrase "fuck you."

This story, totally ludicrous in any version, was popularized on the National Public Radio segment "Car Talk," where it was meant as a joke; many unfortunates, particularly on the Internet, have taken it seriously. It will be debunked.

On the serious side, considerably more etymological information will be presented. The editor is grateful to Anatoly Liberman for sharing the entry (and bibliography) for *fuck* from his magnificent forthcoming etymological dictionary. Liberman argues convincingly that the word is part of a large family of Germanic words having the form f + [short vowel] + [stop], having the base meaning 'to move back and forth' (not 'to thrust', as most dictionaries, and the original edition of *The F-Word,* had it). It is probably a borrowing from Dutch, Low German, or Flemish, but not a continuation of an Old English word. He finds no Indo-European cognates (of Latin *futuo* he notes "It is a strange coincidence that Latin *futuo* is also an *f* word").

On the less serious, but still scholarly, side, we will refer to the hilarious *Studies Out in Left Field: Defamatory Essays Presented to James D. McCawley on His 33rd or 34th Birthday.* This remarkable collection applies the principles of transformational grammar to the analysis of sexual and scatalogical vocabulary. Quang Phuc Dong's "English Sentences Without Overt Grammatical Subject" looks at the oft-questioned basis of "fuck you!," whilst Munç Wang's "Copulative Sentences in English: A Germanic Language Spoken in Northern Delaware" studies the grammaticality (in the author's idiolect) of such sentences as "Micky fucked Michelle's cadaver in the ass" (grammatical), "Bret fucked the mannikin through the hole he drilled in its throat" (of questionable grammaticality), and "Fred fucked the log through a hole that squirrels had made" (ungrammatical). The omission of this classic, first published in 1971, is unforgivable.

Least forgivable of all was the omission of Allen Walker Read's 1934 classic "An Obscenity Symbol," the most important article ever written on *fuck,* despite the absence of that word from the article itself (a not uncommon situation in the field, I might add). The decision of the editor (who even now is hiding behind this circumlocution, but yes, it was me) to forgo a bibliography should not have prevented him from acknowledging this indispensable work.

New Words and Senses

A moderate number of new words or phrases, and a smaller number of new senses, have been added. Several readers suggested the addition of that '70s hit, *zipless fuck* 'an act of intercourse without an emotional connection', coined by Erica Jong in *Fear of Flying*. We had originally decided to omit it since *zipless* was often used on its own to mean 'passionate but emotionally uninvolved', but it does appear often enough as a set phrase to deserve entry. Arnold Zwicky, chief editor of the *Studies Out in Left Field* collection celebrated above, suggested *genderfuck* 'instance of reversal of normal sex roles; (specifically) *transvestism*', a common term whose absence can only be explained using the Johnsonian formula, in answer to a woman who has asked him why he defined *pastern* as the "knee" of a horse, "ignorance, Madam, pure ignorance." Thanks to the diligent research of friends and colleagues, we have pushed this back to 1973 with frequent cites thereafter. Another unfortunate omission was *fuck buddy* 'a sexual partner, esp. a friend with whom one engages in casual sex', which we currently have found to 1983 but have hopes of bettering. To *mercy fuck* and *sport fuck* we now add the even less pleasant *hate fuck*, immortalized as the title of the first album of postpunk band Pussy Galore in 1987 but found in the '70s, and *force-fuck*, apparently coined because the word *rape* wasn't shocking enough. The bizarre lesbian expression *fuckerware party* 'gathering for the group use of sex toys' seems, contrary to expectations, to be real; the definition of *fist-fuck*, originally limited to anal fisting, has been widened (with citations) to allow for vaginal fisting as well. More recent additions are a new sense of *ratfuck* 'a busy party marked by flagrant social climbing'; insults such as *fuckball* and *fuckrag* (popularized in the movie *Scream*); and a number of marginal uses whose admission is being debated, including *fuck-trash* 'loathsome person' and *fuck monster* 'promiscuous person, esp. a woman'.

British and Australian terms, omitted on policy grounds from the first edition, are now being included—and why not, with a word this widespread? *Fuckpig* 'a disgusting person' (according to Partridge, it dates to the nineteenth century, a claim I'd love to be able to verify) is a winner, as is *fuckwit* 'a fool', *fuckwitted* 'stupid', and the absolutely delightful contestant from *Bridget Jones' Diary: fuckwittage* 'stupidity'. *Fucktruck* 'a van or car in which people engage in sexual activity' had been mentioned in the introduction as being Australian (where it has been used since the 1960s), a statement rejected by numerous correspondents who testified to their activities in thusly named vehicles in the U.S. of A.; two people noted that the word was also used for 'a bus on which one can meet prospective sexual partners' (both, curiously, referring to a shuttle between Wellesley College and the Harvard and M.I.T. campuses).

Many of these new items came from suggestions, but most suggestions were ultimately useless. Everyone and his or her brother or sister, it seems, has a favorite *fuck*-related usage. And in most cases, these appear to be expressions doomed to the nonce world. The introduction to the first edition listed several such words, suggested by colleagues, such as *clothesfuck* 'difficulty in deciding what clothes to wear' and *fuckbreak* 'leave of absence from work in order to get pregnant' (two other terms from this section, *fuckload* 'a large amount' and *fuck-muscle* 'the penis', were omitted for insufficient evidence but will now be added). Publication brought a blizzard of ever more outrageous suggestions, including (but not limited to) *fuckadocio, fuck-a-doodle-doo,* and *fuck-aroni,* whose meanings can only be guessed at. Many suggestions also failed to respect the nature of the definitions; several readers commented on the absence of *un-fucking-believable,* which appears under *-fucking-,* infix, or of *fuck book,* which is covered by *fuck,* adj., 'pornographic; erotic'.

Antedatings

As most users of historical dictionaries know, the search for antedatings—citations earlier than those previously known for a word or sense—is a crucial effort. Early examples force us to rethink what we thought we knew about the historical development of language. The original work for *The F-Word* proved that *fuck* was used in a variety of figurative senses far earlier than had previously been believed, and that certain expressions were years or decades older than anyone had realized.

The number of antedatings we have found in the last several years has been small, which is both good (in validating the quality of our original research) and bad (no breakthroughs). The insulting epithets *fuckface* and *fuckhead* were originally first cited in 1961 and 1962, respectively. Several of the citations referred to World War Two, and a euphemistic 1940 example of *fuckfaced* suggested that these terms were in use in the 1940s. Happily, we found solid 1945 citations in an article published in this magazine in 1989—an article we had read, without catching these cites. This article also provided a significant antedating for N.F.G. 'no fucking good', an abbreviation accidentally omitted from *The F-Word* but included in the book's parent work with a first cite from 1977.

The compound *fuck-me* 'intended to invite sexual advances', chiefly exemplified by *fuck-me [shoes]* (with various specific types of shoes), was only attested to 1989. Several reliable sources claimed familiarity to the 1960s and 1970s, and we were able to confirm this with a 1974 citation from the musician David Bowie. The expression *fuck-you money*, unknown to the editor before a reader letter called it to attention, was first cited to 1986, thanks to a search of the Nexis database. A colleague subsequently discovered a 1976 example. *M.F.*, a euphemistic form of *motherfucker*, had been attested to 1964; we found a 1959 example buried in Robert Gold's excellent *Jazz Lexicon*. Finally, the best we had been able to do on *titfuck* was 1986; a Nexis search came up with a *Playboy* example from 1984, which inspired a check of Robert Wilson's 1972 *Playboy's Book of Forbidden Words*, which indeed had it. The second definition of *fuckable*, 'sexually available', with a single 1977 example, was pushed back to 1972 in Bruce Rodgers's *Queens' Vernacular*, which also supplied a first cite for *mouthfuck*, verb.

An important goal of the revision has been to include any "famous" use of relevant forms of *fuck*. In the original version, we were content to have a good smattering of examples from the earliest to the most recent, but as long as the examples were genuine attestations, we were satisfied. (Preference is given to actual examples in running text, then to printed glossarial evidence, and finally to orally collected examples.)

Now we have made an effort to extend our evidence from important or interesting sources. Thus, we have added the famous scene in *Catcher in the Rye*, where Holden sees a "fuck you" graffito and muses on his desire to protect his little sister Phoebe from seeing such vulgarity. Another important citation is from Allen Ginsberg's "Howl," where he has seen "The best minds in my generation destroyed by madness, . . . who let themselves be fucked in the ass by saintly motorcyclists, and screamed with joy." *Bufu* 'a homosexual man', a portmanteau from *butt fucker*, was already in with a first citation from a 1982 Valley Girl dictionary, but we have added the use in the defining text of that subculture, Frank Zappa's "Valley Girl": "Like my English teacher—He's like Mr. Bufu . . . He like flirts with all the guys in the class." Under *fuck up* we have added the well-known opening lines to Philip Larkin's poem "This Be the Verse," the only use of *fuck* to be regularly found in dictionaries of quotations:

"They fuck you up, your mum and dad./ They may not mean to, but they do." And for the literal sense, we learn from Liz Phair that "I want to fuck you like a dog . . . I'll fuck you till your dick turns blue."

The regular program of gathering new evidence, combined with database searches for underattested forms, has delivered an impressive return of citations. We have four instead of two examples of *fubar* in the secondary sense 'drunk'; up-to-date examples for *give a fuck, fuck* 'act of sexual intercourse', *fuckable, fuck-all, fuckboy, fuckfest,* and others; a valuable third cite for *fuck* 'an evil turn of events'; more florid entries in the "stronger, more vivid, or more elaborate curses" section, and newly fleshed-out entries for *fuckee* in both literal and figurative senses. This evidence proves that these terms are all real words, still in current use in the English-speaking world.

We have tried to keep deletions to a minimum, chiefly by not including marginal terms in the first place. Any item with two or more examples may be considered secure; an item from a single non-glossarial source that parallels an existing expression may also be considered secure; an item with only a single glossarial citation would have been kept out unless a confirming example could be solicited. An included marginal term, then, would be one from a single oral or written source that does not parallel another term and appears, in this editor's opinion, to be unlikely. Those that are on the ropes for this revision, include *fuck-plug* 'a contraceptive diaphragm', with a single example from a college student in 1984, a term not subsequently found despite wide questioning and extensive database searching; *fuck* 5.b. 'to trifle or interfere with' (that is, the usual sense of *fuck with,* but without the "with"), found in a single example from a movie; and *friggin in the rigging,* a nautical expression for 'loafing on duty', which is too uninteresting a figurative sense even if it does have some currency beyond the single oral example we have found.

And last of all, but first in the book, we are adding something that no book should be without: an epigraph. The easily offended, who nonetheless choose to pick up this book, will be faced with this before they get to anything juicy:

> *Tis needful that the most immodest word*
> *Be looked upon and learned.*
>
> —Shakespeare, *Henry IV, Part II*

Notes

Identity and Language in the SM Scene

M. A. BUCHANAN

1. *Leathers* is the generic term for SM–related clothing, in this case a leather shirt, vest, and black denim jeans. *Leathers* can also indicate a chain harness, a jockstrap, and a smile, or any other combination that you can think of. *Colors* is the term used for the back-patch worn on a leather vest. It denotes one's organizational affiliation. Colors can also consist of club pins or a club T-shirt.

2. *SM 101* is the term used when giving the we're-safe-sane-and-consensual-and-we-live-right-next-door talk to vanilla people. These talks always emphasize how safe, cuddly, and friendly SM people and practices are and usually involve much flourishing of suede whips and pieces of fur as examples of the kinds of equipment used. While these talks are always technically true, they always seem to leave out the fact that the chief fun in doing SM is in being naughty. As a friend of mine once said after going to a talk on lesbian history, "From the way they talk, you'd believe it was nothing more than a political movement and didn't involve sex at all."

3. *Leatherman* is a term denoting gay and bisexual men who like wearing leather for sexual pleasure and/or doing SM. There are leathermen who only wear rubber but enjoy spankings, and there are leathermen who like to dress up and are horrified if someone wants to tie them up. *Leatherfolk* and *leatherpeople* tend to refer to SM people in general. Straight people usually say that they are "into the scene," which sounds much more circumspect.

4. For the edification of European Americans reading this article, I am now going to reveal a painful truth. Most of the people of color who are my informants have told me that when they were growing up they were told by friends and relatives that white people were all "try-sexuals," that is, they would try anything in bed. In other words, they were seen as the sole source and receptacle of sexual perversion in the universe. I

myself have actually heard black people claim that black homosexuality is caused by white men seducing black men. Fortunately, most of my POC (people of color) informants no longer believe this nonsense, but in many cases this canard has made coming out as gay, into leather, or both, impossible.

5. Although the physiological effects can be excruciatingly arousing—see, for example, the veiled reference to orgasm in Melville's *Billy Budd*—choking, also known as breath control, is considered by most of the SM community to be so dangerous and far out that they rank it in a special category: *edgeplay*. Edgeplay includes any activity that could lead to physical or emotional trauma, or even death. Most practitioners will not even discuss edgeplay in front of novices or "tourists" (newcomers or curiosity seekers) for fear of someone getting hurt or getting some very strange ideas about regular practice and safety protocols. Some practitioners even believe that edgeplay shouldn't be discussed or practiced at all.

6. A *switch* is a person who, depending on the situation, may be willing to play as either a dominant or a submissive in an SM scenario.

7. A perfect example of this exists in Spanish. The standard Spanish words *novio* and *novia* literally translate as "future spouse" or "affianced one." There is no word for "boyfriend" or "girlfriend" in the American English sense. This is because, as a Spanish-speaking friend told me, love relationships between young persons of the opposite sex were expected to lead, until recently, straight to marriage. Card stores in East Harlem have boyfriend and girlfriend cards in the English-language section, but the *novio/novia* cards tend to be more serious in tone than their English near-equivalents.

On Blue Moons, and Others

NICK HUMEZ

1. Pope Gregory XIII's calendar of 1582 was a revision correcting a ten-day error, the result of a lingering imprecision multiplied during sixteen hundred years of the previous Julian calendar, itself a reform under Julius Caesar of the still older Roman calendar, which had gotten out of phase with the solar year by several months. The Gregorian calendar is

essentially the one Westerners use today, with its 365-day year plus an extra day thrown in every four years except at the turn of three centuries out of four. In case you're wondering, there was a February 29 in the year 2000.

2. Two hundred thirty-five lunations of 29.53 days = 6,939.55 days; nineteen years $\times$ 365.25 = 6,393.75 days. Not a bad fit, really.

3. For more information about this delightful publication, send an e-mail to worldwidewords@linguist.ldc.upenn.edu. Quinion himself lives in the British seaport of Bristol, whose venerable maritime tradition is enshrined in, among other places, the touchmark of its silversmiths' guildhall, an anchor.

4. Dating from the same period are the first mentions of the moon being made of green cheese, cited by John Heywood in his 1541 collection of English proverbs but first appearing in print a dozen years earlier in John Frith's *A Pistle to the Christian Reader,* published in 1529: "They woulde make me[n] beleue that the Mone is made of grene cheese." Both blue- and green-cheese moons are clearly intended to mean nonsense. A more rational view of the latter, however, has been offered recently by a child whose name is unfortunately lost to posterity but whose age (six) has been preserved, and who, with charming ingenuity, explained that "For centuries, people thought the moon was made of green cheese. Then the astronauts found that the moon is really a big hard rock. That's what happens to cheese when you leave it out."

5. By contrast, the color of the moon during a lunar eclipse is a faded red; the earth's albedo—the reflectivity of its surface—keeps the moon from being altogether darkened during the hour or so when it is in the earth's shadow. While not as awe-inspiring as the blotting out of the sun at midday during a solar eclipse, the transition of the moon from its silvery fullness to a sickly dried-blood color can inspire a distinct uneasiness, and as the eclipse lasts nearly ten times as long, the cumulative effect can be quite unsettling. On the other hand, lunar eclipses are much more frequent, so one can get used to them, not the case with eclipses of the sun.

6. Shaukat, who is also an engineer and mathematician, has a fascinating Web site at http://moonsighting.com.

7. I am indebted to Jessy Randall of the Library Company of Philadelphia for this term. The Indian government's heroic efforts to stabilize the nation's population growth included widespread distribution of birth

control pills; women were encouraged to keep track of where they were in the cycle by timing it in phase with the moon. An unforeseen effect was that all the women in the program now crowded into the rivers for the ritual bath of purification at the same time, instead of one by one throughout the month.

8. According to Roger "Blue Kiwi" Sharp in his review of Larry Bulmer and Bob Mills' *Dicks Out: The Unique Guide to British Football Songs*.

Assing Around

JESSY RANDALL AND WENDY WOLOSON

1. John Simpson and Edmund Weiner, eds. *The Oxford English Dictionary* (Oxford: Clarendon Press, 1993) 698–9.
2. Ibid.
3. Alastair Fowler, ed. *The New Oxford Book of Seventeenth Century Verse* (Oxford: Oxford University Press, 1991) 707.
4. American Libraries (December 1998): 21.
5. J. E. Lighter, ed., *The Random House Historical Dictionary of American Slang* (New York: Random House, c 1994) 47.
6. We have even heard of a young woman said to have a train up her ass—but we do not know the woman personally and cannot stand by this assertion.
7. There is an old joke that uses this expression to some effect: A "Myra bird," which attacks whatever you tell it to using the command "Myra bird, cracker" or "Myra bird, bathtub," is purchased for a friend's birthday. Upon hearing about the bird's special talent, the friend replies, "Myra bird, my ass." (This joke can be told to children by replacing *ass* with *foot* in the punchline.)
8. Tom Dalzell, *Flappers 2 Rappers: American Youth Slang* (Springfield, MA: Merriam-Webster, 1996) 202.
9. Eric Partridge, ed. *A Dictionary of the Underworld* (New York: Macmillan, 1950) 11.
10. Lighter 38.
11. Ibid.
12. From this usage comes a mildly off-color joke (brought to our attention by friend Nick Humez): Two rakish young boy mice are standing on the corner watching all the girl mice go by. Says the first mouse,

"Wow—will you look at the ass on that one?" To which his comrade replies, "Personally, I'm a titmouse myself."

13. Paula Munro, *Slang U* (New York: Harmony Books, 1991) 51.

14. "The Razor's Edge," *Philadelphia Weekly,* 27.48 (December 2, 1998): 22.

15. Eric Partridge, *A Dictionary of Slang and Unconventional English* (New York: Macmillan, 1984) 29.

Deciphering the Four-Letter Word in a Medieval Manuscript's Satire on Friars

CARTER REVARD

1. I was able to inspect the manuscript (Harley 3362), and here acknowledge the kindness of the staff of the Students Room of the British Library in providing access as well as the marvelous services and facilities for study which make it such a pleasure to work there.

2. *Reliquiae Antiquae* vol. 1, p. 91.

3. A cipher very similar to this occurs in B.M. MS. Sloane 351, fol. 15, from which Wright prints it (op. cit. vol. 2, p. 15). Wright says this MS also is "of the fifteenth century."

4. The definitive history of the obscenity symbol, including its etymology, is now being worked out by several scholars, notably Allen Walker Read. It may well be of Flemish origin. Certainly one would want to know the details of how it entered English and why it came to replace *swive.* It appears that the latter word was indeed perceived as a gross term, and its written appearances seem confined primarily to invective or comic contexts; the first *OED* citation for *swive* is for the gerund *swiving,* used in the "Song of Lewes" (written ca. A.D. 1265) as a term of contempt: The poet says that Richard of Cornwall spent all his treasure on *swiving,* and clearly it was not just uxorious activity that the poet had in mind. Chaucer used *swive* only to describe adulterous or clandestine fornication, and one can see how a word in such a smelly role will easily give way to another more foreign and vigorous: It is much easier and funnier to swear in a foreign language, as Americans have found with the British *bloody,* for instance.

A SELECTION OF OTHER TITLES
ALSO AVAILABLE IN PIMLICO

The Chameleon Poet:
A Life of George Barker

Robert Fraser

'The tale of a poet with a colossal talent...Throughout, it is
scrupulously researched, factually hard-edged, and dextrous
in its grasp of tricky material...This is a remarkable biography.'
Tablet

Eliot wrote of his 'genius'. Yeats thought him the most interesting
poet of his generation. Dylan Thomas envied his power over women.
War trapped him in Japan. In America he conducted one of the most
celebrated love affairs of the century. He fathered fifteen children in
several countries, three during one battle-torn summer. By the 1950s
he was the toast of Soho. George Barker was Catholic and bohemi-
an, frank and elusive, tender and boisterous. In Eliot's phrase, he was
'a most peculiar fellow'.

'Absorbing...a fascinating tribute. His prose is of the best kind –
fluent, lucid and with no 'style' peeping through anywhere.'
Lloyd Evans, *Daily Telegraph*

'It is the great achievement of Fraser's book lovingly to re-present
Barker's best poems. And to make us see that his present reputation is
considerably less than it deserves to be.'
Andrew Motion, *Financial Times*

'Highly readable...it offers a lyricism and linguistic pyrotechnics that
are all his own.'
Vernon Scannell, *Sunday Telegraph*

£16.00   0-7126-9171-5

Trollope

Victoria Glendinning

WINNER OF THE WHITBREAD
BIOGRAPHY OF THE YEAR AWARD

'Majestic, capacious, compelling and clear-sighted.'
Hilary Spurling, *Daily Telegraph*

'Glendinning succeeds, as no biographer has done before, in bringing
him to life on the page...Here, at last, is an Anthony Trollope whom
one can know as a man...The effect is startlingly impressive.' Jonathan
Raban, *Independent on Sunday*

'Enormously enjoyable'
John Mortimer, Books of the Year, *Sunday Times*

'Full of fascinating knowledge about the Victorian age in England...
A great story superbly told.' Augustine Martin, *Irish Times*

'As compellingly readable as any of Anthony's own novels.'
Ruth Rendell, *Sunday Express*

'I came to this biography of Trollope with unreasonably high expectations. They were amply fulfilled...A work as readable, richly shift-
ing and well-shaped as a good novel...compendiously well-informed.'
Caroline Moore, *The Times*

'A brilliant and subtle interweaving of the man and the work; wonderful.' Joanna Trollope, Books of the Year, *Daily Telegraph*

£14.00   0-7126-9790-X

Jonathan Swift

Victoria Glendinning

'A sparkling book...Victoria Glendinning is one of our finest
biographers, diligent, penetrating and alive to every nuance
of character and feeling.' *Daily Mail*

Best known as the author of *Gulliver's Travels*, Jonathan Swift - poet,
polemicist, pamphleteer and wit - is the master of shock. His furious
satirical responses to the corruption and hypocrisy he saw around him
in public and private life have every relevance for our own times. His
black imagination, and his preoccupation with the foulness that lies
beneath the thin veneer of artifice and civilisation, gave a new adjective – 'Swiftian' – to the lexicon of criticism.

Victoria Glendinning, prize-winning biographer, investigates at close
range the main events and relationships of Swift's life, providing a
compelling and provocative portrait set in a rich tapestry of contro-
versy and paradox.

'A full-scale life, a model of the genre, appealing both to the head and
the heart.' *Guardian*

£9.99   0-7126-6262-6

Cyril Connolly: A Life

Jeremy Lewis

'A sparkling biography...stylish and funny...unflaggingly entertaining.' *Independent*

Precociously brilliant in his youth, Cyril Connolly was haunted for the rest of his life by a sense of failing and a romantic yearning to recover a lost Eden. His two great books, *The Unquiet Grave* and *Enemies of Promise*, are classics of English prose, combining wit, romanticism and merciless self-knowledge.

As witty in person as he was in his prose, he was notoriously slothful and greedy; he was married three times and his dealings with women were bedevilled by a lifelong tendency to be in love with two or more people at once.

'In one of the funniest literary biographies I have ever read, Lewis assembles all the excellently entertaining anecdotes about this deeply loved, much mocked, sometimes reviled figure whose departure has robbed the literary world of its social smartness and any worthwhile eccentricity...An excellent, wildly funny and informative biography.' Auberon Waugh

'A biography brimming with energy and enthusiasm...He is a subtle and intelligent critic of Connolly's work, and his sympathy for his subject is unbounded.' *Sunday Telegraph*

£12.50   0-7126-6635-4

Some Sort of Genius: A Life of Wyndham Lewis

Paul O'Keeffe

'**Paul O'Keeffe has written a magnificent biography of Lewis, rich in revealing anecdote, with a dark sense of humour that relishes the many ironies of Lewis's life…This will be the definitive biography of Lewis for decades to come.**' Lawrence Rainey, *Independent*

'A man of undoubted genius,' T.S. Eliot said of Wyndham Lewis, '…but genius for what precisely it would be remarkably difficult to say.' Painter and draughtsman, novelist, satirist, pamphleteer and critic, Lewis's multifarious activities defy easy categorisation. *Some Sort of Genius* is the compelling biography of a major but neglected figure of twentieth-century modernism.

'A massive work of scholarship, painstaking detective-work and exhaustive detail – a biography in the mould of Richard Ellmann's *James Joyce*.' Andrew Taylor, *Literary Review*

'O'Keeffe has done brilliantly in pointing up many of the myths and falsifications which Lewis encouraged, and in uncovering many new facts. He has a relish for detail…which he uses to telling, and often darkly comic, effect. He builds up a rich picture of a bitter and frustrated life.' Matthew Sturgis, *Times Literary Supplement*

£15.00   0-7126-7339-3

Phillip Sidney: A Double Life

Alan Stewart

'**This is a work of great scholarship and fluency, filled with an affection for the subject...An excellent biography.**'
Peter Ackroyd, *The Times*

Courtier, poet, soldier, diplomat – Philip Sidney was one of the most promising young men of his age. Brilliantly conjuring up a sixteenth-century Europe in flux, this fascinating biography reveals an unfamiliar Philip Sidney – his plans to form a pan-European Protestant army, his secret diplomatic negotiations – and unearths for the first time the full extent of his double life.

'A gripping biography...Alan Stewart skilfully guides the reader through the complex power struggles of the Virgin Queen's court and out onto the bigger stage of European politics.'
Mark Sanderson, *Time Out*

'A thoughtful and erudite biography...committed and sympathetic.'
Frank McLynn, *Irish Times*

'A stylish and searching biography...a fine account.'
Charles Nicholl, *Sunday Times*

'An impressive achievement.' Anne Somerset, *Daily Mail*

£12.50   0-7126-6548-X

Thackeray

D. J. Taylor

'An excellent biography…accomplished, responsible, imaginative.' Victoria Glendinning

Vanity Fair, published in 1847–8, made William Makepeace Thackeray famous. Behind him lay an extraordinary life – an intense, Anglo-Indian childhood, dominated by the figure of his mother; a fortune lost by his early twenties; a disastrous marriage to a wife who went mad and left him to bring up their two small daughters in near penury. Thackeray's early career was a struggle.

But as D. J. Taylor shows in this incisive new biography – the first major study for twenty years – his later life was no less troubled. A tortuous, platonic love for the wife of a close friend, bitter literary quarrels and an obsession with earning enough to keep his family combined to produce a complex, touchy man, fearful of publicity. Worn out by work and beset by illness, he died at 52, sadly aware that the brilliant novels of his maturity – *Pendennis*, *The History of Henry Esmond* and *The Newcomes* – could never scale the peak claimed by *Vanity Fair*.

'Outstanding…On every page of this book there is evidence of a formidable critical and imaginative intelligence at work.'
Evening Standard

'Dazzlingly good' *Independent on Sunday*

£12.50   0-7126-6246-4

Essential English for Journalists, Editors and Writers

Harry Evans
Fully Revised and Updated by Crawford Gillan

Essential English **has for generations been the bible of any aspiring Harry Evans.' Alan Rusbridger, Editor-in-Chief,** *Guardian*

Essential English is an indispensable guide to the use of words as tools of communication. It is written primarily for journalists, yet its lessons are of immense value to all who face the problem of giving information, whether to the general public or within business, professional or social organizations.

'Harry Evans is one of the great newspaper professionals of his time, and his book should be a standard text for every journalist.'
Max Hastings, Editor, *Evening Standard*

'Every journalist in Britain should read this exceptional book. Harry Evans is a master of our trade and a master of how to use the English language.' Piers Morgan, Editor, *Mirror*

'English is the world's most used and abused language. This book is on the side of the angels. It should become an essential textbook for every journalist.' Paul Dacre, Editor, *Daily Mail*

'Great editor: great teacher of editors.'
Peter Stothard, Editor, *The Times*

£12.50   0-7126-6447-5

Week-End Wodehouse

P. G. Wodehouse

'**Mr Wodehouse's idyllic world can never stale. He will continue to release future generations from captivity that may be more irksome than our own. He has made a world for us to live in and delight in.' Evelyn Waugh**

Week-End Wodehouse — required reading at country house parties in the late Thirties — remains one of the best introductions to the work of a writer who, in Hilaire Belloc's words, 'nearly always approaches, and often reaches, perfection'.

All the old favourites are here: Drones Club stories, Mr Mulliner stories, stories of Jeeves, Lord Emsworth and Ukridge. But this hugely entertaining selection also includes generous extracts from the novels and non-fiction writings.

Just as in its original edition, *Week-End Wodehouse* is introduced by Hilaire Belloc and wittily decorated with illustrations by Kerr.

£10.00   0-7126-5034-2

Order more Pimlico books from your local
bookshop, or have them delivered
direct to your door by
BOOKPOST

Robert Fraser
The Chameleon Poet: A Life of George Barker   0-7126-9171-5   £16.00
Victoria Glendinning
Trollope   0-7126-9790-X   £14.00
Victoria Glendinning
Jonathan Swift   0-7126-6262-6   £9.99
Jeremy Lewis
Cyril Connolly: A Life   0-7126-6635-4   £12.50
Paul O'Keeffe
Some Sort of Genius: A Life of Wyndham Lewis   0-7126-7339-3   £15.00
Alan Stewart
Philip Sidney: A Double Life   0-7126-6548-X   £12.50
D.J. Taylor
Thackeray   0-7126-6246-4   £12.50
Harry Evans
Essential English for Journalists, Editors and Writers 0-7126-6447-5   £12.50
P.G. Wodehouse
Week-End Wodehouse   0-7126-5034-2   £10.00

FREE POST AND PACKING
Overseas customers allow £2 per paperback

PHONE: 01624 677237

POST: Random House Books
c/o Bookpost, PO Box 29, Douglas
Isle of Man, IM99 1BQ

FAX: 01624 670923

EMAIL: bookshop@enterprise.net

Cheques (payable to Bookpost) and credit cards accepted

Prices and availability subject to change without notice.
Allow 28 days for delivery
When placing your order, please mention if you do not wish
to receive any additional information

www.randomhouse.co.uk/pimlico